# BUILDING CHARLESTON

# BUILDING CHARLESTON

TOWN AND SOCIETY
IN THE EIGHTEENTH-CENTURY
BRITISH ATLANTIC WORLD

*Emma Hart*

The University of South Carolina Press

Hardcover edition published by the University of Virginia Press, 2010
Paperback edition published by the University of South Carolina Press, 2015

www.sc.edu/uscpress

Manufactured in the United States of America

24 23 22 21 20 19 18 17 16 15
10 9 8 7 6 5 4 3 2 1

Library of Congress Cataloging-in-Publication Data
can be found at http://catalog.loc.gov/.

ISBN 978-1-61117-658-2 (paperback)

This book was printed on recycled paper with
30 percent postconsumer waste content.

*For Daniel, Klara, and Lily*

# Contents

# Illustrations

# Acknowledgments

Writing this book has taken rather a long time, and over the years I have accumulated many debts. The manuscript began life as a PhD dissertation at the Johns Hopkins University under the exemplary supervision of Jack P. Greene. Jack's enthusiasm for my topic, frustration with my poor grammar, and demands to know "what the point" of my work was, resulted in a thesis that was the firm foundation for a book. I should also like to thank my second reader, Mike Johnson, and the members of the Graduate Seminar in Colonial American history for their many useful comments.

On leaving Johns Hopkins and arriving at the University of St. Andrews, my dissertation began the arduous journey from thesis to book. Along the way, Cathy Matson, Joyce Chaplin, Trevor Burnard, Phil Morgan, and an anonymous reader for the University of Virginia Press all read (and in some cases reread) complete drafts of the manuscript. I should like to thank each of them for taking the time to look at my work, and for providing the observations and criticisms that allowed me to formulate and to refine my arguments. Without their input, this book would, quite simply, never have made it into print. Also invaluable were discussions with Max Edelson, Ben Carp, and my colleagues at the University of St. Andrews, especially Hamish Scott, Bruce Lenman, and Rab Houston. Dick Holway and Raennah Mitchell at the University of Virginia Press have also been instrumental in bringing the book to fruition.

I could not have undertaken this project without financial support from a variety of institutions. A graduate fellowship from Johns Hopkins University, a grant from the Early American Industries Association, a Madelyn Moeller fellowship at the Museum of Early Southern Decorative Arts (MESDA), and funds from the University of St Andrews all aided the completion of my research.

I also wish to thank the archivists at the South Caroliniana Library, the

South Carolina Historical Society, the South Carolina Department of Archives and History, and the Library Company of Philadelphia, for their friendly assistance while I undertook lengthy periods of research. Particular thanks are due to the staff at the Museum of Early Southern Decorative Arts, and especially to Donna Rothrock and Sally Gant, both of whom provided help and hospitality during my long stays in Winston-Salem. Some material in chapter 2 appeared in *Global Perspectives on Industrial Transformation in the American South,* edited by Susanna Delfino and Michele Gillespie, and is reprinted here by permission of the University of Missouri Press (copyright © 2005 by the Curators of the University of Missouri). And parts of chapter 4 appeared in my article, "'The Middling Order are Odious Characters': Social Structure and Urban Growth in Colonial Charleston, South Carolina," in *Urban History,* vol. 34, no. 2 (August 2007): 209–26.

Finally, I owe many debts to family and friends. Daniel has had to endure my obsession with Charleston ever since we met, and his willingness to read and comment on endless drafts went above and beyond the call of spousal duty. My parents, my brother Mike, Mariana Dantas, Sebastien Biot, and Cathy and Chris Cardno also provided much needed friendship and support along the way.

# BUILDING CHARLESTON

# Introduction

Towns, wrote Fernand Braudel, "are like electric transformers. They increase tension, accelerate the rhythm of exchange and constantly recharge human life."[1] With their extraordinary concentration of people, their shared closed spaces that force inhabitants of different colors, classes, and nationalities to collide with one another, and their plethora of commercial and cultural possibilities, cities have often made a special contribution to the character of societies. Even if rural life remained the norm in the Western world before the twentieth century, imparting a character and a dynamic all its own, towns still had the ability to concentrate forces for change, to reinvigorate the countryside, and to connect individuals to economic and cultural entities larger than themselves. This book is about one such "electric transformer"—Charleston, South Carolina—and the ways in which, as it "recharged" human life, it influenced the development of a colony and the nature of that colony's relationship to the larger British Atlantic world.

As the fourth-largest town in mainland British America, and by 1775 one of the forty largest in the English-speaking world, Charleston had grown, over the course of the eighteenth century, into a major metropolis. Although there were British and American towns that were larger, it was Charleston's spectacular growth—its population increased fourfold within half a century—that placed it among the ranks of the most dynamic urban places in the empire, its rate of expansion outstripping Boston's and almost equaling that of New York between 1700 and 1775. Within British North America, only Philadelphia achieved a more impressive population increase.[2]

"Charles Towne" had been part of Carolina from the colony's earliest, Proprietary days. Initially situated to the southwest of its present location, the town was moved in 1678 at the behest of the colony's Proprietors. At its second founding, the "Grand Modell" grid plan, conceived by Carolina's Proprietor Lord Anthony Ashley Cooper provided a tidy template for future growth.

At first the town's population increased quite slowly, but after 1730 even a succession of epidemics, hurricanes, fires, and earthquakes could not halt its rapid expansion. During the second quarter of the eighteenth century, the construction of numerous public buildings gave Charleston a more stable character. Settlers were mostly successful at building their homes according to the footprint of the Grand Modell, resulting in an easily navigable town that possessed a regularity admired throughout the colonies. Orderly expansion beyond the planners' original grid was achieved either by draining and reclaiming marshland on the south side of the peninsula on which the town stood, or by laying out new streets in an area, commonly called "Charles Town Neck," to the west of the center. The first to seize upon the opportunity for expansion was Captain George Anson, who allegedly won a tract of land in a game of cards, divided it into lots, and sold it in parcels to eager developers. By the third quarter of the eighteenth century, other major landowners on this western edge of the town were similarly involved in speculative projects to improve their property with new houses.[3]

The steady pace of expansion established by 1750 was a reflection of Charleston's numerical superiority over other towns founded by the colony's white settlers. Although a number of urban places existed in early South Carolina, none achieved the size and stature of the capital. Both Port Royal/Beaufort, to the south, and Georgetown Winyaw, to the north, grew to a modest size, but neither came close to successfully challenging the capital's supremacy. Likewise, efforts to create a series of townships on the frontier during the 1730s failed to produce sizeable urban settlements. Indeed, it was not until the expansion of settlement and farming in the backcountry in the 1760s that the marketing needs of new colonists began to make inland towns viable. Throughout the colonial period, Charleston was the epicenter of urban life in the Low Country and increasingly a point of reference for the South Carolina backcountry and for Georgia, North Carolina, and Florida.[4]

The town's enduring importance to the colony was reflected in the size of the urban population. The proportion of urban dwellers, when compared to the total for all South Carolina inhabitants, held steady at about 10 percent (12 percent of the white population) through the entire colonial period. It was not until the 1790s that Charleston's growth failed to keep pace with the region's rural expansion, its share falling to 6 percent at the time of the first U.S. Census. Within its hinterland, Charleston actually accommodated

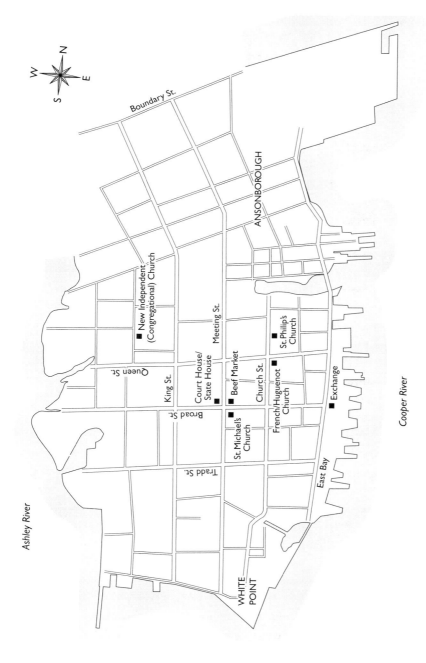

Fig. I.1. Street plan of Charleston. (Map by Bill Nelson)

a slightly higher proportion of settlers than did early America's other major towns, whose populations represented fewer than 10 percent of the total population of their regions. Further, the proportion of Carolinians resident in the town was on a par with the proportion of residents in Britain's more rural regions, such as Lowland Scotland; there, the concentration of urban dwellers within large provincial centers like Edinburgh, in conjunction with a lack of smaller towns in outlying rural areas, resulted in an overall settlement pattern similar to that of the eighteenth-century Low Country. In terms of both its size and its standing within its region, therefore, Charleston brought the Low Country into broader British Atlantic demographic trends.[5]

Charleston's demographic development may have followed a well-trodden path, but, to date, historians of Charleston have mainly chosen to emphasize the town's unique aspects. Concentrating on the plantation as the "dynamic instrument of colonization and economic development," scholars have laid most emphasis on Charleston's special experience as a town raised up by its total subordination to the surrounding staple economy.[6] Without doubt, the startling expansion of rice and indigo cultivation did mold the character of South Carolina's chief metropolis. Most obviously, as planters and merchants focused the trading of their bulky staples there, the city grew into a major port, one through which not only rice and indigo, but also slaves and British manufactures flowed. This economic activity supported the creation of a wealthy planter-merchant elite, a group whose selection of the town as a seasonal home further underwrote Charleston's growth. Highly visible on the cultural and political, as well as the economic, scene, this elite manipulated the town to suit its needs, making Charleston the epicenter of the group's grip over the colony's ruling Assembly, and a playground in which to pursue a genteel and luxurious lifestyle.[7]

Planters' enthusiastic embrace of slave labor also shaped Charleston in very important ways. Half of all townspeople were enslaved Africans, and as a succession of excellent studies has demonstrated, these black residents were central to the town's character. Dominating the marketplace, gathering to socialize in public spaces and dram shops, and living and working within the household complexes of white Charlestonians, slaves and free blacks influenced every feature of daily life in this slave society's chief metropolis.[8] In the same way that the failure of urban settlement in the colonial Chesapeake was intimately linked to the expediencies of tobacco production, the success of the metropolis in the Low Country was indicative of the needs of rice and indigo, and of its growers.[9]

The consequence of a narrative that lays such an unremitting emphasis on the importance of the region's staples to Charleston's rise is that Charleston is now firmly viewed as a southern town, distinctive from the earliest decades of settlement. Even though Carl Bridenbaugh's classic *Cities in Revolt* uncovered many commonalities between Charleston, Philadelphia, New York, and Boston, recent scholarship has consistently made a distinction between between Charleston and its northerly neighbors. As a result, the South Carolinian metropolis stands outside of the processes that, historians have argued, dominated the landscape of colonial America's "urban crucibles." Jacob Price has contrasted Charleston's economic function with that of its mainland colonial counterparts, contesting that its lack of maritime industries made it more of a shipping point than a true port town. Gary Nash located the colony's northern seaports at the "cutting edge" of the social, political, and economic upheaval that gave rise to the most-radical elements of the American Revolution, but did not include Charleston in his analysis. Although the diversity and dynamism of growing towns in the northern colonies has placed them at the center of the narrative of eighteenth-century colonial British America, Charleston and many of its inhabitants have remained on the margins of the action.[10]

My exploration of colonial Charleston was born of a set of interrelated questions about this current view, not only about the role of Charleston within its immediate environment, but also about wider debates involving the colonial British American city. In the specific case of this southern colony, I wondered, should the plantation so dominate our understanding of a region where a significant proportion of the population lived in a town? Was Charleston itself, as a separate urban place, really so unimportant in influencing South Carolina's character? This question seemed particularly pertinent, as Caribbean towns such as Kingston and Port Royal, Jamaica, and Bridgetown, Barbados—also situated in slave societies—have, since the 1990s, been bestowed by historians with more autonomy than Charleston in the shaping of their respective locales.[11] Could the power of the plantation and the staple economy successfully sweep all before it, removing this considerable town from the larger urban dynamic that united its contemporaries? Studying South Carolina's colonial era from a Charleston perspective, this book tests the staple-dominated narrative of southern development, asking whether it is always logical to emphasize the importance of cities and commerce only in regard to early America's *northern* colonies.[12]

I also had broader questions about the suitability of viewing America's towns as exceptional New World cities. Carl Bridenbaugh's seminal study of the colonial city compared America's five largest seaports to their metropolitan counterparts, arguing that by the 1760s they had become extraordinary because they were "the superiors of all the cities of Britain save London." Subsequent historians have also placed an exceptional view of the American town at the heart of their narratives, stressing the importance to urban change of processes and events specific to the New World. Thus, the story of colonial urban life has mostly been told within a framework that emphasizes how, after 1750, war and trade brought economic inequality and social strife to America's towns, this discontent then seamlessly feeding into the radical political protests that fueled opposition to British taxation measures and, eventually, to the Revolution itself.[13]

However, extensive scholarship on the British eighteenth-century town has in the meantime made it clear that assumptions regarding both the superiority and the exceptional nature of Britain's colonial counterpart may be difficult to sustain. Across England and Scotland, provincial towns were experiencing an "urban renaissance" in which an expanding market economy, increased population, social upheaval, and cultural and physical renewal were transforming the urban environment.[14] In documenting these processes in a British context, such studies thus reveal that, during the eighteenth century, dramatic socioeconomic change, rapid growth, conflict, and increasing political radicalism were not unique to the American town. In view of this convergence of urban experience, I wondered whether we should be writing narratives of colonial urban life that emphasized so heavily the exceptional aspects of New World settlement. Especially given the recent trend toward viewing early America as a component part of a larger British Atlantic world, would it not be useful to examine colonial urban society within this broader framework?[15] This book, therefore, also aims to produce a history of Charleston as a British Atlantic town, by thoroughly connecting the urban process in the Low Country to that taking place elsewhere in the eighteenth-century English-speaking world.

By recounting Charleston's colonial experience in the light of these questions, I first describe a previously unconsidered relationship between colonial South Carolina and its largest town. Concentrating on the domestic repercussions of urban growth reveals that Charleston was a principal element in the shaping of Low Country society from the late 1730s onward. Rather than being putty in the hands of an Atlantic staple economy, the expanding town and its inhabitants became an equal force in the making of colonial South Carolina. No facet of the colony's eighteenth-century evolution was left untouched by the presence of such a large urban place. The town had an impact on the culture and the geography of the region's marketplaces. The physical growth of Charleston and its varied businesses also brought wealth and innovation in sectors outside the control of the plantation economy, such as housing construction and manufacturing. Following the initial flush of success of staple agriculture, the colony therefore experienced a second, post-1740, wave of economic development as the town came into its own.

Furthermore, just as rice was not the foundation of every inhabitant's economic world, race was not exclusively at the root of all conflicts and divides among South Carolinians. Whereas Charleston's Caribbean contemporary, Bridgetown, had a large free black population and relatively few free white inhabitants, the South Carolina town was home to very few free blacks before the Revolution but did have a sizeable free white community. Thus, although Charleston's enslaved population marked the town out from its northerly counterparts, its free population was comparable to theirs. After 1740, as the town's growth began to influence South Carolina's larger development, the structure of this urban white society was significantly altered. Giving rise to a "middling sort" (as contemporaries labeled this new class), the town nurtured a social group different from both the planters and the plain folk who populated rural South Carolina.[16] Since chattel labor lay at the heart of this middling sort's ability to make a good living in the urban economy, they were happy to live with the institution of slavery in their midst. Still, however much this urban middling sort perpetuated the rule of white over black, they did not join in a united front with South Carolina's planter-merchants in the name of increasing the size and power of this elite. Instead, the possibilities of the urban economy meant that members of Charleston's middling sort frequently rejected the opportunity to "turn planter," even when they might have been able to afford to do so. At the same time, middling tradesmen were quite willing to break ranks with planters; for example, they often accused their superiors of putting the social order at risk with their luxurious and dissolute life-styles, and of being unwilling to reform the morals of Charleston's poor whites and enslaved blacks.[17]

This story of Charleston's sway over colonial South Carolina reverberates beyond the confines of the eighteenth-century Lower South. In particular, the manner in which the growth of urban society affected social structure in early South Carolina offers new perspectives on the process of class-formation in colonial America. In the first instance, it uncovers a middling sort in a slave society. It also emphasizes how the existence of stark racial divisions did not necessarily mean that the colonial South was home to a united white population.[18]

However, the emergence of this middling sort between 1740 and the Revolution is also at odds with larger assumptions regarding class in early America as a whole. As C. Dallett Hemphill has argued, colonial historians have developed a "bourgeois blind spot" in their discussions of social structure, and nowhere is this truer than in regard to the city. Although early America was once thought of as a "middle-class" society in which all occupied an equally wealthy middle ground, the applicability of such a configuration has long been out of fashion in scholarship on the colonial urban environment. Current ideas of urban social structure, while emphasizing growing inequality, divide up the population into opposing groups on a strictly binary basis—elites and lower sorts, merchants and artisans, blacks and whites, men and women, slave and free.[19]

Charleston's middling sort, however, refused to conform to such a binary model. Their presence gave urban white society in South Carolina a tripartite character. Their identity was not forged exclusively through struggle with a conflicting group of South Carolinians, but was instead wrought from their economic, cultural, and political responses to living in a flourishing urban environment. Middling householders first came together as they expanded their economic pursuits beyond their main trades and, as families, created diverse enterprises unrestricted by their primary interests. When communities were forged across occupations, social structure ceased to be based mainly on profession. Together, middling traders then carried the values of hard work, discipline, and prudence that had served them so well in the economic arena into the cultural and political spheres. Ultimately, it was such values that marked them out from elites and from plain folk and lay at the root of disagreements with their superiors on matters of domestic governance. By the third quarter of the eighteenth century, Charleston nurtured a middling sort with an identity of its own and an emerging awareness of its distinctiveness as a group.

In this study of plantation society, the utility of class as a category of analysis relies on our ability to untether ourselves from a model of social relations that focuses on a two-way conflict between patricians and plebeians. Such definitions, long favored by colonial America's urban historians, relied on a "vision of class," supplied by the historian E. P. Thompson, that "remained wedded to a conception of social change and political consciousness arising out of the economic immiseration associated with the late eighteenth and early nineteenth centuries." In place of this older model, the present study deploys a more flexible, nonlinear definition, in which a class was formed when the shared political, cultural, and economic opportunities open to a group of people bound them together at the same time as it set them against other social groups in their immediate environment. In eighteenth-century Charleston, the growing city provided the conditions for the creation of an economically successful urban middling sort that would at once help to define the social structure of colonial South Carolina and fashion an autonomous identity for itself, an identity that clashed with those of poorer and wealthier whites when middling political and cultural goals proved unattainable.[20] Furthermore, Charleston's failure to harbor a nineteenth-century middle class comparable to that which developed in America's northern cities illustrates how this eighteenth-century middling sort was a particular product of its time and place rather than a stage in a process whereby two opposing parties struggled toward a new social order.[21]

Finding such a middling sort in an eighteenth-century southern city may be surprising in a colonial American setting, but it is entirely predictable in the larger context of the British Atlantic urban environment. Over the past two decades, scholars have been uncovering the story of Britain's urban middling sorts—a group that emerged with the explosive growth of towns in the eighteenth century. These British and American commonalities speak to the power of the evolving town of this era to alter the society in which it existed. Whether in a colonial slave society or in provincial England, a growing town had certain universal implications for the milieu in which it had taken root. Thus, explanations of eighteenth-century early America as an exceptional society, or indeed as a society that was ardently emulative of a monumental British cultural model, cannot fully capture the nature of the relationship between the metropole and its colonies. While South Carolina's large slave population undoubtedly made the colony exceptional and its elite demonstrated a strong penchant for the emulation of London fashions, Charleston's middling sort was comprised of "provincial citizens of an Empire in which provincials would play an increasingly large role."[22] In other words, they inhabited one province of an urban British Atlantic world.

Regarding Charleston as such a provincial town reaches beyond the story of its middling sort to advance our general understanding of the early American urban form in both a South Carolinian, and a colonial, context. In the first instance, viewing the urban economy within a provincial framework reveals new dimensions and nuances. Commensurate with their focus on staples and transatlantic markets, historians have tended to regard all colonial urban economies as being principally shaped by their function as ports, characterizing them on the basis of their being oriented to the east and to overseas trade.[23] However, profiling Charleston's economy within the context of the wider range of towns that united to form a single British Atlantic urban system reveals a more sophisticated picture. Not simply a colonial city, a port city, or even a plantation city, Charleston was equally a provincial town—a place that flourished as a result of its ability to bring a diverse range of goods and services to a demanding local population. With the advent of a consumer society, provincial towns like Charleston became important nodes in a system that emerged when urban environments specialized in particular economic functions and then worked together as part of a larger, "diffuse and polycentric" structure, delivering goods and services to surrounding rural populations. Within this network, manufacturing towns concentrated the large-scale processing of raw materials, port towns possessed economies dominated by the maritime industries, spa towns focused exclusively on the leisure sector, and provincial towns proved their worth as convenient local centers for the consumption of luxury and essential goods and services.[24]

At the same time, Charleston's success as provincial player in a large urban commercial network suggests that we might reevaluate our understanding of colonial economic development in the eighteenth century. Scholars of early North America interested in economic change have often centered their investigations on a transformation, fueled by elite merchants and manufacturers mobilizing entrepreneurial capital, which mostly took place north of Virginia. Such groups, furthermore, are often presumed to have created their market economy at the expense of yeomen farmers, artisans, and small producers, who then became the victims of a new and aggressive commercial society.[25] However, concentrating on Charleston's function as a provincial facilitator of a British Atlantic consumer society uncovers how the town's trading families were not casualties of economic change, but rather leading protagonists in a pre-Revolutionary, southern shift toward a more commercial, market-oriented system. Although often ambivalent to the luxurious lifestyle they were selling, traders and artisans were nevertheless cognizant of the many business opportunities opened to them by an advancing consumer culture. In pursuit of financial security for their families, middling artisans in the luxury and service sectors established manufacturing networks in order to smooth out production, and cut costs by sourcing their own raw materials; by diversifying into other facets of the leisure economy, trading wives kept schools and opened coffeehouses, bowling greens, and taverns. Through such practices, these non-elite tradespeople made a major contribution to the evolution of the larger South Carolina economy, even before the Revolution.[26]

As Charleston's role as a hub of consumption suggests, provinciality is also important to our understanding of colonial urban cultural development.[27] Provincial towns throughout Britain flourished because the urban environment was uniquely able to provide the full range of amenities necessary to perform the polite behaviors associated with the emergence of consumer society. Towns accommodated the assembly rooms, taverns, racecourses, and parks in which wealthy and middling consumers acted out their newfound gentility. While London remained at the epicenter of fashionable society, provincial towns (along with spa towns) soon also became very important as cultural centers, to the degree that after 1750 they began to sponsor the appearance of distinct provincial genteel identities. Just as the urban economic system had become polycentric—with towns working together as partners rather than being merely disciples of the center—so had urban culture.[28] Since it fostered the creation of a South Carolinian provincial gentility, and a distinct middling culture, the Low Country metropolis evolved within a similar paradigm. As Charleston and the metropole entered into a cultural dialogue, South Carolinians could count themselves as provincial innovators as well as metropolitan emulators.

Finally, reading Charleston as a provincial British Atlantic town brings new insights into the local political scene in colonial America, adding another dimension to our understanding of early Revolutionary protest. During the eighteenth century, much of the town's sophisticated reputation stemmed from its participation in a broad movement for urban improvement. In towns across the English-speaking world, citizens were investing in new public buildings and establishing novel regulative bodies in the name of bettering their surroundings. Prominent in this quest for the enlightened town were those trading folk who had recently found success in the urban economy. For them, building projects furnished both a source of income and the possibility of local political power. But rising interest and influence among middling townspeople often brought with it conflict over whose urban agenda should prevail and, ultimately, who should govern.[29] Like their English compatriots, Charleston's elite and middling sort both embraced the cause of civic improvement, with the consequence of their enthusiasm being the extension of such clashes to this New World town. Then, as middling townsmen quickly linked the failures of the governing elite on the civic stage with their perceived deficiencies as leaders in the imperial arena, these provincial disagreements became an important motivation behind radical protest after 1764.

This study of Charleston's era as a provincial British Atlantic town begins with an investigation of the forces that converged to bring it into being before 1740. Placing the well-known story of the discovery and rise of plantation agriculture alongside other natural and human forces, in chapter 1 I trace how, despite Carolina's uncertain start, urban settlement was a central aspect of the colony's character right from its very beginnings. I then go on to focus on the economic, social, cultural, and political aspects of Charleston's growing influence after 1740.

Turning first to the town's marketplaces, in chapter 2 I explore Charleston's maturation as a provincial commercial hub. Favoring the town over rural commercial outlets in their consumption habits, South Carolinians from across the Low Country sponsored the development of Charleston into a marketplace capable of fulfilling their material needs. In response to these demands, tradesfolk set up in large numbers, creating an urban economy in which imported British goods and locally manufactured wares combined to answer the needs of the local population. Increasing its influence over the circulation of goods in the Lower South as it grew in stature, Charleston became even more important as it developed a range of marketplaces attractive to every type of consumer. Like its provincial counterparts elsewhere, the town engrossed trade by offering outlets as diverse as open-air markets, auctions, luxury shops, warehouses, and street-traders, where every South Carolinian had the opportunity to trade in any sort of goods. By becoming the epicenter of market activity, the urban marketplace also came to influence the commercial customs of the Low Country, introducing newer, and typically urban, relationships among buyers and sellers. Ultimately, the story of Charleston's commercial rise was as important as the influence of the area's staple crop over the dimensions of the region's marketplaces.

Chapter 3 continues the investigation of Charleston's economic sway with a look into the urban construction industry and housing market. Asking how houses and commercial premises got built, how they were bought and sold, and who owned them, I show how the business of building a town brought wealth and innovation to the region and economic opportunity to particular groups within South Carolina society. Specifically, with Charleston's emergence as the region's commercial hub came a demand for urban homes and business premises. Ready to answer this demand were tradesmen in the building industry who, by purchasing slaves, adapted to the local labor market and created sizeable business concerns. Soon, Charleston's construction sector was industrialized to a level similar to its British provincial counterparts, with wealthy general contractors running enterprises that not only undertook to build for particular clients but also raised houses on a speculative basis with the aim of turning a profit. These construction entrepreneurs were joined by those Charlestonians outside of the trade who realized that buying rental properties in the city represented a rewarding and secure investment. Overall, Charleston's physical expansion created new sources of wealth in South Carolina and stimulated economic development in areas entirely outside of the plantation sector.

Although property speculation and landlord activity proved attractive to Charleston's seasonal planter population, it was an economic opportunity especially favored by the urban tradesmen who lived and worked in Charleston all year around. The most successful among these tradesmen showed a penchant for buying up multiple city lots, transforming themselves into the landlords of wealthy planters and poor whites alike. Chapter 4 focuses on this group, embarking on the story of how Charleston's expansion supported the emergence of a middling sort and hence the creation of a particular class structure in the Low Country. However, investment in urban property was merely one element in the economic portfolio of those "independent trading households" who used the talents of the entire family and its slaves to exploit the opportunities of the urban environment. A principal characteristic of this middling sort—in Charleston and in other English-speaking provincial towns—was its ability to innovate in the main business while transcending the boundaries of the trade of the male household head, achieving financial security through involvement in an array of commercial pursuits. In the process of exploiting the urban economy in this way, middling households forged economic and social ties with one another, eventually coalescing into a distinct group whose urban-centric economic goals simultaneously bound them together and differentiated them from the wealthier planter-merchants above and the poorer whites and free blacks below.

The distinctiveness of this middling class was also expressed in the cultural arena, and chapter 5 explores how Charleston, as a British Atlantic provincial town, facilitated the emergence of separate cultural identities among middling, elite, and poorer colonists. Although Charleston was a stage on which elites were able to trumpet their successful adherence to certain metropolitan standards of gentility, it was equally a landscape that aided the creation of a provincial gentility—one that reflected the identity of planters as a distinct provincial elite in a larger British Atlantic world. The town's tradespeople and its special landscapes were the chief assistants in the creation of this provincial gentility. Some tradespeople were then happy to participate in the genteel lifestyle that they sold, but others preferred to take advantage of the flexibility of the urban environment to pursue the values and community that they had forged through work. Thus, Charleston's middling sorts became more distinctive when they favored charitable societies and dissenting religious values over balls and drinking clubs. Ultimately, Charleston fostered the creation of a plethora of urban cultures that rubbed up against each other in the close confines of the cityscape—a situation that reflected the cultural environment of other towns in the British Atlantic.

Friction also characterized the political environment fostered by the town, a topic addressed in chapter 6. Historians have typically viewed Charleston as the seat of a colonial assembly that, in equal measure, promoted harmony among Carolinians and discord between crown and colony. Ruling elites also maintained domestic consensus as they used the construction of a clutch of prestigious public buildings—known as the "four corners of the law"—to stamp their authority on a potentially querulous slave society.[30] However, looking more closely at the process of creating and maintaining Charleston's public spaces reveals that, in the domestic political arena, elites were increasingly running up against a middling faction who had succeeded in gaining control of the instruments of urban government. Once installed on Charleston's commissions and on its grand jury, these tradesmen, who were already prominent in the town's charitable and dissenting religious scene, began to criticize the unwillingness of elites to devote time and resources to creating better order in the town. Such protests reflected the principles embraced by this group in their economic and cultural lives, bolstering their distinctive identity. At the same time, this conflict was to affect South Carolina's response to the Revolutionary crisis between 1764 and 1776, causing a rift between urban radicals and more conservative patriots over the question of the colony's reaction to British attempts to tax America.

The conclusion to this colonial story provides a brief look at the fortunes of Charleston during the Revolution and its immediate aftermath. As in rural South Carolina, war brought chaos to Charleston. In particular, the occupation of the town by the British between 1780 and 1782 neutralized its economic and political importance and divided its middling sorts. Disorder and strife continued to plague the urban community in the years immediately following the British evacuation and American victory. However, within a short time, pre-Revolutionary economic, social, cultural, and political trends reemerged, restoring Charleston to its customary role in South Carolina. Yet even as the city continued to develop along familiar lines, forces were at work elsewhere in the new state that would eventually shatter its central role. With the westward drift of settlement and the relocation of the capital to Columbia, Charleston's glory days were over. While, in the North, middle classes formed the backbone of nineteenth-century urban society, in Charleston, the middling sort became the subjects of King Cotton.

# "To plant in towns"

## Charles Towne at the Founding of Carolina

T HE NARRATIVE of Carolina's early colonization is a familiar one in the context of England's New World settlements. Although the colony took an unusually long time to achieve stability, the events, people, and processes behind its founding followed the usual trajectory of the Old World's move westward to the "empty" lands of America. Profit slowly triumphed over principle, and whites gradually accumulated control over blacks and Native Americans. Two groups of white adventurers were chiefly responsible for initiating the occupation of Carolina. The first group, an assemblage of eight Lords Proprietors who had been granted land by Charles II, was behind the logistics of settlement and the drawing up of the territory's template for government, the Fundamental Constitutions. With most of these Proprietors never visiting Carolina, however, it was up to a second collective of Europeans—mostly consisting of Englishmen with Barbadian connections, and a party of French Huguenots—to people the new colony.[1]

These early white claimants to the territory of Carolina shared the initial motivations of others who led Europe's settlement of North America. Like their compatriots, they embarked on their New World project to implement beliefs and principles that they had been unable to realize in their Old World. For Carolina's eight Proprietors, such principles, embodied by the Fundamental Constitutions, centered on emerging ideas of governance too radical to implement in England. For the colony's Huguenot settlers, arriving in waves toward the end of the seventeenth century, it was the religious toleration endorsed by the Constitutions that drew them from an intolerant Catholic France to a colony in which they could freely establish their own churches.[2]

However, those settlers with ties to the British Caribbean island of Barbados — settlers often known collectively as the Goose Creek men — were less devoted to the political or religious principles of their co-colonists. Leaving the Caribbean from a lack of economic opportunity, the Barbadians arrived in the Carolina Low Country intending to re-create the lucrative commercial society familiar to them in the empire's southernmost reaches, and also characteristic of the nearby colony of Virginia. The exclusive commitment of these men to profit clashed with the more ideological stance of the Lords Proprietors, and it was this long-running conflict that lay behind Carolina's troubled early history. Contravening the system of land distribution so that they might grab the best territories, the Goose Creek men relentlessly pursued their own agenda of settlement.

Also ignoring the Proprietor's policies and regulations concerning the Indian trade, the Barbadians chased profits through such commerce to the degree that armed conflict broke out between the two parties, reaching its zenith during the 1715 Yamassee War. Finally, the Goose Creek faction objected to the dissenting principles embodied by the Constitutions, instead seeking the primacy of their religious institutions. Receiving little support from metropolitan authorities, who were of course supportive of the Church of England, the embattled Proprietary government gradually lost ground to its opponents. With most of the original Proprietors either dead or disengaged from their colonizing project, Carolina eventually became a royal colony in 1729, with a standard system of British colonial rule through governor, royal council, and a Commons House of Assembly. Over the first half century of Carolina's settlement, principles of political experimentation and religious freedom had largely lost out to the profit motive and the might of England's official church.[3]

The quest for riches also triumphed when colonists confronted the need for labor on their extensive new plantations. With the experience of previous English settlers in New England, the Caribbean, and the Chesapeake at hand, Carolina's Proprietors had planned for a colony built on long-term settlement and cultivation of the land rather than on the easy extraction of mineral wealth. Thus, on arrival, the majority of the colonists got down to the business of commercial agriculture. In this task, the Barbadian settlers found particular success, not only because they brought with them knowledge about cultivating crops in a hot climate, but also because they imported the enslaved Africans necessary to undertake the hard project of improving the "wilderness." Quite unusual in the British American context, Carolina was a colony based on slave labor from its very beginning, and, as successive historians have documented, Africans were a critical component of Low Country society from founding onwards. As expert keepers of livestock, and as essential hands in the production of naval stores such as tar, pitch, and staves, slaves were central to the range of economic activities that kept the colony afloat in its first decades. While their precise role is hotly debated, it is also clear that slaves were critical to the successful cultivation of rice—the crop that after 1700 made Carolina a success despite the political instability that had initially threatened to destroy the enterprise.[4]

Although the narrative of Carolina's settlement had its particularities, in the end the precedence of profit over principles placed the colony in the mainstream of colonial British American society. And along with this triumph of materialism came a familiar power dynamic between Carolina's European settlers and the nonwhite people with whom they shared their new world. Initially, Native Americans proved to be more than a match for white settlers. However, disease, faltering supplies of deerskins, and indebtedness to traders meant that, following the Yamassee War of 1715, Europeans in the Low Country were able to pursue their economic goals with less heed to the wishes of Catawbas or Cherokees. As Native Americans retreated westward, African slaves came to be the predominant nonwhite presence. With their knowledge of rice cultivation and their perceived ability to thrive in a subtropical climate, blacks were condemned to a lifetime of bondage so that their white masters might enjoy the status of mainland America's wealthiest residents. Slaves nevertheless managed to carve out areas of economic and cultural autonomy for themselves, in 1739 even mounting the sizeable Stono Rebellion. Reaction to the uprising by the government in Charles Towne, however, resulted in a new slave code and the brutal repression of any transgressions of whites' authority. As had already occurred in many other coastal regions of colonial America, the English soon found themselves in better control of their domain.[5]

What was unusual about Carolina throughout these first decades of its existence were the many different milieux that influenced the nature of the colonizing enterprise. In most of England's territories the natural environment proved to be the principal force acting upon the settlers, since (in contrast to the Iberian model of colonization) the metropolitan government did not direct the actions of colonists or insist upon the creation of urban settlements. In the Low Country, the "virgin" territories claimed by the Lords Proprietors as their own when they received their charter from Charles II in 1663 played a major part in dictating the direction of the enterprise. This potential agricultural land held a powerful attraction for those settlers who had made the journey to these southern reaches of England's New World. The process of acquiring that land from its Native occupants then figured largely in white–Indian conflicts and, once secured, these tracts proved to be the route to wealth for those Carolinians able to survive the ravages of the environment long enough to develop their plantations.

A second influence, the Old World background of England's first adventurers, was also vital to the nature of their initial colonizing efforts. In Virginia, the economic expectations of the metropolitan Virginia Company directed the pursuits of Jamestown's inhabitants. In New England and Pennsylvania, ideologies and ideas formed by founders in the Old World were highly influential to the colonies' first decades. And as L. H. Roper has recently highlighted, events on both sides of the Atlantic influenced the decisions made by Carolina's Proprietors about their new territory. Both the claustrophobia and the competition of life in the Court and Parliament of the king, and the imagined tracts of empty, fertile, lands loomed large for the Earl of Shaftesbury and his fellow Proprietors as they shaped their colonial enterprise.[6]

More unusual in the English context, however, there was yet another backdrop for the opening acts of Carolina's history: the urban setting of Charles Towne.[7] This town—or, rather, village, in the decades before 1700—struggled as much as Carolina's first plantations. Once relocated to its final home at Oyster Point, it had streets and squares but few people willing to make a home on them. It had a harbor, but few ships arrived to weigh anchor in it. However, Charles Towne was the center of the Goose Creek men's political power in the young colony, and also the hub of the small amount of transatlantic and domestic trade being conducted in these early years. When new settlers arrived, they came to Charles Towne. Early on, the town would also be home to the first churches established by Anglicans, Huguenots, and Congregationalists. The urban environment continued to increase in importance as it received support from certain groups of settlers and, eventually, encouragement from a strengthening economy. Together, these stimuli colluded to make Charles Towne a central force in the colony of South Carolina by the 1740s.

Although there was much that was typical about Carolina's founding, the colony was thus distinctive because its beginning featured a triangle formed by rural New World, town, and mother country. Right from the start, all three of these locations would interact—as would the humans who moved through them—to create the character of Carolina. The conflict between English Proprietors and New World settlers is well documented, as are the processes by which these settlers established a rural plantation economy. Less understood is Charles Towne's place in the narrative of Carolina's founding and of the colony's growth.

## Laying the Groundwork for Urbanism

How did South Carolina end up with a town at its heart, when its close neighbors, the Chesapeake colonies of Maryland and Virginia, had remained predominantly rural? The answer did not lie solely with the nature of the colony's staple economy. Before an economic raison d'être had been found for Carolina, an urban aspect to the seventeenth-century colony was secured by the beliefs and preferences of its founders. Responsibility lay, first, with the most enthusiastic Proprietor, Anthony Ashley Cooper, the first Earl of Shaftesbury. Shaftesbury had taken less interest in the enterprise at its inception, but toward the end of the 1660s he proved himself to be its strongest cheerleader, hoping that a successful colonization project might become his legacy. The major manifestation of Shaftesbury's rejuvenated enthusiasm was his authorship of a founding document for the colony. When they drew up their Fundamental Constitutions in 1669, the Earl of Shaftesbury and John Locke set in motion a second beginning for Carolina. Although moves toward settlement had begun in 1663, the Constitutions offered a new template for the basic structures of government and society in the colony. Among early America's more idealistic founding documents, the Constitutions were used by Shaftesbury and Locke to test out radical ideas of governance. Designed to promote an ordered, yet enlightened, society of nobles and commoners, of the sort endorsed by the neo-Harringtonians, the document envisaged a social structure that had proved unrealizable in England, even through civil war. However, Shaftesbury's Fundamental Constitutions were innovative for another, less commented on, reason: they were the first English colonial founding documents to make secular urban settlement an obligatory feature of a society. The Constitutions thus became the vehicle by which their authors might impose their belief in the importance of the modern town on an entirely rural New World.[8]

Shaftesbury's commitment to urban settlement, and the reasons behind it, emerged first in his private letters. There, the earl explicitly stressed that Carolina adventurers should "plant in towns," a form of settlement that, he believed, would immediately make his colony into a more successful and civilized society than Virginia, which he judged inferior to New England precisely because it lacked urban places. As he wished his towns to serve both a social and an economic purpose in an otherwise "uncivilized" New World, Shaftesbury further expressed the desire that urban settlement should conform to the model offered by the classical town, which at this time was believed to be the most advanced example available. Thus, when mulling over his plans for Charles Towne, the earl thought carefully about the width of the streets and alleys, and the size of house plots, explaining that although buildings would be "never so mean and thin at first yet as the town increases in riches and people the void spaces will be filled up and the buildings will grow more beautiful."[9]

The Fundamental Constitutions then elaborated on Shaftesbury's privately articulated wishes. In a departure from other such documents of the era, which were preoccupied with the simple establishment of settlement or the achievement of a specific religious goal, the Constitutions stipulated that it was of "great consequence to the plantation that port-towns should be built and preserved." This regulation was given economic support by the granting of an urban monopoly on the landing of imported goods, with further authority stemming from a structure of incorporated government for each town. Every settler who was granted a rural tract would also receive a piece of urban land in Carolina's chief town. At the same time, the colony's High Steward's Court was given the power for "setting out and appointing places for towns to be built on in the precincts, and the prescribing and determining the figure and bigness of the said towns, according to such models as the said court shall order; contrary or differing from which models it shall not be lawful for any one to build in any town."[10] In short, the creation of classical, regular towns with political and economic importance was a central element in the vision of the Fundamental Constitutions' authors. Because Shaftesbury believed that the cooperation of farmers and city traders was the recipe for a successful Carolina, he was determined to legislate against an entirely rural settlement that would only serve as a "hindrance to towns."[11]

A primary motivation for Charles Towne's creation, Shaftesbury's strong interest in towns was continually reinforced by his metropolitan experiences. Until the summer of 1666, keeping a place at court and handling its many intrigues were foremost in Shaftesbury's mind. In the autumn of that year, however, other preoccupations of Londoners were suddenly eclipsed by the devastation caused by the Great Fire. The effects of this inferno, and of the plague that accompanied it, are legendary in the annals of English history. Thirteen thousand buildings burned, leaving many homeless and destitute. Preachers bemoaned Charles II's profligate ways, blaming him for provoking God into punishing his kingdom. It comes as no surprise, therefore, that the Great Fire had direct consequences for Shaftesbury's personal situation. The earl was entirely caught up in the circumstances created by the disaster, and in the immediate aftermath he was kept busy drafting in laborers to eradicate dangerous hot embers. With fears circulating that the conflagration had been a Papist conspiracy, Shaftesbury also devoted a portion of his time to protecting a servant to the Portuguese ambassador who had been accused of starting the fire.[12]

However, it was the events following the Great Fire that really propelled Shaftesbury's urban vision: in subsequent months and years, he witnessed the creation of a brand new, modern London that transformed metropolitan society. One of the most visible benefits of reconstruction was the creation of a more classical townscape to replace the ramshackle, timbered buildings that had been destroyed by the fire. Legislated into existence by the 1667 "Act for Rebuilding the city of London" (subsequently followed by a further act of 1670), this classical vision was an improvement already accessible to Shaftesbury as he drew up his Constitutions. The London Act boldly declared, "in regard that building with brick is not only more comely and durable, but also more safe against future perils of fire," that all edifices should henceforth be made from "brick or stone." Finishing with detailed instructions on the desired mathematical relationship between house and street, the act was replete with the precise guidelines needed to achieve the symmetry and uniformity required by the classical home and townscape.[13] Before London's rebuilding had even begun, the English statute books revealed to Shaftesbury the nuts and bolts of a "modern" city. It was in the light of such developments that Shaftesbury elaborated on his initial 1669 urban ideal for Carolina with the 1680 implementation of his "Grand Modell," a town plan whose regularity clearly drew on the principles guiding the capital's Act for Rebuilding and the work of its chief supervisor, Sir Christopher Wren.

Shaftesbury's continued commitment to urbanism was also a reflection of the fact that the reconstruction of London had proven to be a dramatic stimulus to economic growth and development in the metropole. In order to raise the new types of building enumerated on his statute book, Charles II was forced to end the monopoly of some of the London guilds, thus setting in motion major economic change among the capital's building trades. Seeing a free market opportunity, tradesmen flooded into London, refashioning themselves as construction entrepreneurs by buying leaseholds on mortgage, then developing the land with housing on a speculative basis. Led by these "general contractors," core working practices among all of England's building artisans began to change. Whereas landowners had previously called in individual bricklayers, carpenters, and plasterers on discrete accounts, master craftsmen made themselves into the managers of extensive projects at their own financial risk, and ultimately for their own profit.

By the first decades of the eighteenth century, contemporaries lavished praise on the new urban landscape. Laid out before Shaftesbury's eyes was the stimulation that an expanding town could bring to an economy.[14]

Between the settlement of Virginia, New England, and Jamaica, and that of Carolina, the Great Fire helped in England's transformation from a struggling postwar society into a cultural and economic leader. Such transformations encouraged Shaftesbury to transfer an idea to the New World that was already being successfully realized in the Old. In the belief that towns might do for his society what they were doing for Restoration England, the Proprietor wished to extend to his Carolina the benefits of the revivified urban environment that surrounded him in London. Hence, rather than pursuing the example of his predecessors, Shaftesbury set an example for his successors. Most notable among his followers was William Penn, whose 1681 "Charter for the Province of Pennsylvania" showed a parallel concern for towns as political and economic centers in his own, Quaker enterprise. A wealthy Londoner, Penn had also experienced the Great Fire and witnessed firsthand the revival of the city following the destruction, and although urban development in his Pennsylvania colony ultimately followed a different trajectory, the roots of town settlement there were embedded in a similar background.[15]

Shaftesbury's idea of an urban Carolina was critical to the creation of Charles Towne, but the Proprietor's distance from his New World territory meant that he lacked the ability to take practical steps toward his vision. Fortunately, there were others among the colony's early settlers who were willing to lend their support to the urban project. Early on, the arrival of the dynamic Governor John Archdale in 1695 resulted in the implementation of new policies to encourage urban growth through "sobriety and vertue as well as trade," an aim clearly founded on Shaftesbury's earlier ideas that towns were not merely central to the economy, but also to society.[16] At the same time, Carolina's initial colonists were also ready to see the logic and the necessity of urban settlement. Although few among these early settlers were familiar with recent developments in London, they had experienced the effects of growing towns in their own colony or country.

Carolina's Barbadian immigrants, for example, came from a society that was home to one of the British New World's largest towns. In 1680, Bridgetown had 3,000 residents, but it was subsequently to experience its major period of growth, and by 1712 its inhabitants numbered over 10,000. In the course of three decades, the town had become Barbados's primary commercial entrepôt, hosting a large community of merchants, maritime workers, and service providers. It was thus little surprise that Carolina's Goose Creek men further guaranteed Charles Towne's future when, rather than allow the deerskin trade to be conducted in the rural parts of the colony, they pushed through a 1707 act to concentrate it in the colonial capital. This act had the effect of privileging the role of specialist urban merchants who could mediate between the town and the colony's interior to collect and ship skins, thus securing the fortunes of a notable proportion of Charles Towne's population. As a result, over half a million skins left the colony through the town between 1706 and 1715.

Numbers in the town were also dramatically boosted by the arrival of a large number of French Huguenot refugees. With many urban-dwelling craftsmen and merchants in their number, the Protestants began arriving as early as 1679. However, the largest influx came in 1687, when six hundred arrived in Charles Towne. Some settlers targeted the French Santee area some sixty miles north of the town, drawing up detailed plans for their own urban settlement—Jamestown—on the river's edge. Most Huguenot merchants and tradesmen, though, chose to base themselves in an existing urban environment where opportunities for trade were more established.[17]

Soon, the French Protestant community had built their principal place of worship in Charles Towne and had begun to achieve prominence on the commercial scene. Tradesmen like Huguenot watchmaker and jeweler Nicholas de Longuemare placed their faith in the young urban economy, setting up some of the town's earliest businesses. De Longuemare's records of his work between 1698 and 1707 show that he labored alone repairing the clocks and watches of the Low Country's residents, making sets of mourning rings, gold buttons, and brass weights, and fashioning the occasional set of cutlery. Work came into his shop only sporadically, with a "busy" month yielding four customers and a quiet one none at all. De Longuemare dealt with this low demand by also establishing himself in the business of silk importation and by developing a cattle ranch on a nearby suburban tract. Although demand for his luxury services obviously remained weak, De Longuemare nevertheless stayed on in Charles Towne. Many of these early townspeople further demonstrated their commitment to the urban environment when they invested in the lots marked out in Shaftesbury's Grand Modell. Early records show that 161 settlers purchased 236 lots before 1700. The largest investor was politician, merchant, and Barbados man, Jonathan Amory, who owned seven of the town's more than three hundred tracts. Huguenot settlers also showed themselves to be eager buyers, with at least seven investing in town lands.[18]

Through the actions of the Proprietors, and the predilections of settlers who subsequently came to the colony, urbanism was a reality in South Carolina from the first decades of its history. Before a successful staple economy existed, Shaftesbury had conceived of a society civilized by the presence of towns. Working in line with a growing urban movement in England, and implementing his ideas in the light of the experiences of previous New World settlement enterprises, the Proprietor was successful in ensuring that his beloved Carolina would have an urban character to complement its rural focus. Very early on, Shaftesbury's plans were supported by the choices of those French and Barbadian settlers who came to Carolina, and even though both groups of incomers found little to their liking in the Fundamental Constitutions, they were nevertheless sympathetic to Shaftesbury's urban vision.

## The Logic of Urban Growth

Elsewhere in the British Atlantic world, the efforts of men like the first Earl of Shaftesbury, the determination of town residents, and favorable economic conditions, meant that at the dawn of the eighteenth century, the drive for urban renewal was spreading rapidly. In Britain itself, provincial towns such as Warwick and Northampton built on the innovations ushered in by London's Great Fire. Touring the nation between 1690 and 1700, Celia Fiennes was often astonished by the advanced state of the provincial urban landscape. On her arrival in Newcastle, Nottingham, and Warwick, Fiennes meticulously detailed the broad streets, the brick homes, and the classical house fronts that she repeatedly encountered. Across the Atlantic, this dynamism was matched by Charles Towne's immediate successor, Philadelphia, where there were already 2,500 residents in 1700. Contemporary paintings of Penn's capital depicted an impressive cityscape complete with finely conceived places of worship and sumptuous town houses. English Caribbean towns like Bridgetown, Barbados, were also now thriving, even though the temporary nature of the built environment often failed to reflect the new wealth of their inhabitants.[19]

In all of these places, urban growth was underwritten by a strong economy. Bridgetown's rapid ascent had come in the wake of Barbados's sugar revolution, the increase in trade of the staple through the port prompting the expansion of the urban service sector. A lively trading economy meant that Philadelphia had garnered almost 8,000 inhabitants by 1734, climbing to 9,500 by 1741. At the same time, between 1650 and 1750, the urban population of England increased by some 5 percent as the early stages of industrial revolution and the expansion of the empire stimulated town and city economies. In particular, western coastal cities like Glasgow and Liverpool were beginning to forge ahead on the back of the tobacco and slave trades, and Manchester flourished as its textile industries grew. In both Britain's provinces and in colonial America, strong economies firmly rooted in international trade or domestic manufacturing had proved to be the key to urban growth.[20]

Certainly, there were signs from 1700 onward that Charles Towne was not untouched by this transatlantic movement for change. Early urban improvements came as Carolina's Proprietors gradually yielded in their struggle with the colony's other main governing faction, the Goose Creek men. An important by-product of the growing supremacy of the latter group was the establishment of the Anglican religion as the official faith of the colony in 1701. In legally asserting the dominance of the Church of England, colonists created a situation in which religious government would stand side-by-side with secular bodies in the rule of Carolina. Initially, the victory of the Goose Creek men in the spiritual arena had little impact on Charles Towne. However, in 1706, five years after the drawing out of parishes, the assembly moved to brand this Anglican superiority into the townscape in the most obvious way possible, by establishing a committee to raise money for "a new church built of brick in Charles Town."[21] The church brought to the Low Country the elements of a new classical style of ecclesiastical architecture, pioneered by Sir Christopher Wren with his rebuilding of London's City Churches and perpetuated in the first decade of the eighteenth century with the completion of St. Paul's Cathedral and the commissioning by Queen Anne of a further fifty new churches.[22]

Yet, while the strength of the Goose Creek faction introduced some "modern" features to the townscape, the party's disagreements with the Proprietary authorities simultaneously prevented further "improvements" from taking place. In 1720 the crown dispatched its first envoy, Governor Francis Nicholson, to take control of the colony, which, after the coup of 1719, now stood awkwardly poised between the King's rule and Proprietary regulation. Nicholson was determined to bring Charles Towne's authorities into line with up-to-date modes of civic government. As a result, in 1722 he proposed to incorporate the town and appoint a self-perpetuating council of nineteen men, who would regulate its commerce and its population. At this juncture, however, viewing Nicholson's efforts as part of a ploy to fleece them of control over the colony's affairs, the Goose Creek men succeeded in having the incorporation act declared illegal by the Board of Trade. Charles Towne thus remained unincorporated and outside of the customary template for governance of the English-speaking urban environment.[23]

However, a lack of good government was far from the only disadvantage still facing Charles Towne. Carolina's climate and its numerous native peoples proved to be a further stumbling block to Europeans' ability to develop their town. The colony suffered one of the worst disease environments in mainland British America; between 1680 and 1720 it was rare for adult men to survive past sixty and common for them not even to make it into their fifties. Within the town itself, disease and disaster ravaged those settlers plucky enough to pursue their livings there. In 1698, first smallpox, then an earthquake, and finally a large fire, decimated Charles Towne. With barely a moment to recover from this first onslaught, townspeople were subsequently hit with a yellow fever epidemic, and a damaging hurricane in 1699. Efforts by the Proprietors to encourage more settlers from Britain failed as stories about the poor prospects on offer filtered back to the Old World.

At the beginning of the eighteenth century white settlers then faced further challenges when Carolina's Native people confronted Europeans' growing control of trade and territory. In 1715 the outbreak of the Yamassee War caused some one hundred settlers to be massacred at Beaufort, and hundreds more to abandon their new plantations. As Ashley's "civilizing" Grand Modell was hemmed in by ever more substantial fortifications against Native attack, the conflict drove home Charles Towne's colonial situation. Rather than being able to focus on the raising of classical brick townhouses or the paving of broad streets, Charles Towne's inhabitants were instead throwing what resources they had into the building of palmetto-log batteries, which would have been visible from most points within the town and hence a daily reminder of their fragile situation.[24]

Political conflict, Native American determination to resist European dominance, disease, and disaster all intervened to prevent growth in Charles Towne's population. Temporarily, these circumstances also stymied existing settlers' efforts to build a strong economy, which in turn meant that demand for town-based services remained low. During the first twenty or so years of settlement, Carolina's inhabitants made their livings through two principal pursuits, neither of which resulted in substantial levels of trade and wealth. First, the raising of livestock and the beginning of a trade with the West Indies in beef and pork helped some settlers to get on their feet. Whites were assisted in this pursuit by the increasing number of black Carolinians, many of whom were old hands at the open-grazing style of cattle farming most suited to the untamed Low Country landscape. These activities were accompanied by the post-1680 growth of the Indian trade, which provided Carolina merchants with deerskins for export to Britain. Such pursuits kept colonists afloat but

Table 1.1

**Number of tradespeople arriving in Charleston, by decade, 1670–1739**

| Trade | 1670–79 | 1680–89 | 1690–99 | 1700–09 | 1710–19 | 1720–29 | 1730–39 |
|---|---|---|---|---|---|---|---|
| Blacksmith | 1 | — | 6 | 3 | 1 | 6 | 8 |
| Bricklayer | 2 | 1 | 1 | 5 | 1 | 6 | 14 |
| Carpenter | 10 | 5 | 13 | 10 | 11 | 27 | 52 |
| Gunsmith | 1 | — | 2 | 1 | 1 | 3 | 3 |
| Shipwright | 2 | 2 | 4 | 4 | 3 | 8 | 15 |
| Cabinetmaker | — | — | 1 | — | 1 | 2 | 8 |
| Coachmaker | — | — | — | — | 1 | 1 | 1 |
| Clocksmith | — | 1 | — | — | 1 | 2 | 4 |
| Silversmith | — | — | 3 | — | 3 | 3 | 13 |

*Source:* Index of Artisans, Museum of Early Southern Decorative Arts, Winston-Salem, NC. First mention of each Charleston artisan included in this database was noted by trade and decade.

did not lead to spectacular riches. With the colony lacking exportable goods, the quantity of trade conducted with England and the West Indies through Charles Towne failed to reach the scale of that being conducted in colonial British America's other young towns. Overall, cheap land remained one of the few reasons for settlers to go to Carolina—a place where one stood as much chance of dying of tropical fevers as of making a living.[25]

With little demand for the services of an urban economy, town businesses remained small and simple in structure, not expanding beyond the proportions of de Longuemare's enterprise, and certainly not embracing the innovations apparent on the London scene after the Great Fire. Few tradespeople were attracted to Charles Towne, and its economy was not lively enough to encourage any speculative building by general contractors (see table 1.1). Townspeople looking to build—like the executors of Elizabeth Sindrey's estate—were forced to direct the project themselves using any skilled men they could find. Thus, the labor required to build Sindrey's shops and warehouses came from individual indentured servants and slaves belonging to William Rhett, a family friend. White carpenters Charles Crouch, Matthew Toole, and Charles Brewer labored alongside hired slaves following the orders of the Sindrey executors. Materials were purchased by the executors and given to the builders, who were paid according to the number of days that they had worked on site. The methods used to build the Sindrey shops and houses were strongly reminiscent of increasingly extinct British custom—not of new innovation. No written plans of the proposed buildings were mentioned, and no general contractor or architect was employed to organize the labor or buy the raw materials for the project. Instead, William Rhett took on the management of the building himself.[26]

It was during Charles Towne's earliest, difficult decades that some tradesmen chose to abandon urban settlement altogether, quickly giving it up in favor of a planting career. Like the other white settlers who were starting to arrive in the Low Country, they had realized that cheap land held out the best prospects of advancement. Shipwright Percival Pawley was one such arrival. Pawley first appeared in the Low Country in 1698, and was distinguished in records as a shipwright of Charles Towne. However, the precarious urban economy, and the sorry state of shipbuilding in the province, led him almost immediately to acquire a series of rural tracts in Berkeley County, and by 1714 the former shipwright was describing himself as a planter—a status then readily claimed by his descendants. As these former craftsmen, professionals, and merchants left the town for the countryside, Charles Towne became devoid of the sorts of people whom Daniel Defoe described as men and women of a "middle station"—people who formed the bulk of city-dwelling, entrepreneurial inhabitants driving the expansion of the urban economy in Britain and taking advantage of the opportunities on offer in colonial America's more thriving cities of Boston, Philadelphia, and New York.[27]

For a while, at the turn of the seventeenth century, Charles Towne's expansion was slow and halting, and the town remained unremarkable on the English Atlantic urban scene. As the eighteenth century advanced, however, greater economic stability came to Charles Towne. At last, circumstances were conspiring to support the growth of the urban settlement promoted by Shaftesbury and many of Carolina's settlers. Now, the young staple economy provided encouragement to the project started by the Proprietor. The 1715 Yamassee War had certainly hemmed in Charles Towne's residents, but it also punctuated the end of a decade that had generally seen more economic growth than any period of Carolina's history until then. Across the turn of the eighteenth century, exploration of the possibilities of cheap land, coupled with the skills of black slaves, set whites on the road toward a successful agricultural economy. After 1695 land grants increased rapidly in number, as did the numbers of Africans being imported into the Low Country. By the late 1690s rice had risen to become Carolina's chief commodity, and between 1698 and 1702 exports of the crop experienced a 20.7 percent annual compound growth rate. Rice production continued to expand at an astonishing pace until 1740. The take-off in rice exports came at the same time as the Board of Trade's decision to offer bounties on naval stores, extending a financial lifeline to Carolinians who had ample natural resources to supply the timber, pitch, and tar valued by the mother country. Thus, the 1730s also saw further growth in exports of turpentine, rosin, corn, peas, leather, and lumber. Because a large proportion of these goods were being sent not to the metropole, but to elsewhere in the British American world, Charles Towne was also becoming a stopping-off point in the colonial coastwise trade. Sides of leather went to Boston, Philadelphia, and the West Indies, and barrel staves and other processed timber kept Jamaica, Barbados, and Antigua in building and packing materials.[28]

Increased exports also made for a rise in the quantity of goods flowing into Carolina through Charles Towne. The period between 1738 and 1742 witnessed the highest value of imports per capita of the white population ever—over £6 sterling, as opposed to the low of £2.92 twenty years previously. Town-dwelling merchants were now beginning to see their profits rise as ever wealthier planters clamored for the luxuries and necessities that they were bringing to the colony. Few commodities were more sought after by free whites than the African slaves who were now arriving in Charles Towne in ever greater numbers. From the point at which naval records commence, in 1717, until commerce was temporarily halted in 1738, the number of people arriving from Africa and the West Indies increased constantly.[29]

This traffic in slaves doubly bolstered Charles Towne's position in the Low Country, for as well as making money for white merchants and planters, it increased the number of Carolinians with a preference for the urban environment. As they were sold on to eager plantation owners at Charles Towne's wharves, most Africans' first experience of the town was brief and unhappy. Yet, from an early stage, this rising black population showed a strong determination to evade the controls put in place by their plantation masters, something they could best do by going to Charles Towne and using its marketplaces and social spaces to carve out some economic and cultural independence. As a result, the black population of Charles Towne doubled between

1690 and 1700, and from that point onward, took off on an upward curve. The authorities were quick to appreciate such developments. Indeed, their complaints about the slaves' predilection for town life only served to underline how blacks were supporting the town's growth, as they frequented it to trade goods, to socialize, and to exchange information.[30]

Accompanying the increased pace of economic life came a greater demand for the goods and services that customarily congregated in the urban environment. Such demand was given a boost by one of the greatest misfortunes to befall eighteenth-century Charles Towne—the destructive fire of December 1740. With the need to rebuild shops, homes, and warehouses destroyed by the inferno came plentiful employment for house carpenters and bricklayers arriving in the colony. Some town merchants, desperate to get their businesses back on course, exhorted metropolitan correspondents to send men in these trades out to Carolina as quickly as possible.[31]

However, more steady demand stemmed from the increased volume of shipping in the port, as the arrival and departure of a vessel potentially required shipwrights and carpenters to repair the hull, blockmakers and blacksmiths to fix pumps and metalwork, butchers to supply food for the crew, and sailmakers and ropemakers to repair torn sails and worn rigging. At the same time, those engaged in trade needed places to store their wares and to house themselves and their families. Charles Towne's skilled workers were particularly well placed to respond to this increased demand because of the easy availability of slave labor. All tradesmen who left inventories during the 1730s owned one or more slaves, and by the early 1740s many had found prosperity through their skilled, chattel workers. Charles Towne's white shipbuilders were especially quick to recognize the advantages that accompanied slave ownership, explaining how they had "with care and pains . . . trained up those slaves to be useful to them in the exercise of their trade, and to be necessary for the support of them and their families, when by age or infirmity they became incapable of labour." When challenged by the ruling authorities (during a dispute about unfair working practices) about the disadvantages brought to bear on non-slaveholding shipwrights, they asserted that, given the quantity of naval and merchant vessels now constantly occupying Charles Towne's busy port, "there was business for three times the number of ship carpenters." By the 1730s the number of free white traders working in port-related trades had begun to increase, their businesses also growing larger in size.[32]

Indeed, there is much to suggest that during the 1730s and early 1740s settlers were demanding more of the Charles Towne economy than it could provide; urban growth was having difficulty in keeping pace with the colony's dramatic economic success. First, the import sector of the urban marketplace was not mature enough to achieve the smooth delivery of required goods to customers, and such erratic linkages caused great frustration among local buyers and sellers. Merchant Robert Pringle complained that the town had had "no ship from London for these four months past and severall articles of dry goods are very scarce at present." The trader later reiterated the point to his brother, Andrew, in London, observing that with poor trading connections and a quickly expanding population, "there never was so great a demand or encouragement for dry goods." The lack of wares available for purchase was further compounded by transatlantic misunderstandings that resulted in the export of the wrong types of product to the Low Country. The mismatched market meant that Pringle's correspondence was replete with complaints about winter woolens too warm for a subtropical climate and beaver hats sent when the market was already flooded with similar products.[33]

Since many sectors of Charles Towne's domestic economy were equally lacking in their ability to answer the demands made by the increased number of customers, when imported items were scarce or unsuitable, consumers had to do without the essentials of life. The few tallow chandlers and soap boilers working in Charles Towne at this time could not fulfill demand, and colonists were left unwashed and in the dark when supplies of soap and candles failed to arrive from New England. Likewise, customs lists of this era show that for every finished good that was exported to the colony from Britain (stockings, bridles, and metalwares, for example), there was another item (bricks, fabric, window panes, paint components) that needed processing in Charles Towne by artisans who were still relatively scarce. During the 1730s, for example, only fourteen bricklayers arrived in the town to service the population.[34]

Faced with such shortages, Low Country settlers complained about the exorbitant prices they had to pay for the poorly made goods, bad service, and tardy delivery of the few wares produced by Charles Towne's craftsmen. Merchant Robert Pringle had attempted to have a suit of clothes made for himself in the town during the 1730s, but resorted to his London tailor because "the workmanship [was] very bad." Initially, there were many occasions on which a Charleston manufacturer lost out to a London colleague when elite settlers who could afford to send to Britain for goods placed their orders in the metropole. As late as 1743, residents were still complaining that the town lacked even the most basic of artisan services. In that year, Pringle again suffered, when a shipment of grindstones arrived in Charles Towne with no holes cut into the center; as there was no one in the town with the skills or tools to cut them, they were rendered useless.[35]

However, the 1740s saw the number of tradesmen arriving in the town increasing dramatically, their presence making a big difference to the depth and breadth of the Charles Towne economy. Tradesmen who had previously been able to make a living even though they had offered substandard goods were now forced to resort to underhand tactics in order to beat off waves of new competitors. Unhappy at the arrival of a number of very able rivals, in 1739 Daniel Bourget, a baker who had for a number of years enjoyed the lion's share of trade in the town, joined with his fellow baker George Helm in a devious plan to drive the new competition out of Charles Towne. However, the scam was scuppered when Helm admitted to the *South Carolina Gazette* that

Mr. Daniel Bourget's great justice and generosity (in advertising that the price of bread having been very high he will for the future sell 3 lbs bread for 2 and 6) ought not to be forgotten, and take butterflies for angels, I here under-written do assure the publick, that the said Bourget had no other motive to be generous but this, viz., that if I would join with him in making bread so heavy, as that new beginners (of which there was two lately come in) should not be able to carry on the trade, they then must inevitably break or go off, and then, we having the whole trade in our own hands, should by degrees bring down the weight of our loaves as we should think fit.[36]

Despite the efforts of men like Bourget, Low Country customers of the 1740s increasingly found that the Charles Towne economy fulfilled their demands. Writing to a London saddler from whom he had been receiving exports, one merchant explained that "there are now severall of your trade in this town and some of them have very good business, so that there is not now the encouragement to import saddlery from England that has been formerly as they make saddles &c. in town, especially for country people cheaper than they can be imported."[37] Charles Towne—and the services it had to offer—now played a vital role in the daily life of South Carolinians.

Yet demand for services was not the only force drawing tradespeople, the backbone of urban economy and society, to Charles Towne. At this particular moment, in the 1740s, shifting local circumstances further enhanced the attractiveness of the urban environment. Most importantly, a new developmental phase in the plantation economy significantly diminished its allure to new arrivals. In the first instance, the late 1730s marked the point at which the core zone—the lands easily accessible from Charles Towne—became entirely occupied by existing settlers. Now, newcomers who wished to enter the plantation business would have to either pay the higher prices for already developed lands, or settle for a tract more than forty miles from the town, in close proximity to potentially hostile Native Americans, and a long and difficult journey from the comforts of the city. This was a situation that could easily put off less adventurous tradesmen, who now had to weigh such disadvantages against the growing potential of the urban economy.[38]

Also pushing new settlers toward the town, however, was a sharp depression in the rice economy. Following the high point of rice exports in 1740, circumstances conspired to produce a decade of stagnation and decline in the Low Country's staple sector. Compounding an already downward trend in prices after 1740, King George's War tipped the rice economy into depression, pushing up shipping costs and suppressing European demand for the commodity. With the accompanying reduction in the need for African labor, merchants in the slave-importation business also faced hard times. In such unpromising circumstances, those planter-merchants who stayed afloat did so by creating economies of scale or, as some were doing by the 1750s, diversifying their enterprises into the new crop of indigo. For newcomers to the Low Country, therefore, multiple barriers to the easy creation of a profitable plantation enterprise were now in place. No longer an easy option, agriculture favored those who had accumulated enough expertise, land, and capital to weather the crisis of the 1740s. At the same time, it appears that there was still abundant opportunity within the urban economy, which was running to catch up with the demands of those settlers who had managed to establish their rural enterprises prior to the downward turn in the staple economy. After some eighty years of settlement, circumstances were finally colluding to make Charles Towne as attractive a destination for new arrivals as its founder, Lord Ashley, had hoped it might be.[39]

Far from an ideal supported by the few, the Charles Towne of the 1740s had been transformed into a town demanded, and needed, by the majority of settlers. As a religious and cultural center, and as an economic hub for white and black South Carolinians, it was playing an ever larger role in colonists' daily lives. This was the role imagined for Charles Towne when it was conceived by the colony's Proprietors, who, immersed in England's late-seventeenth-century urban renaissance, believed that their new society would be successful only with towns at its heart. But even with the support of Shaftesbury, Carolina's Fundamental Constitutions, and the colony's settlers, Charles Towne initially foundered, even as other towns in the English (and from 1707, British) Atlantic world continued to flourish. Disease, political conflict, the strength of the Native American population, and the poverty of the early economy all colluded to prevent the town—and the colony—from enjoying the wealth characteristic of contemporary English American planta- tion societies. As such "obstacles" (as the Europeans viewed them) were over- come over the course of the eighteenth century, the colony, and the town, began to enjoy more success. With rice climbing its way up the customs lists of colonial products arriving in Britain's ports, with Carolinians consuming ever more British manufactures, and with blacks becoming an ever larger per- centage of the Low Country population, Charles Towne ascended the British Atlantic urban rankings. And as it grew in size, so South Carolina's chief town grew in stature, increasing its influence over the Low Country and carving out a place for itself in a transatlantic urban commercial system.

# 2

❧

## "A floating market"
### Commercial Growth, Urban Growth

P REOCCUPIED with his relatively new roles as monarch and as English-
man, it is unlikely that the day in 1729 when George II formally became
South Carolina's chief ruler went down in the sovereign's diary as a
noteworthy highlight of his week. More than most colonies, Carolina was a
developing territory that appeared to justify the Crown's policy of "salutary
neglect." Rice exports and slave imports had both increased with the mini-
mum of intervention from the British authorities. So, after a difficult decade
spent facing down the final challenges of a Proprietary regime, a succession of
royal governors were left in peace to tussle with a troublesome South Carolina
House of Commons. As long as rice planters continued their profitable ways,
periodic "descriptions" of the progress of the colony proved enough to keep
the empire's governing body, the Board of Trade, at bay.[1]

However, had the king availed himself of the opportunity to take a really
close look at the naval records sent to him from Charleston, or indeed to read
the lengthy reports produced by the colony's governors, he would have noticed
that South Carolina was now home to a town that was growing as rapidly as
the staple economy itself. Charleston's position, of course, was bolstered by
the residence of the governor and the regular sitting of the upper and lower
houses created to assist him in the running of South Carolina. What effect

did such a vibrant urban environment have on South Carolina's character and its path of development? Beginning with a look at the evolution of the urban marketplace, the following discussions reveal Charleston's centrality to colonial patterns of economic, social, cultural, and political change.

Charleston had, of course, found success, because it emerged as a bustling hub of trade and the beating heart of a productive staple economy with an inherent need to truck and barter its raw materials for manufactures. Transatlantic trade made Carolina and its chief town into wealthy places—among the wealthiest in Britain's first empire. Between 1730 and 1780 more than 40 percent of the South's slaves arrived at Charleston, and the majority of the Low Country's rice crop cleared through its port. On the back of increased trade and rural population growth, Charleston itself soon began to enjoy the rates of expansion that had previously been the preserve of other American, Caribbean, and British towns. Although it was never the largest town in the mainland colonies, it was during this era that Charleston's rate of growth outstripped Boston's and equaled that of New York.[2]

Because of its situation at the mouth of two large rivers, Charleston had the makings of a successful port town, and like all of its New World counterparts and some of Britain's west-facing coastal cities, transatlantic commerce made a significant contribution to its premier position in the economy. The profile of the business community evolved to meet the needs of rice growers who found face-to-face dealing in a physical marketplace to be the best way to sell their crop. This particular manner of conducting trade marked South Carolina out from its main southern counterpart, the Chesapeake, where commerce was depersonalized, as tobacco was shipped from remote plantation landings to distant Glaswegian merchants. In the Low Country, planters' more personal encounters with English factors at the town wharves directly shaped the market culture of the colony, the commercial reputation of the individual producers quickly becoming synonymous with the quality of the rice and indigo they offered.[3]

If we place this narrative of a solely staple-driven market evolution alongside the actual experiences of Charleston's residents, however, a contradiction emerges. Although Charlestonians recognized that the port had a pivotal role to play in their commercial endeavors as planters, and in the slave trade, they also knew the town to be much more than a market fashioned only by the call of the Atlantic. In his 1751 survey of South Carolina, Governor James

Glen had observed how the Cooper River that flowed from the backcountry and into the Atlantic at Charleston was "a floating market . . . bringing down country produce to town, and returning with such necessarys as are wanted by the planters."[4] It can not be assumed, however, that these "necessarys" were only rice, slaves, and British goods. Indeed, the experience of colonists like Isaac Hayne, a planter in St. Paul's Parish, reveals that Charleston was also relevant as a domestic marketplace supplying a wide range of goods and services. As well as selling his rice and buying slaves or British manufactures in town, Hayne spent much of his time in the shops of the tradesmen who renovated his coach, supplied clothing and freshly butchered beef, painted his portrait, and fixed his broken shoe buckles.[5]

Without exploring the nature of these other market activities, we cannot understand their pivotal contribution to the growth of Charleston as a commercial center. After 1740, the arrival of traders, and the willingness of residents to patronize their businesses, fashioned Charleston into a provincial service center that flourished because it was an urban nexus in a British Atlantic "empire of goods." The growth of this marketplace was partly a consequence of the increasing quantity of British imports brought to Charleston by the town's merchants and factors. However, newly imported goods formed only one facet of trade. Simultaneously, a whole host of less visible markets, centered on artisan shops, auctions, and small retailers, evolved to bring the town to prominence in South Carolina. Overall, Charleston grew because it united in one place the fruits of an emerging consumer society. Thus, the contours of its commercial scene were also determined by trade conducted in a large range of goods across an equally extensive variety of marketplaces. Although the town thrived as a port, it also became important as a regional service center with multiple layers of markets and many different marketplaces. At the same time, the eclectic nature of the interactions that took place between buyers and sellers in this domestic sphere influenced the market culture of the region, placing it squarely within a larger, British Atlantic, paradigm.[6]

## Making a Domestic Market

Between the establishment of a profitable rice trade and the dawn of Revolution in the 1760s, Charleston's marketplaces experienced continuous development. Some aspects of this change were directly linked to the transatlantic trading systems focused on the town. From the 1750s on, evolving relationships between English merchants, South Carolina planters and traders, and local factors led to shifts in the organization of Charleston's overseas trading community. Merchants became more numerous, and their businesses more diverse. Some traders specialized in the export trades to the West Indies and Southern Europe, while others focused on the slave trade. Soon, a few very successful merchants had engrossed the traffic of people from Africa. At the same time, the commerce in dry goods also became more sophisticated, and by the early 1760s merchants began to import their own cargoes of British manufactures into the Low Country.[7]

With increasing quantities of luxuries and necessities arriving from the mother country, Charleston embarked on its development as a retail center and a hub of consumption. The town was growing into a place that serviced both the needs of South Carolinians and the needs of their staple crop. This development was evident in the increasingly sophisticated stores that lined Charleston's main commercial streets—East Bay, King Street, and Tradd Street. At the end of the 1720s, for example, the premises of Scottish merchants Nisbet and Blackwood offered a relatively limited range of ready-made stockings and gloves, tea, rum, sugar, and other groceries to their customers. But as Charleston's marketplaces grew in complexity, the choice of wares in premier retail establishments became simply staggering. When he died in 1771, dry goods merchant and shopkeeper Thomas Corker had a stock valued at over SC£13,000 (£1,860 sterling).[8] Corker's wares included a breathtaking variety of silks, patterned linens, India calicoes, woolens, and Hollands; manufactures such as playing cards, buttons, bundles of violin strings, and oil cloth umbrellas; an assortment of patent medicines, such as Greenough's tincture for teeth; as well as more mundane items like pewter kitchen ware and workmen's tools.[9]

The heavy patronage of city merchants like Corker came to be a feature of the consuming lives of most wealthy South Carolinians who left a record of their purchasing habits. The daybook of James Poyas, a storekeeper, recorded the regular visits of elite Horrys and Manigaults to his establishment for all manner of dry goods and groceries. Likewise, the expenses of the Bakers of Archdale Hall, fourteen miles from Charleston, and those of the Hartleys of Buck Hall, thirty miles north of the town and close to Georgetown, demonstrated a firm reliance on a selection of town stores for everything from tea sets to soap to "coarse shoes." As more and more ships unloaded their wares at Charleston's wharves, Carolinian consumers did not wait for a country store to open up in their neighborhood, but traveled to the town where they could now present their plantation produce for sale at the wharfside and make purchases from the wide array of British manufactures on offer.[10]

Yet the presence of increased numbers of merchants, be they factors or traders on their own account, was no longer the sole raison d'être for the city's existence. Although the sectors of the urban economy involved in manufacturing and processing goods were slow to develop during the 1730s, after 1740 they began to take more responsibility for Charleston's growth. Forward linkages from a growing rural population certainly encouraged the town's expansion, but it was equally the activities of manufacturers and service providers that made the urban marketplace a reality. The role of these people in defining Charleston's markets is harder to uncover than the part played by wealthy merchants. A lack of surviving documents means that it is not possible, for example, to calculate a per capita output for tailors, cabinetmakers, or house carpenters. However, their presence was essential in a preindustrial economy that demanded the performance of a wide range of manufacturing and servicing tasks in situ.[11]

Following the take-off in the influx of skilled white settlers from the late 1730s onward, Charleston's manufacturing and service sector steadily expanded in depth and breadth, to the point where it became a central pillar in colonists' consuming lives. Where there had been about 170 overseas merchants in Charleston between 1762 and 1767, by the 1760s there were roughly 400 skilled white men and women (plus their slaves) plying their trades in the city. Atlantic commerce was no longer the only stimulus to urban growth.[12]

As Henry Laurens's plantation empire grew, for example, his business began to rely heavily on the Charleston economy for its expansion. Making a central contribution to the running of Laurens's enterprises was the ensemble of tradesmen who worked to maintain the fleet of boats used to transport rice, wood, and imported goods from plantation to town. Preparation for a voyage usually involved some repair to a vessel; in order to make the *Montague* fit for its journey to Kingston, Jamaica, in April 1769, for instance, Laurens had to call in shipwright George Powell to make a new mast, William Hinckley for new sails, Barnard Beekman for blockmaking, and butcher Jacob Boomer to lay in food for the crew. Such "refitting" was repeated, by similar groups of

Table 2.1
**Skilled whites arriving in Charleston, 1670–1790**

|      | *Luxury & Service Sector* | *Manufacturing & Construction Sector* |
|------|:-------------------------:|:-------------------------------------:|
| 1670 | 2   | 18  |
| 1680 | 4   | 10  |
| 1690 | 11  | 23  |
| 1700 | 2   | 24  |
| 1710 | 13  | 16  |
| 1720 | 21  | 51  |
| 1730 | 85  | 114 |
| 1740 | 101 | 122 |
| 1750 | 133 | 81  |
| 1760 | 225 | 130 |
| 1770 | 156 | 149 |
| 1780 | 155 | 168 |

*Sources:* Extrapolated from data contained in the Index of Artisans, Museum of Early Southern Decorative Arts, Winston-Salem, NC; issues of the *South Carolina Gazette*, 1732–1800; and Charleston County Inventories, 1670–1800, Charleston County Public Library, Charleston, SC.

Charleston tradesmen, tens of times over the course of Laurens's working life in the Low Country. At the same time, Laurens also turned to Charleston's tradesfolk to construct, as well as to repair, the infrastructure of his plantations. In the course of establishing rice production at his new Mepkin enterprise, for example, Laurens summoned skilled townspeople for help in constructing the basic machinery necessary to process the crop. In early 1771, he paid the carpenter Stephen Shrewsbury SC£200 to build a "hammer machine" at the plantation. Laurens also decided to get slave shoes for all of his plantations from the Charleston cordwainer Patrick Hinds, buying over 360 pairs from that local manufacturer in the space of three years.[13]

Other planters came to be equally reliant on the urban market as they laid down the infrastructure for a profitable enterprise. John Harvey commissioned the Charleston firm of Miller and Cannon to build the four sets of vats necessary for his move into indigo production. William Harvey kept bricklayer Jacob Axson and his employees in work for a month as they paved his yard and raised buildings at the plantation. Richard Bohun Baker required the services of a Charleston blacksmith seven times in 1762. The smith com-

Table 2.2

**Recorded instances of patronage of Charleston service and manufacturing enterprises, 1710–1800**

| Service purchased | Proportion (%) (N = 540) |
|---|---|
| Personal needs (clothing, shoes, hairdressing) | 26 |
| Luxury and household goods (furniture, silver, upholstery, coaches, etc.) | 32 |
| Infrastructure and construction, excluding house building (ships, saddlery, carpentry) | 27 |
| Food and services (carting, bakery, gardening, soapmaking, candlemaking) | 15 |

*Sources: The Papers of Henry Laurens;* James Laurens account book, 1767–1775, South Carolina Historical Society; Rawlins Lowndes receipts, Pinckney Family Papers, 1086.03.01, South Carolina Historical Society; South Carolina Judgment Rolls, 1710–1800, South Carolina Department of Archives and History; Judge James Waties Papers, South Caroliniana Library.

pleted a number of jobs for Baker, including the securing of his property with gatehouse locks and the supplying of new parts for his ploughs. On another occasion, Baker had a gun restocked by Charleston gunsmith John Scott, the charge of SC£11 being a fraction of the cost of a new gun imported from Britain. Time and again, the establishment of a plantation might require specialist skills that were readily available in town, but less frequently on offer in the countryside (see table 2.1).[14]

Overall, however, the business of servicing the plantation enterprise made up only a quarter of recorded transactions. Constituting half of all dealings were the multifarious household needs—both luxury and essential—of South Carolina's white settlers. Butchers, clergymen, apothecaries, and merchants spent largely at the shops of Charleston's tradespeople for riding chairs, silver trinkets and coat buttons, pewter ware, and all sorts of household furniture, from fine mahogany dining tables to more serviceable pine chests. Planters were also likely to spend money on locally made household and personal goods, and from the 1750s onward they willingly bypassed the cumbersome process of importing custom-made items from London by placing their orders with local craftspeople. During this decade, the eight purchases that Richard Baker made from Charleston's manufacturers included a portrait from the local artist Jeremiah Theus. In the following ten years, Baker placed over sixty orders with artisans for brand new luxury goods. Among other things, the family commissioned local workers to make a silver punch ladle, silver sauce boats, numerous dresses and suits, a dressing table, a close stool chair (commode), a pair of card tables, new boots and shoes, turned banisters for their house, silver table spoons, and a large chased coffee pot. This patronage continued on into the 1770s, when Baker had three more portraits painted by Theus at a total cost of SC£113.15.0. During the 1760s alone, the Bakers spent over SC£330 with the local tailors, shoemakers, staymakers, and mantuamakers who clothed the couple and their two children. The planter's surviving receipts from these thirty years only included one from a London tradesman.[15]

Indeed, South Carolinians from every part of the colony were willing to hand over responsibility to local manufacturers for commodities central to their self-fashioning as an elite. Even though metropolitan tailors often found it difficult to cater to the needs of the distant colonial customer who inhabited an unfamiliarly hot climate, some South Carolinians continued to call on them into the 1730s, because an unfashionable outfit might call into question one's gentility or status. Records reveal, however, that across the middle of the eighteenth century Charleston's clothiers had become competent enough to win the business of many colonists for whom much depended on the right attire. Just over a quarter of the total recorded visits to town craftsmen were to tailors, mantuamakers, milliners, perukemakers, or shoemakers. Fashioning outfits from British cloth that they had supplied themselves, Charleston tailors suited up gentlemen, attorneys, assemblymen, and the richest merchants in cashmere and superfine silk outfits. At the same time, local milliners and mantuamakers created fancies for wives and daughters from the fabrics, feathers, and ribbons that they ordered in from Britain.

The debts owed by clients to two Charleston tailors reveal the extent to which South Carolinians relied on local manufacturers to transform imported cloth into usable apparel. When he died in 1745, the tailor Alexander Smith was owed money by 344 different people. They represented a cross-section of white male society, and Smith had outfitted everyone from esquires, planters, merchants, and Indian traders to harbor pilots, ship's captains, tavern keepers, shoemakers, and "the purser of the Phoenix." Although some customers came from Charleston itself, other hailed from far-away rural Georgia. The smallest debt owed to him was just SC£1, the largest SC£250. Smith had loyal clients, like the Huguenot silversmith Moreau Sarrazin, who was fitted up for a suit with silver buttons in 1734, and who owed a further SC£46 when his tailor died eleven years later. It appears, moreover, that the popularity of Charleston's tailors only increased as time went by: forty years later, fellow town tailor Alexander McCormack had accounts owed to him by 157 clients at his death, with the "good debts" and the "bad and doubtfull" debts totaling SC£10,413. McCormack's customers similarly included eminent merchants and artisans from Charleston, as well as planters from the rural reaches of the colony.[16]

White settlers, however, were not the only customers encouraging the expansion of the town's domestic marketplace. Goods commissioned by the South Carolina government for sending to Native Americans show that Charleston's tradesmen were also important players in the colony's Indian trade. At its height during the Seven Years War, the government spent 28 percent of its annual budget on goods for Native Americans, and a substantial proportion of these monies ended up in the pockets of the town's traders, who made and mended guns, provided saddles, and supplied medicines, clothing, silver breastplates, and bullets. The Indians' demands, like those of the white colonists, could be met only when imported goods were merged with the processing and manufacturing abilities of those craftsmen who formed the basis of Charleston's domestic economy. And with Native Americans now constituting part of their clientele, the tradesmen were able to extend their sphere of influence beyond the town's hinterland and backcountry.[17]

As the urban market lodged itself in the economic landscape of colonial South Carolina, its central position became reflected in the increased manufacturing capacity of Charleston's tradesmen. From the mid-eighteenth century onward, coaches were built in the town for the first time, wigs made from scratch, silver flatware and hollow-ware hammered out, jewelry assembled, woodcarving for picture frames and interiors completed, tinware made, all sorts of saddlery done, hides tanned, large quantities of windows, doors, and house frames prefabricated, and even violins made. When he died at the end of a lengthy Charleston career, tinsmith George Ross's shop was cluttered with the latest tools and materials used by craftsmen of his trade in towns throughout the British Atlantic world. Punches, rivets, creasing hammers, soldering irons, 21 pounds of bar coppers, 19 pounds of lead, and 74 pounds of iron wire were used by Ross to turn out the 483 individual items of his own making—from colanders to coffeepots—that stocked his shop. A number of these items were still in the process of manufacture, including one "lot of unfinished lanterns" and another "lot of saucepan handles."

The increased stature of these domestic manufacturing and service trades even made its presence felt on Charleston's East Bay—the stronghold of the large merchant houses. Although the majority of tenants on this wharfside thoroughfare were wealthy traders, the street was, by the 1750s, also home to milliners, a druggist, a dancing school, a physician, bricklayers, and attorneys—all businesses more appropriately described as service or leisure establishments, not the mainstays of the seafront of a major port.[18]

At the same time, Charleston's tradesmen began to dominate subsidiary markets. Even the wealthiest consumers frequently elected to visit a local business to repair an existing possession rather than buy a replacement, and Charleston's tradesmen were much valued in the local marketplace for their ability to update and renovate household goods. Cabinetmakers carved new feet for tables, reattached brass escutcheons and hinges, refinished veneers, and repaired decorative cornices. Goldsmiths and clockmakers were called upon when silver cutlery got bent, watch glasses shattered, and china became chipped or broken. Planter Richard Baker's records reveal that 40 percent of his dealings with local workmen involved the alteration or repair of items such as dresses, silver, furniture, or shoes. Indeed, owners went to some lengths to keep their possessions serviceable; Benjamin Perry, for example, extended the life of his coach for a total of fifteen years by having local coachmaker Richard Hart re-cover the steps, attach a new harness, refinish the leather seating, put in a new carpet, and paint and varnish the exterior.[19]

Without doubt, the manufacturing sector that emerged in Charleston after 1740 was not as extensive as that in other British Atlantic cities like Manchester or Philadelphia that were concurrently developing into leading industrial centers. However, the town still had a vital role to play in determining the character of the larger South Carolina economy with which it interacted. Most importantly, the expansion of the service and manufacturing sector brought Charleston into line with other provincial urban economies of the eighteenth-century English-speaking world. As with Charleston, elsewhere in the urban British Atlantic some provincial towns were, by mid-century, flourishing purely because they could supply services and luxury goods from local,

national, and international markets to the customers in their regional hinterlands. By the third quarter of the century, various English provincial towns
of Charleston's size were home to a larger-than-average proportion of free-
men providing luxury goods and services—clothing, furniture, silverware,
toys, dancing and singing lessons—to the local population. Often, the economic profiles of such towns had changed considerably since the previous
century, when small regional industries such as leather and textile processing
had dominated. As these cottage enterprises faded away in the face of competition from new, larger manufacturing centers like Manchester and Birmingham, provincial urban economies found themselves on the crest of a wave—
if they could accommodate themselves to this new, international, consumer
market. Hence, as the westerly coastal town of Chester was eclipsed by Liverpool, and the Shropshire town of Shrewsbury fell into the shadow of Birmingham, they continued to thrive by answering the consuming needs of the local
gentry and middling sorts.[20]

Critically, the emergence of Charleston as such a center within the Low
Country suggests that, in response to the demands and expectations of local
consumers, it had developed an autonomous manufacturing sector that
answered a similar call. Patterns of growth in British imports especially reveal
how local industries expanded to form a complementary relationship with
the transatlantic trade. Since the kinds of businesses that were found in towns
of Charleston's size were not generally disposed to processing raw materials,
but made their way by assembling basic components manufactured elsewhere, rising imports of British goods accompanied an advancing domestic
economy. With simultaneous growth occurring in both sectors, the types of
goods imported shifted to accommodate the reality of Charleston's expansion; certain British manufactures disappeared from Carolina import lists as
the town's economy grew to answer the demands of Low Country consumers.
Most notably, the need for ready-made garments practically dried up as tailors set up their shops, imports of cabinetwares crested in the 1740s but soon
petered out, and the demand for British saddles failed to take off as Charleston's saddlers established themselves as the suppliers and repairers of tack to
white and Native American customers. Yet, because Charleston was only a
provincial manufacturing and service center, decreases in the trade in some
wares were accompanied by sharp increases in the import of mass-produced
items from the empire's industrial hubs: earthenware, glass, and silk contin-

## Table 2.3

### British manufactures sent from London and outports to Carolina, 1735–1765 (5-year intervals)

| Years | Number of ready-made garments | Value of cabinetware/ joinery (in £ sterling) | Dozens of shovels shod | Number of saddles | Amount of wrought silk (pounds/ounces) | Number of glass and earthenware pieces, excluding window panes |
|---|---|---|---|---|---|---|
| 1734–35 | 3,993 | 0 | — | — | 90/0 | 48,640 |
| 1739–40 | 420 | 10 | 74 | 1,256 | 1,454/9 | 139,823 |
| 1744–45 | 2,370 | 0 | 41 | 498 | 544/0 | 90,198 |
| 1749–50 | 677 | 200 | 92 | 479 | 1,478/3 | 55,325 |
| 1754–55 | 74 | 7 | 6 | 995 | 3,416/0 | 54,996 |
| 1759–60 | 0 | 24 | — | 1,212 | 8,175/0 | 57,936 |
| 1764–65 | 45 | 70 | 13 | 852 | 3,462/4 | 192,688 |

*Source:* British National Archives (formerly British Public Record Office), Colonial Records, Customs 1.

*Note:* These goods have been selected in part on the grounds that their unit of measurement was not pounds sterling. Such a selection should minimize any variations in figures that might result from the rising or diminishing cost of the items.

ued to pour into the colony in vast quantities from those specialist industries in the Staffordshire potteries and London's Spitalfields.[21]

Between 1740 and 1780, therefore, Charleston achieved commercial importance to South Carolina because of its ability to deftly coordinate the trade in British imports and the market for locally made, finished, or repaired goods and services. Just as the provincial consumers of Shropshire could take a day trip to Shrewsbury safe in the knowledge that they would be able to obtain exotic silks, have fashionable handles fixed to an old chest of drawers, be fitted for a new suit, and collect a pipe of Madeira wine, so South Carolina's wealthy residents could expect the same array of services in their principal town. Widespread patronage of new businesses from consumers throughout the Low Country, and the arrival of new traders and manufacturers attracted to this busy marketplace, had fashioned the town into a notable center of manufacturing and processing. That Charleston should fulfill this function might appear natural to the modern eye, yet in the early modern British Atlantic world the ascendancy of the provincial service town was a relatively new phenomenon. What is more, the town's rise to such a position had not been achieved solely under the aegis of the staple merchant or factor, but equally had occurred because Charleston's tradesmen and women had insinuated themselves into the consumption habits of colonial South Carolinians.

## Beyond Workshop and Wharf: The Geography of the Market

Charleston did not take a lead role in the shaping of South Carolina's markets merely because of its increasingly busy manufacturing and merchant concerns. The town's influence as a provincial service center also stemmed from its hold over the arrangement of the market in the Low Country. The center of just about every level of trade in South Carolina, Charleston's economy was composed of multiple layers of markets and market-places focused in a single location—the town. The result of this influence was a very complex marketplace that was specific to the British Atlantic urban environment as it developed in the eighteenth century.

Charleston's role within South Carolina's markets has frequently been viewed by historians as that of a staging post for the Atlantic economy. Rather like a collective of the separate plantation landings that hosted the outflow of tobacco and the influx of British manufactures into the Chesapeake, the town is described as a waypoint on the way into, or out of, South Carolina. Thus, Charleston served as a nucleus for the operations of the Low Country's rice aristocracy. For example, Henry Laurens's commercial empire was orchestrated from his Ansonborough house in the town's suburbs, making the residence a central node for his international trafficking of goods and people. The structures established by Laurens, however, were but one artery in a much larger circulatory body that had Charleston at its heart. Although individual households in the town certainly acted as the headquarters for rice empires, the town independently stood at the center of a larger market system. The twin trades in new goods and domestic manufactures and services were the pillars of this system, but the urban environment also harbored more complex structures. Charleston had room for market places that operated away from both workshop and wharf, and as it came to lie at the center of these many other markets in the period after 1740, so South Carolina became thoroughly integrated into the diffuse system that united English-speaking provincial towns in a single, well-oiled, market machine. Charleston's special abilities to accommodate these emerging systems then made the colony into a true commercial province in a British Atlantic world of goods.[22]

Within the consuming empire, a huge range of goods changed hands in an equally eclectic assemblage of marketplaces. In Charleston, as in other cities, a Wedgwood Queensware dish might be ordered directly via a town factor, purchased from the store of a Charleston shopkeeper, or snapped up at a house sale. Likewise, a good cheese could be found at the grocer's, in Charleston's general stores on the East Bay, in the open air provisions market, or even at auction. On the whole, therefore, markets were not readily distinguished by the types of goods that they sold.[23] Rather, it is easier to approach the anatomy of the Low Country's commercial scene from its geographical aspect, just as it is by understanding the physical (and sometimes social) boundaries of each marketplace that we can grasp how Charleston became a central site in the trading lives of so many residents of the Lower South.

In the first instance, Charleston increased its commercial influence when it became the epicenter of a regional urban system. Planters who lived some distance from the town relied on it for goods and services, and other small towns and trading posts within the region therefore developed in reference to Charleston. Within South Carolina, the growth of Camden from the 1750s onward was the clearest example of this process. As settlement expanded into the backcountry, and planters diversified into wheat, it had become clear that Charleston was too distant to fulfill their needs satisfactorily. Through the efforts of men like Joseph Kershaw, the town's main investor and owner of a wide variety of its enterprises, Camden grew to answer this demand. By the 1770s, the town functioned as a backcountry processing center selling dry goods, gathering and grinding wheat into flour, and accommodating travelers on their way through the colony. But importantly, these were all processes that occurred in support of Charleston's place as the major market of the region. Kershaw's store was a branch of his Charleston-based business, travelers were on the road that led to Charleston, and crops processed at the town's wheat and grist mills were then sent on to Charleston for export elsewhere.[24]

Although a colonial capital in its own right, Savannah also increasingly operated as a satellite of the Charleston market, with the influence of its northerly neighbor quite visible across many aspects of its trade. Tradesfolk who had failed to make a go of their businesses in Charleston attempted to reestablish themselves in Savannah; much Georgia land was sold in Charleston auctions; and the *Georgia Gazette* reported the arrival of British goods in Charleston as a matter of course.[25] Savannah's provisioning market also developed a deferential relationship to its superior contemporary, and in 1764 the *Gazette* carried a report that "a Gentlemen here has got a fishing smack built upon new principles to bring all the variety of fish with which this coast abounds to Charlestown market; and we hear if he meets with proper encouragement he proposes to extend his design so as always to have a quantity on hand sufficient to supply every demand, and at any hour—A project highly for the advantage of the inhabitants and which every friend to the town will wish to succeed."[26]

Within this regional hinterland, Charleston-based dealers both sent goods out to sell at these satellite trading posts and bought up produce collected from the countryside. By the 1760s, even the smallest backcountry trader relied on Charleston, and not on the individual merchants and factors who often orchestrated trade in the Chesapeake or Northern colonies. Thus, an innkeeper and storeowner in Rowan County, North Carolina, derived his stock from Charleston, drawing generally on the urban market rather than dealing exclusively with a single merchant or factor.[27]

As it was climbing to the top of the Lower South's markets, Charleston was also in the ascendant as a center of the colonial coastwise trade. Being practically equidistant from the British Caribbean and New England, the town was ideally located midway between the two geographical extremes of Britain's New World, and from the late 1730s onwards it emerged as a key stopping-off point in the trip along the Atlantic seaboard. Early on, Charleston's importance was limited to British merchants and ship owners, who carried half of all the molasses, rum, beer, bread, and flour that the town imported, along with the vast majority of wine, sugar, and slaves. So, although it represented a shipping point, the urban economy itself did not actively sponsor the growth of this coastwise system. However, this state of affairs was to change dramatically in the following thirty years as South Carolinians began to finance and enjoy the fruits of its continued expansion. So, whereas in 1762 British ships still carried the majority of slaves and wine into the town, American ships dominated in all other commodities. Almost all flour, bread, and rum arrived in Charleston on American ships, as did over 80 percent of beer. Further, Charleston-based ships carried half of all beer, bread, and flour brought into the colony, along with 40 percent of all sugar and a third of all rum. A mere four years later, Charleston traders had increased their share of trade into the colony even further, and 70 percent of all flour, 60 percent of beer, and half of all sugar came into South Carolina on their ships.[28]

While becoming a key hub in the importation of provisions from other British American colonies, Charleston also took up a central role as an exporter of South Carolina's own produce. Lumber, staves, shingles, corn, and leather destined for both the West Indies and the Northern colonies all left South Carolina through Charleston in ever-rising quantities.[29] There is some evidence to suggest that these unprocessed goods were increasingly accompanied by some town manufactures. Cabinetmaker Thomas Elfe, for example, had an ongoing relationship with the firm of Legare & Greenwood, who commissioned pieces from him for their customers. Over a period of four years, the merchants ordered twenty-three items from Elfe, including a "mahogany desk for George Grafton" and a "dressing table for Mr. Field." Tinplate workers Bolsover & Sherman advertised that they could supply merchants with "tin-ware, by the quantity, as cheap as can be imported." And it seems that Isaac Motte & Co. may well have taken them up on this offer, as the tinsmithing partnership appeared among Motte's contemporary receipts. Also coming into the colony through Charleston, it may be noted, were quantities of Philadelphia pottery, recently unearthed by archeologists in at least three downtown lots abutting that city's wharves.[30]

The strength of Charleston's position as a hub of this coastwise trade was further bolstered by its importance to the growth of a resale market in British goods. Without official statistics, the extent of these dealings is much harder to document, but there can be little doubt that the town was a major center for the recirculation of British imports. Robert Pringle's correspondence with fellow merchants in Boston, Antigua, and Philadelphia reveals that during the 1740s he regularly exchanged parcels of fabric, china, metal wares, and cocoa that had failed to sell in Charleston for wares initially imported elsewhere. Some twenty years later, Newport merchant Aaron Lopez dispatched his brother Moses to Charleston, where he oversaw a commercial empire built as much around reselling as it was around importation.[31] This resale trade, however, was not the preserve of the most successful merchants. The business could easily be conducted on a small scale with little capital, and this meant that it was particularly attractive for those townspeople who made their main living elsewhere but sought extra income in other areas of the urban economy. These might well have been the benefits that brought carpenter James Verree into the reselling trade, and by the 1750s he had established connections with traders in both Philadelphia and New York, with whom he exchanged rice, indigo, and scrap metal in return for beer, bar iron, feathers, oznabrig, and gravestones.[32]

Probably lacking a wealth of transatlantic business connections, how did Verree, a small-time trader, manage to get hold of the eclectic variety of goods that he sent to his contacts in the Middle Colonies? Verree's stock depended on the fact that Charleston did not merely win primacy by coordinating a regional market, but it also harbored an increasingly diverse commercial landscape within its own limits. Allowing the town to cater to a wide range of social groups, these marketplaces further sustained Charleston's development as a provincial service center. Behind tradesmen like Robert Pringle and Thomas Corker, whose global traffic in new imports represented the highly visible face of Charleston merchandizing, lay a network of smaller stores that catered to the many other Low Country consumers who did not have the credit, the "commercial friendships," or the cash to buy firsthand. These Charleston traders sold goods that had not been newly imported or recently made at all, but had come from the unsold stock of larger stores—items characterized by one wealthy town merchant as being not "fresh and good in quality, but rather appear to be old shopkeepers that have often been handl'd."[33] One such trader was Thomas Gates, his small shop likely being located in an alley or lane rather than on one of the town's more prestigious thoroughfares.

Gates's inventory cast him as a shopkeeper, but his stock added up to little more than a few loaves of sugar, some brooms, and some wine. John Patient was in a similar position at his death in 1761—his wares consisting of a few books and some stockings. The value of Patient's SC£146 estate was supplemented only by SC£188 worth of credits owed him by other Charleston traders.[34] Although their stock was relatively measly compared to that of the rich import merchants, such shopkeepers nevertheless permitted South Carolinians from across the social spectrum to access the commercial scene.

Since the items that they sold were often "nearly new," shopkeepers like Gates (as well as resellers such as Verree) were as much a product of Charleston's multiple markets as they were its creators. In particular, such traders and their customers were dependent on the flourishing of yet another urban marketplace—the vendue sale or auction. Licensed by the town authorities, Charleston's vendue masters charged a commission to bring everything from a working plantation to the shop goods of a bankrupt trader to the auction block. As sellers took the opportunity to dispose of anything with a value, the auctions sponsored the creation of secondhand markets similar to those operating in the metropole. There, the increase in urban retail outlets was accompanied by the daily trade in used clothing and household goods, allowing a much wider swath of society to access the ever larger world of goods. By extending these alternative markets to the Lower South, Charleston's vendue created a "democracy" that contrasted with rural parts of the American South—and undoubtedly parts of the North—where consumers' choices were limited by the monopoly of merchant-owned stores selling only new goods. Quite simply, the vendue reflected the exclusive ability of the town to underwrite a truly British Atlantic empire of goods, where there was not only more to consume, but where more were able to consume it.[35]

Charleston's vendues thus played a critical role in the consuming lives of a broad range of South Carolinians. The vendue became very useful for merchants like Robert Pringle, since, when faced with an unsalable item, they could be certain of shifting it at auction, albeit at a low margin of profit. Between 1743 and 1745 Pringle resorted to the "publick vendue" on numerous occasions, selling Manchester cloth, nails, blubber, cocoa, low-grade rice, ribbons, pots, axes, butter, and sugar. Vendues made up of goods from the estates of deceased or bankrupt persons were also common, yielding an Aladdin's cave of secondhand wares to eager consumers who fell on everything from bound editions of *The Spectator* to battered iron frying pans. At the vendue of

the estate of Elizabeth Mackenzie, a Charleston shopkeeper, other small traders snapped up job lots of ready-made petticoats, needles, and thread. When
estates were being auctioned for debts, widows even bought back as many of
their own possessions as they could afford.[36]

Furthermore, as wealthy planters and merchants made fortunes, accumulated possessions, and then died, Charleston also became the center of a more
exclusive secondhand market based around the resale of luxury household
furnishings. Advertisements for sales of such goods were a weekly feature
of the South Carolina newspapers, developing in sophistication until they
described what would be under the hammer in tantalizing detail: for sale
after the departure of Egerton Leigh from the city in 1774 was "elegant household furniture—a mahogany bedstead, fire grates, carpets, histories, tapes-
try, library bookcases, pistols and fine painting by the most eminent hands
in Europe." Indeed, the extent to which elite South Carolinians relied on
Charleston's "nearly new" market—and not on British imports—for prestige
possessions is underlined by the fact that in 1765 Egerton Leigh had instructed
Henry Laurens to purchase similar household furnishings from the auction of
a Mr. Graeme's possessions. Thus, buyers at this 1774 sale were quite probably
purchasing not secondhand, but thirdhand goods.[37]

The vendue was especially popular with South Carolina's women; wives,
spinsters, and sole traders, as well as female slaves on errands for their mistresses, were often to be found among the bidders. Women were also ubiqui-
tous in every other retail space in Charleston, from the chaos and stench of
the fish market to the refined interiors of the best jewelers on Tradd Street.
Put together, this array of commercial outlets was successful at offering equal
consuming opportunities to male and female consumers. But there is little
evidence that any of these places welcomed the presence of black citizens trying to buy and sell on their own accounts, and in this respect the eclectic trading spaces of this British Atlantic town did not avail every South Carolinian of
the new "empire of goods."[38]

Yet, as has been well documented by other scholars, the Low Country's
slaves were not about to obey the customs and regulations of their white masters, and in the end it was Charleston's burgeoning popularity as a center of
the slaves' market that transformed it into a complete British Atlantic marketplace. The Low Country's slaves used the town's spaces to buy and sell
groceries, dry goods, prepared foods, and local produce. Enslaved and free

blacks also dominated the city's fish market, and made up a large proportion of its butchers. That this market constituted a source of perpetual annoyance to the town's authorities did not make it any less a pillar of Charleston's economy. In carving out a space where hucksters could hawk all manner of goods to anyone who cared to buy—blacks included—the town's blackmarket men and women added a depth and texture to Charleston's role as an urban trading center that would otherwise have been absent. Through their drive to sell and barter, slaves and free blacks replicated the informal and illegal aspects of many an urban marketplace across Britain, and truly put the last piece in the complicated puzzle that made up the eighteenth century world of goods.[39]

In hosting these multiple layers of trade and accommodating so many different types of marketplace, Charleston became the equal of other major British Atlantic towns such as Liverpool and Philadelphia. The ubiquity of slaves as traders and as wares, along with the large quantities of rice and indigo passing through, certainly singled out this urban marketplace as unique. Yet, at the same time, Charleston functioned in the same way as other eighteenth-century towns to create a provincial bazaar rich in trading opportunity for a broad swath of South Carolinians. Providing a variety of commercial arenas that outstripped the possibilities inherent in the rural Chesapeake to the north, Charleston's influence rapidly spread to draw the whole region of the Lower South into its web.

## Market Cultures

Profiling the colonial marketplace by examining its physical attributes or the types of wares proffered for sale reveals much of its character, but early America's markets were also distinguished by the culture of commerce forged by those men and women who traded within them. Thus, the market relationships fostered by rice and indigo shaped many commercial customs and identities in the Low Country. South Carolina planters stood before factors and agents who judged their characters and reputations against their claims about the crop that they brought to market. Even in the distant mother country, planter's reputations were fashioned by the opinions of metropolitan merchants about their product. Yet, with the growing importance of South Carolina's own manufacturers and service providers, the home market also began to influence the commercial *culture* of the region, and intricate relationships were soon established between town traders and their customers.[40]

In the eighteenth century, on the other side of the British Atlantic, the nature of commercial exchange in the burgeoning towns was experiencing a period of change and uncertainty. This transformation in the customs of the market was documented by contemporary commentators, including Daniel Defoe. In his *Complete Tradesman*, Defoe devoted the best part of his pamphlet to explaining the etiquette of the "commercial friendship," pressing home the behavior, the conduct, and the care, that was required on the part of tradesmen to win over the patronage of their often socially superior customers. Defoe stressed the strength of the bonds that characterized such a relationship once forged, but also the ease with which they might be severed by a false move: "A tradesman's reputation is of the nicest nature imaginable; like a blight upon a fine flower, if it is but touched, the beauty of it, or the flavour of it, or the seed of it, is lost, though the noxious breath which touched it might not reach to blast the leaf, or hurt the root; the credit of a tradesman, at least in his beginning, is too much at the mercy of every enemy he has, till it has taken root, and is established on a solid foundation of good conduct and success."[41] Once this "solid foundation" had been established, customers might be depended upon to devote themselves to a tradesman, and Defoe used the example of a lady who would only patronize "her mercer." However, it was still possible for this committed commercial friendship to founder on the rocks of rumor or bad behavior, and a tradesman could lose the loyalty of his clientele to one of the many competitors clamoring for attention in an increasingly eclectic urban retail environment.[42]

As historians have noted, such "commercial friendships" did exist between business correspondents in colonial America, and were characterized by long-term relationships among British merchants and the Chesapeake's wealthiest tobacco lords. Since they were a universal fact of eighteenth-century business, their prevalence in the American South is to be expected. What is of greater concern here is the precise texture of these "friendships"—in particular, how they were affected by the growing dominance of diverse urban markets, crammed with choices, tradesmen, and shopkeepers. Throughout the urban British Atlantic world, the commercial friendship came under pressure from the glut of consuming possibilities and the growing array of media through which reputations might be forged or destroyed. Most notably, burgeoning presses, active in many British Atlantic provincial towns from the 1720s onward, provided an entirely new arena in which to "manage" commercial reputations. Overall, reliance on urban markets meant that more and more consumers and suppliers had to operate in an environment like that described by Defoe: one of increased uncertainty, where bonds might be made and broken on any number of counts. Indeed, such issues of unfamiliarity were particularly emphasized in a New World town, where recently arrived settlers were an unknown quantity who sometimes manipulated their anonymity to the great disadvantage of those who had dared to trust them.[43]

Because elite Low Country consumers were part of an urban market that was as sophisticated as any that could be found in Britain's flourishing provincial towns of the era, the relationships between South Carolina's buyers and sellers were also forged along newer, as opposed more traditional, lines. The character and culture of trade became reliant not only on enduring commercial bonds made over rice, indigo, and slaves, but also on deals struck on household furniture, suits of clothes, and new window frames. This domestic market culture was wrought in the furnace of a novel and fast-changing urban market.

Like their British contemporaries, Charleston's tradesmen increasingly courted their "friends" (customers) through the medium of print. Often, a printed endorsement by an established member of the town's commercial community was used to assure potential customers of a good reputation; by serving notice that he had "started off in Mr. Bonsall's shop" but was now striking out on his own, whitesmith John Cleator managed to link himself to one of Charleston's wealthiest master metalworkers. Coach painter Thomas Philips likewise explained that he had been "invited to this city by a number of friends, and some of the principal coachmakers." Similarly, gunsmith Edward Tash took the trouble to introduce the successor to his business, assuring his clientele that the new man was "late from LONDON" and could be "recommended as a person every way suitable for the trade . . . having had great experience therein."[44]

At the same time, tradesmen were quick to use the newspaper to quash gossip that might prove damaging to a carefully assembled reputation. Clockmaker Richard Clark specifically placed a notice to put an end to the rumor that he had left the province and would not be taking on any more business. Likewise, Richard Singleton informed customers that he had not reneged on his partnership with fellow metalworker Charles Harris, but had never signed such an agreement in the first place. Most likely, these defenses were prompted by attacks from fellow manufacturers who realized the importance of public reputation and identified the destruction of character as a way in which they might eliminate their closest competitors.[45]

As the urban marketplace became more diverse and depersonalized, Charleston's tradesmen also selected the newspaper as a forum in which to generate confidence in their product among readers who were potential customers. When business owners sought to assure the public of their reliability, claims were usually made about the quality or cost of a product. Carpenter Thomas Legare was typical when, in 1740, he advertised: "As people have complained of the extravagant price of coffins, he will furnish country and city funerals as cheap as possible." Tailor John Ward likewise promised that his suits, at SC£45–SC£50 for cloth and workmanship, were "near as cheap as can be sent from England." What is more, Ward noted, gentlemen could expect a quality product for their money, as he had "just imported in America from London a fresh assortment of superfine broadcloths, fine trimmings etc., bought upon the best terms by as good a judge as any in England." And in 1765, upholsterer John Mason boldly published a list of set rates for various services in the newspaper, no doubt in an effort to impress potential clients with his absolute honesty and transparency.[46]

By indulging in such tactics, Charleston's tradesmen were merely drawing on methods popular across the urban British Atlantic. Thus, where Scottish cabinetmaker and upholsterer Francis Braidwood boasted to his Edinburgh customers that "he is just returned from London with an elegant and fashionable assortment . . . which he will sell upon such terms as will entice him to a share of the public favour," his Charleston opposite number, Solomon Smith, promised that he could offer goods "in the newest taste in London." Likewise, Charleston gardener Robert Bennett sold his seeds "at an easy expense," while Edinburgh nurseryman William Boutcher peddled the same product "at the lowest rates."

Tradesmen on both sides of the Atlantic also sought to win consumers' favor by stressing the advantages of establishing a "commercial friendship" in the nearest town. In Edinburgh, "commissions from the country" were "punctually answered," as they were in Charleston, where "commands from the country" were "duly executed and gratefully acknowledged."[47] Many Low Country business owners highlighted that they "would endeavor to oblige those in town and country," and would ride out to gentlemen's plantations if necessary. Carver John Parkinson explained that "orders from the country will be immediately complied with, and their work packed up with the greatest safety"—a guarantee that an English carver would not be able to make at a distance of four thousand miles. As well as being reliable, tradesmen elucidated that they were also very competitive on cost, with services available not just on "reasonable terms," but "cheaper than can be imported," "as cheap as in London, lowest prices," or on "as reasonable terms as can be done in South Carolina."[48]

Through these public pronouncements of price, quality, and reliability, Charleston business owners strove to show they could fulfill their obligations in the construction of secure domestic "commercial friendships" that, because of their urban situation, suffered from the same insecurities as their British contemporaries. But, as Defoe had stressed, such measures only constituted one part of the equation, for it was important that a tradesman's promises should reflect reality, enabling his customers to have the confidence to return for future purchases. From the private scribblings of Charleston consumers, it becomes clear that, while some tradesmen were successful at laying a "solid foundation of good conduct and success," others failed to win the trust and patronage of the Low Country's consumers. Those South Carolinians who needed to call on the services of the urban tradesman found that, although they were able to rely on some individuals, a good "commercial friendship" often remained elusive. Despite the soothing words spoken by tradesmen in the *South Carolina Gazette,* consumers often struggled to find their way in the new reality of the urban marketplace.

For Henry Laurens, trusting relationships were only slowly established. During the 1740s Laurens still tended toward placing most of his faith in individual metropolitan manufacturers, with whom he had cultivated good relations. Writing to business partner Francis Bremar from London, Laurens mentioned a number of manufacturers there whom he thought "worth [the] acquaintance" of the latter. Laurens included the names and addresses of hatters, gunsmiths, hosiers, upholsterers, cordwainers, tinsmiths, and tailors whom he knew and whom he therefore felt could be relied upon to send quality goods to South Carolina customers. As the eighteenth century progressed, however, these London contacts faded into the background as Laurens gradually gained confidence in an array of Charleston tradesmen. Overall, craftsmen whom the merchant felt to be "honest and sensible," or "industrious," in their work could rely on him for his support of their ventures.[49]

When such a relationship had been successfully created, Laurens was enthusiastic in his support both of existing local businesses and of tradesmen who intended to set themselves up in Charleston. In 1773, John Daniel Henrie, a German cooper, embarked on the long journey to the New World, and any apprehensions he might have would have been assuaged by the note he carried, telling Charleston merchant John Lewis Gervais to "advice [him] the proper steps to be taken in order to escape extraordinary expenses, to get into business and to find out certain friends of theirs." Laurens's recommendations also worked in reverse, on the other side of the Atlantic. When tailor Walter Mansell decided to go on a buying trip to London, a letter from Laurens to the merchants Rogers & Dyson went with him, stating that "he has follow'd the taylors trade here for some time with great success—he intends to make a purchase of cloths and other things in his way and may possibly apply to you for some of them as we told him that you can supply him on as good a terms as any men in London." The Laurens brothers also helped out Charleston coachmaker, Thomas Hutchinson, by sourcing and importing raw materials for his business on their ships from London.[50]

Indeed, Laurens's patronage of a good "commercial friend" knew no bounds, and the merchant's ardent support of Charleston's shipwrights meant that he was prepared to advertise their skills as far afield as Britain. Looking for someone to fulfill an order from Bristol for a ship in 1771, he immediately sought out the advice of John Rose, "the great great shipwright who came in recommended to me with a broad ax on his shoulder in the year 1749, and who has since acquired a fortune . . . by his honest Industry." Although Rose had retreated to his plantation by this time, Laurens expressed the hope that he might come out of retirement to take the commission or else recommend someone for the job. In this complex urban economy, however, bad words were often spoken and the ties of "friendships" severed. In the same breath that Laurens thanked fellow planter John Coming Ball for his "hint about the carpenter" whom Laurens had just employed on his plantation, he also informed Ball that "after [the carpenter] has performed a month's work he will be dismissed." It comes as little surprise that, on one occasion, Laurens, seemingly desperate to avoid the "tricks of the town" practiced by Charleston's tradesmen, sent for a carpenter and bricklayer direct from Britain.[51]

The terms on which Laurens built relationships with local tradesmen were not unusual, and other elite Low Country consumers also negotiated a complex web of reputations and recommendations quite different from the trusty alliances enjoyed by their Virginia neighbors. When in need of a new coach, merchant William Ancrum immediately sent for a Mr. Hall because he had heard through friends that the craftsman was "famous for the manufacture of

riding chairs." However, Mr. Hall was just one of the many retailers and craftsmen encountered by Ancrum in his consumption of necessaries and luxuries,
as he patronized an eclectic collection of builders, tailors, jewelers, tinsmiths,
and carpenters in search of the best price and a good product. Ancrum and
his contemporaries had learned that, while it was possible to develop reliable
relationships with individual tradesmen, it was also wise to take advantage of
the choice on offer in an urban environment, especially if a particular individual did not live up to his or her promises.[52]

In addition to Charleston's capacity to coordinate the buying and selling of
products from across South Carolina, the Lower South, colonial America, and
the metropole, the town also held a position at the vanguard of a new scheme
of urban marketing in the New World. Because of the town and its traders,
Low Country consumers truly met with a British Atlantic empire of goods
when they entered the fray of Charleston's shops, auctions, and open-air markets—a material empire shaped not simply by the British manufactures that
arrived as part of the Atlantic trade, but also by the tradesmen and the markets harbored by an expanding town. The unique and novel character of this
British Atlantic material world stemmed from the coordination of these many
different nations and provinces of goods into one global entity.

So great was the town's triumph in uniting a plethora of markets that a
succession of non-importation boycotts, war, and British occupation failed to
undermine its value in this respect. Desperately trying to find a pair of new
shoes as she was about to flee Charleston along with the withdrawing British troops in 1783, the Loyalist Louisa Wells recounted how she had expertly
negotiated the town's many marketplaces and "obtained three eighths of a yard
of black serge . . . purchased a pair of clumsy shoe heels of a Jew in an obscure
lane . . . and found out a Negro shoemaker who said he could make for ladies."
Wells's shoes—although shambolic to a middling woman who liked to keep
up with the fashions—were nevertheless indicative of the town's effectiveness
as a modern marketing center; the British imports had run out, but the web
of other markets that converged on Charleston could still supply everything
Wells needed to avoid cutting an undignified figure as she boarded her ship
to New York. Like her urban compatriots across the English-speaking world,
Louisa Wells could depend on the town to meet her consuming needs.[53]

Untangling the knot of trading systems that converged on the city underlines Charleston's singular importance to the character of commerce in South

Carolina. Not simply a market or a culture dictated by the successful growing of a staple, after 1740 the growth of the urban economy and its role as
the domestic marketplace, made a vital contribution to commerce within the
colony. While the town was a conduit for the Atlantic trade, it was also a place
where manufacturers and tradesmen developed businesses. Their activities
created a market system dependent on the town, which in turn meant that
Charleston was much more than an exceptional colonial city in the plantation
south; it was also an English-speaking provincial town, coordinating a range
of markets in a manner that was commensurate with developments in urban
function across the eighteenth century British Atlantic world. Charleston was
a southern city at the heart of a staple economy, and a province in a multilay-
ered "empire of goods."

However, Charleston's influence did not merely make itself felt in the
arena of commerce. Trading wealth and growth also provided the impetus for
other processes, laying the foundation for an urban economy that might make
a more diverse contribution to South Carolina's development. How a successful and growing town, once up and running, could then start to exert its own,
independent, influence over the region at whose center it lay involves deeper
issues, including, in particular, how this large town brought sources of wealth,
entrepreneurial activity, and innovation to the Low Country that were absent
in more rural parts of the South. Ultimately, the urban economy came to have
a distinct role in South Carolina's growth and, moreover, stimulated transatlantic processes of economic and social change in the Low Country.

# "Stupendous works"

## Building Urban Dynamism into the Low Country

BETWEEN 1730 and 1780, with Charleston emerging as the Low Country's commercial entrepôt, the demand for both urban homes and business premises increased. A successful agricultural economy and a thriving urban marketplace were making Charleston into an attractive destination for New World immigrants, and these many arrivals needed housing. The town's fast growth proved so remarkable that, reporting on the state of Charleston in the 1760s, the *South Carolina Gazette* heralded "the stupendous works now nearly completed by Mr. Christopher Gadsden Esq. at the North end of this town . . . which is reckoned to be the most extensive of the kind ever undertaken by any one man in America." Gadsden's achievements were accompanied by development in White Point, at the end of the Charleston peninsula, "which for many years was almost a desolate spot, [but] is lately almost covered with houses, many of them very elegant." Furthermore, the newspaper announced, "in other parts of the town, it is computed, that within five years, upwards of 300 houses have been built, and are building."[1]

As we have seen, similar dramatic growth in London, and in Britain's provincial towns, emerged as one of the cornerstones of urban dynamism in the metropole from the late seventeenth century onward. London's vitality, along with urban population growth, further destructive fires, interest in new classical architectural forms, and the appearance of newly wealthy town dwellers looking to invest their business profits, colluded to stimulate considerable evolution in these urban landscapes. Together, such changes were an important spur to both industrial and consumer revolution, as they ushered in more capitalist practices in the building industry, increased the complexity of mechanisms of credit, and made ordinary townhouses as well as country mansions into fashionable accessories. As they benefited wealthy tradesmen, these developments also impacted the social structure of Britain as a new urban commercial class—separate from the rural gentry—frequently anchored their newfound wealth in property speculation.[2]

Charleston's overall expansion was a consequence of South Carolina's flourishing economy, and, as Russell Menard has observed, the capital accumulated by its residents from trade became a vital source of finance for the continued expansion of the staple sector. But a settler who came to Carolina seeking a living through the staple economy—whether by growing or selling the staple, or by importing or buying slaves and British goods—contributed only indirectly to the actual increase of the town. On the ground, Charleston was growing because of the activities of skilled settlers, interested colonial officials, and slaves, who all put their minds and their hands to the business of actually constructing an urban landscape. Just as a planter improving his land or a merchant investing in his ocean-going fleet made colonial America a wealthier place, so the activities of these groups contributed to economic growth in the New World's more urbanized regions.[3]

In the Low Country, urban settlers made the town into a considerable source of income and capital, and Charleston became an engine of regional growth in the same way as its urban counterparts elsewhere in the British Atlantic. At the same time, the distribution of this new, urban, wealth among certain sectors of the population encouraged the emergence of groups within the Low Country who did not primarily identify their fortunes with rural land, but rather with town lots. Often, such settlers were not as wealthy as the great planters who were beginning to dominate South Carolina's coastal parishes, and the riches they contributed to the overall economy not as great, but they nevertheless had a marked impact on the structure of Low Country society.

Through its very development as an urban landscape, therefore, Charleston shaped the socioeconomic character of the Low Country. What is more, as those Charlestonians who had activated such processes of urban growth were working mostly within a British paradigm, they operated according to the habits of their metropolitan counterparts. Ultimately, Charleston's dynamic potential was enabled not only through the ambitions of these urban settlers, but also through their extension of the legal, financial, and economic innovations fomenting in towns across Britain. As these innovations took root in the Low Country, becoming entangled with Low Country circumstances in the process, they acted further to bring South Carolina into the embrace of an urban British Atlantic of growth and wealth.

## The Legalities of Urban Innovation

One of the major indicators of innovation in the British building industry in the years after the Great Fire of London was a quickening pace of change in the laws governing land purchase and house construction. Whereas earlier builders had raised new houses much as they pleased, rising interest in architecture and a growing concern for fire safety and regularity in the urban landscape led to the promulgation of acts regulating such matters. At the same time, aspects of the common law governing the sale and ownership of land were adapted and used in new ways as speculative buyers and house builders became familiar figures in the urban landscape. These shifts reflected how, on an evolving metropolitan scene, the gradual demise of a regulated economy manifested itself both through new types of statue law and through the organic evolution of certain aspects of England's customary legal structures.[4]

South Carolina's Proprietors, while probably *au fait* with some of these most recent trends in late seventeenth-century urban planning, did not go further than laying out their "Grand Modell" for Charleston. The Earl of Shaftesbury had not dictated the legal footing on which settlers might purchase town lots, nor had he taken responsibility for putting up houses himself. The methods by which the town would grow physically were (within the parameters of a broadly similar English background) left to chance. Settlers' responses to this initial opportunity—and to the ongoing challenges that the building of a town threw in their path—were, therefore, highly revealing. Their decisions not only demonstrated where the Charleston townscape fitted into these wider patterns of urban development, but also signaled the character of the young urban economy in relation to its provincial counterparts elsewhere in the British Atlantic world. By introducing key facets of the

economic and social changes that were shaping the mother country's built environment in the decades after Charles Town's devastating 1740 fire, Charlestonians brought the region into British Atlantic urban processes and laid the
legal foundations of a dynamic and "modern" property market.[5]

The relevance of shifting legal structures to the ownership, trading, and
development of urban land in the Low Country has not previously been of
great interest to historians. The relationship of South Carolinians to the flexible English common law, however, is well documented on a broader level. To
accommodate to the institution of slavery many new legal precedents were
established by settlers, making the law into an effective tool for the subjuga-
tion of blacks; under the South Carolinian version of the criminal law, whites
could murder blacks without fear of imprisonment. On the other hand, South
Carolina women, having as little control over their property as did their British counterparts, labored under a shared disadvantage as they sought financial
security for themselves. In the pursuit of an "ordered" society, South Carolina's
white male settlers thus demonstrated that they were adept at manipulating
or replicating long-held common law custom in their New World. Charleston's staple-sponsored expansion, however, drew these same white men into
an array of English legal novelties—novelties that would prepare the way for
a British Atlantic urban landscape full of potential as an important source of
wealth, capital, and income in the Low Country.[6]

The more innovatory aspects of property law were first implemented in
the South Carolinian response to the major fire that broke out in the town in
1740. Until the 1730s, Charleston house builders had used local wood to construct almost all but the most expensive houses, making the townscape look
somewhat temporary in nature and wholly vernacular in style. Contemporary
depictions reveal a town quite similar to its colonial contemporaries, Philadelphia and New York—places that had begun their expansion in a similar
era. As well as giving the town an "old-fashioned" appearance, the densely
packed wooden buildings were conducive to the rapid spread of fires, and it
was not long before Charleston suffered the same fate as its colonial counterpart, Boston. One morning in November 1740, flames swept through the
commercial heart of the town causing thousands of pounds worth of damage
as the fire destroyed homes and consumed the imported goods and the bar-
rels of rice that lay in Charleston's warehouses.[7]

When such conflagrations had occurred in Britain, they had ruined livelihoods, but had also provided a prime opportunity for British civic authorities to make their towns part of the process of urban renewal, and it appears that Charleston's government viewed their town's disaster similarly. Indeed, their response to the inferno almost precisely mirrored responses in London, Warwick, Northampton, and Blandford Forum, making Charleston part of a transatlantic group of towns that would use destruction to lay new foundations for urban construction.[8] As was the case for all the charred metropolitan towns before it, the first reaction of Charleston's authorities was to quickly promulgate an "Act for regulating buildings . . . in Charleston." With the fortunes of established merchants, like Robert Pringle, in ruins, and the town's population now expanding quickly on the basis of the rice and slave trade, a rapid response was essential to the continued success of the colony. However, the decision to use the law to determine the future path of Charleston's development was also critical because it remade the townscape in a British Atlantic mold, ensuring that future construction would conform to the new agenda that had been set by the Great Fire of London in 1666, and subsequently perpetuated in a variety of provincial settings.[9] Long an idea in the mind and the model of a long-dead Proprietor, a common urban British Atlantic townscape would, in the wake of the 1740 fire, begin its journey from theory to living entity.

Comparing the text of the Charleston Fire Act to the 1667 London Statutes for Rebuilding shows that Low Country legislators wrote their document with the British example in mind. Not only did the overall structure of the act align with the most important opening sections of the London version, but the colonial assemblymen actually transcribed large chunks of the metropolitan statutes into their legislation for Charleston. Comprehensive regulations, such as the article stating that "no building whatsoever shall be hereafter erected or built in Charles-Town (except as hereafter is excepted) but such as shall be pursuant to such rules and orders of building, and with such material, and in such way and manner, as are herein after particularly appointed," were lifted directly from the original statute, as was the preamble specifying brick and stone as being "more comely and durable" materials for construction.[10]

Critically, these precise sections of the London statutes represented two of the most important ideas to emerge in house-building practice after the Great Fire: namely, that the ideal street was created by the imposition of a standard house front, and that this front should be built in brick or stone

rather than timber or wattle. Articles regarding matters as detailed as internal house structure and the positioning of shop stall boards were also adopted
into the Low Country's fire statutes from the London original. The expansion
of Charleston—and the interruption of that growth by fire—had forced the
Low Country authorities to confront the question of how they wanted their
town to look. They responded by seeking out recent precedent in the mother
country and, in the process, encouraged active Low Country participation in
significant developments in urban planning.

Statute law, however, represented only one facet of the way in which legal
instruments promoted new methods of urban construction and property
ownership in Britain. As a flexible and evolutionary entity, the common law
was equally caught up in such shifts as it too was redefined to accommodate
developments in the metropolitan property market. One of the most visible
of these changes was the emergence of new types of property title. Although
freehold and ninety-nine-year leasehold continued to be popular methods of
ownership, the faster pace of the land market demanded more adaptable titles
that would facilitate shorter periods of ownership for those wishing to own
land only to develop it with houses and sell it on. This new type of title was
increasingly known as a "building lease." Building leases, deployed widely by
developers in the growing towns of Britain, allowed the owner of the property
to let it out to a builder on the understanding that the latter would develop the
plot and receive any profits from his efforts until the lease was up. Thus, the
owner did not need to recruit builders or pay them, and the builders themselves would make a profit through renting out the finished house for the
duration of their lease.[11]

The now rapid growth of Charleston, combined with the reduction in
existing housing stock wrought by the 1740 fire, had increased demand for
new homes, workplaces, and warehouses to new levels by the second quarter
of the eighteenth century. Writing to their British contacts, Charleston merchants explained that there would be plenty of work available for any bricklayer or carpenter who chose to immigrate to Carolina.[12] For building artisans already in the Low Country, meanwhile, the sudden rise in demand now
made speculative construction as attractive a proposition as it had been in
the Old World—a development highlighted by the appearance of the building lease in the Low Country metropolis. One of the earliest such agreements
was between the carpenter John Vaun and Francis Guichard, the "clerk pas-

tor of the Church of French Protestants." Taking a fifty-year lease on a city lot at a yearly ground rent of SC£10.4.0, Vaun agreed to "erect and build upon the said part of the said lot . . . a good firm and substantial brick house of good materials and of at least fifteen feet in front," and to keep it in good repair. A year later, having built the required house and two additional tenements, Vaun advertised the properties for let, expecting that they would be "entirely suitable for a carpenter or a private family."[13]

Later instances show that building leases subsequently became a popular method of urban land development in Charleston. Planter Richard Beresford leased an East Bay lot to builder Frederick Kaufman for nineteen years on the understanding that within two years the latter would "build . . . a dwelling house, 14ft x 20ft and fence in the property."[14] An adapted form of the building lease was deployed by merchant Christopher Gadsden, who in 1769 divided up his town lands into lots and put them up for private sale. Although purchasers bought a freehold title, they nonetheless had to "promise to improve [the lots] within a year or eighteen months." However, buyers would be assisted by Gadsden, as he would allow them to "have their timber, bricks, lime and other materials for building said lots, landed at either of his wharves . . . FREE OF CHARGE."[15] Thus was urban construction in the Low Country established as a profit-making enterprise, rather than simply as a means to put a roof over one's head.

New types of ownership title and the rebuilding act had encouraged Charleston builders to construct according to new British methods, starting a process by which innovative modes of financing town development were introduced to the Low Country. But these legal shifts catered specifically to those involved in the raising of houses. Importantly, other developments in property law transformed urban land into an attractive investment for a much wider range of town dwellers. Under the English common law, city property was beginning to be treated in such a way as to make it a flexible, yet secure, asset that could be used as collateral for present loans, or as a guarantee for a family's future. In particular, the late seventeenth and early eighteenth century witnessed developments in mortgage law relating to a mechanism known as the equity of redemption. The equity of redemption was a branch of the law that "minimized the possibility that landowners would lose their land when they mortgaged it in order to raise cash, or used it as security for the debts they incurred." Therefore, a piece of property could be mortgaged out by its owner for cash, but that owner still ultimately held the title, and any failure to pay his debt would probably not result in immediate loss of the land. This law, while originally developed to safeguard the rights of the English aristocratic landowners when they ran into hard times, also became important to urban land speculators from the 1670s onward as they borrowed against land to sponsor development of their property or fund other business activity.[16]

From 1740 onward, the equity of redemption became likewise enshrined in South Carolina law, where specific reference to it was made in deeds relating to the mortgaging of urban land. Consequently, the English legal mechanisms that had transformed town land into an attractive investment for eighteenth-century Britons also assisted its commoditization in the Low Country.[17] The security provided by the equity of redemption meant that the blacksmith James Lingard was not in as much trouble as he might have been when he could not fulfill a SC£3,500 obligation to the merchant Hopkin Price. To solve his financial problems, Lingard mortgaged one of his holdings in Church Street, thus enabling him to pay back the debt in installments. The butcher Melchior Warley, merchant John Wagner, and artist Jeremiah Theus also resorted to similar tactics, and when they were unable to honor their debt, totaling SC£3,400, to various Charleston tradesmen, they mortgaged their jointly owned lot and tenement on King Street.[18]

Transatlantic shifts in land law had helped to make Charleston's town lots a secure asset against which money could be borrowed, potentially releasing extra capital into the Low Country economy and securing settlers' fortunes in a cash-poor society. So while the development of the rural economy was initially what fueled the majority of wealth creation and financial innovation in the Low Country, the concomitant growth of Charleston had stimulated a quite different set of processes that were new to the region but, ultimately, were an extension of novel forces at work elsewhere in the urban British Atlantic.

## The Law in Practice

The introduction of these dynamic aspects of property law was all very well, but they needed to be put into practice if Charleston was going to become a functioning part of an urban British Atlantic—and if it was going to develop into a place that would help to create wealth in the Low Country. Fortunately, in the decades before 1783 such legal tools were widely seized upon by an ever larger group of town dwellers—artisan builders. Their flourishing was underpinned by the continuing success of the rural economy, and the constant stream of free and enslaved people arriving in the town in response to the opportunities on offer in the countryside. But as the numbers of builders expanded and they professionalized, their activities served both to broaden and to deepen in new and unique ways the Low Country's entanglement in a transatlantic world of urban development.

As previously noted, before the 1730s, town-building artisans—along with their counterparts in other trades—were few in number and worked in small, uncomplicated enterprises. This state of affairs contrasted strongly with the increasing dynamism of the British building industry in this first quarter of the eighteenth century, where high demand for new housing was pushing working practices in a capitalist and entrepreneurial direction in a number of key areas.

First, greater professionalization among the ranks of carpenters, bricklayers, and plasterers led to the appearance of the self-styled "building undertaker" or "general contractor." These men directed employees drawn from all the trades in house construction, and they would often also assume responsibility for the supply of materials. This additional control made it easier for the master builder to rationalize the construction process and calculate profits. In order to achieve this efficiency, the contractor, in contrast to his predecessors, would have been literate and numerate, which would allow him to calculate costs and direct building according to the latest classical architectural styles. As a result of this increased professionalization, it became more unusual for land owners who wished to build on their town lands to put themselves in complete charge of the project. Thus, although a substantial number of land owners did choose to execute certain aspects of housebuilding under their own steam—wealthy, educated gentlemen might draw up their own house plans according to the latest style manual, for example— it became more and more common for jobs to be handed over to contractors. Building had become much more about profit and entrepreneurship than it ever had been before, and as a result, the "industry" was becoming distanced from the non-specialist.[19]

Following the economic and fiery ravages of the 1740s when war succeeded conflagration and brought some merchants and planters into a very "low state," the strong demand for new houses in a fast-growing Charleston began to affect the scale of its building industry in much the same way as it had done throughout Britain's provinces. Fairly rapidly, the Low Country building industry began to display the dynamic aspect of its English-speaking brethren. The number of builders working in the town quickly escalated, and records show that over seven hundred free white bricklayers and carpenters worked in eighteenth-century Charleston.[20] Along with the slaves owned by master artisans, construction workers formed an important and numerous group in the urban economy. Together, these tradesmen made a substantial contribution to house-building in the town, and the structure and principles that guided them in their work reveals much about how houses were built in Charleston, and about how this process in the Low Country increasingly incorporated the innovative procedures being implemented elsewhere in the urban British Atlantic.

Between 1730 and 1783 a professionalized building industry emerged to take charge of house construction in Charleston and in the surrounding Low Country. White master craftsmen, styling themselves as general contractors or as building undertakers, stepped in to execute projects for Low Country clients. Rather than employ individual craftsmen to complete discrete jobs of work on a town building site, as William Rhett had done in 1712, clients began to call on a manager whom they could trust with the entire contract. Attorney Charles Pinckney settled on just this course of action when in 1750 he bought a city house and lot that was in a state of some disrepair. In order to revive the property, Pinckney called in carpenter/contractor John Williams. Using a simple scale elevation (see fig. 3.1) and a sketch of the design to be implemented for a new Dutch dormer roof, Pinckney conveyed the outline of the proposed work to Williams. Pinckney supplemented this drawing with a written "Memorandum of carpenter's work to be done." The memorandum—essentially a contract—contained many detailed demands. The doors on the first and second floors were required to have six panels, and the windows were to have plain window seats under them.

However, the contract also left much to the imagination of Williams. The final design of the roof was to be "as shall be judged best," and although the stairs were to be built "without ramp or twist," the shape of the banisters was left open to interpretation. Furthermore, the memorandum closed with a formulaic statement often inserted into such contracts, namely that "the whole

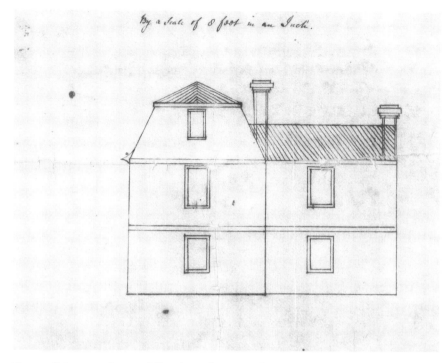

Fig. 3.1. "Memorandum and Sketches: Elevation of a House," by Charles Pinckney, February 19, 1750. (Courtesy of South Caroliniana Library, University of South Carolina)

[should] be completed and finished in a workmanlike, handsome and substantial manner." Although there is no way of knowing in what ways the finished house differed from Pinckney's original plan, the accompanying accounts show carpenter Williams executing his commission with the authority of a contractor. He found all of the necessary materials for the job and organized the slave labor, only presenting Pinckney with a bill once it had been completed. Thus were Pinckney's gentlemanly dabblings in architecture realized by Williams' expertise.[21]

John Williams was clearly a building contractor in the mode of his British counterparts: not only did he act as a manager of Pinckney's project, but his ability to translate his client's ideas into reality rested on his literacy, numeracy, and familiarity with scale drawings and plans. By the 1760s, Williams was a common figure in the Charleston building industry. Peter Manigault regularly employed the construction partnership of Gordon and Young to build city tenements and to work on his own townhouse. In 1765, when Manigault set about the construction of a substantial city house for the then absent Ralph Izard, the attorney again used the services of a general contractor. Manigault took the lead in the overall design of the house and kept Izard abreast of the work with letters and plans of his future residence. Having drawn up a ground plan and dipped into the early phases of planning, however, Manigault handed over the project to house carpenter and contractor Daniel Cannon, who managed the necessary labor and materials and saw the house through to its completion.[22]

As the building contractor established himself as a familiar figure in the Low Country, the relationship between him and his client slowly became formalized. In Charleston, as in Britain, the eighteenth century witnessed the introduction of procedures that ensured that both parties signing a building contract might have recourse in law should one of them fail to fulfill their obligations. The custom for tradesmen to be paid individually, "by the measure," fell out of favor, and it became more common for the general contractor in charge to receive a lump sum, usually paid in installments throughout the period of construction. As the role of the building undertaker became more widespread, so did the instances where a pre-agreed price was paid to this superintendent. Over time, this method of payment came to be known as "by the great."[23] This binding agreement made it much easier for a contractor to calculate costs so as to yield a profit: house-building had become a business for capitalist entrepreneurs and not a mere necessity for landowners looking to put a roof over their heads.

By the third quarter of the eighteenth century, most Charleston contractors were working "by the great." One such contract was drawn up in May 1770 between the bricklayer and carpentry firm of Axson & Gaborial and the planter William Clay Snipes. Before a witness, Axson & Gaborial agreed that they would build a Charleston residence for Snipes, "with outhouses and other appurtenances agreeable to a plan given in and signed by the said John Gaborial." The house was "to be finished in a compleat perfect workmanlike manner on or before 6th November 1770," with Axson & Gaborial receiving half of their SC£3,500 fee when the house was "inclosed," and the other half when it was completed. For their money the partners undertook to provide "all the materials and workmanship," and to pay a penal sum of SC£500 if the building was not completed on time. The agreement was clearly couched in formulaic terms, implying that its writing was a familiar process for the builders. Furthermore, this was a language that recurred throughout contemporary documents, with contractor Thomas Robinson noting that he had built a shed "as per agreement" for Luke Stoutenburgh, and Ann Middleton similarly recording an "agreement with Andrew Gordon for building [a] house."[24]

If the emergence of the building contractor occurred for economic reasons, it also partly came about as a result of the demands made by the popularity of the classical building style endorsed by Fire Acts of the period, Charleston's included. Such styles required high levels of knowledge and skill, as the symmetry and regularity inherent in a building's interior and exterior barred the non-expert from their successful execution. Although many could learn how to raise an irregular wooden house, few could plan a brick Palladian villa or create the intricate moldings that finished every room and chimney-piece. Even if a house was plainer, literacy and numeracy were still essential to measuring out a regular plan. With his access to materials and men, and his knowledge of classicism, the building contractor was, therefore, crucial to the creation of the classical Charleston that rose from the ashes of the 1740 conflagration.

In particular, contractors were critical to wealthy Charlestonians seeking to create a prestige town residence. One of the most impressive of these eighteenth-century structures is the Miles Brewton house. Standing at number 27, Church Street, this building is often described as the greatest surviving example of the Palladian style in colonial America. With its large portico and majestic flight of steps ascending to the main entrance, the Brewton house stood in stark contrast to the dusty street and its neighboring brick and wooden buildings; it had a splendor designed to bolster the reputation of Miles Brewton Jr., slave trader and son of the Huguenot silversmith Miles Brewton Sr.

Leading the construction of Brewton's monument to trading wealth was Richard Moncrieff, one of Charleston's more successful cabinetmakers and building undertakers. At the time of Brewton's contract, Moncrieff was in partnership with another builder, Kinsey Burden, and it is likely that both would have been involved in the organization of the considerable labor and materials that were required to undertake this substantial project.[25] Although it is not possible to know the precise nature of the works undertaken by these master builders, a public dispute over the credit for the carving and carpentry work does reveal the extent to which they had conceived and controlled the project. Using the *South Carolina Gazette* as his mouthpiece, carver Ezra Waite challenged the assumption that it was Kinsey Burden, Moncrieff's partner, who had crafted *all* of the house's interior woodwork. In his advertisement, Waite styled himself as a "civil architect, house builder . . . and carver," and he claimed to have had a hand across all of these areas during the course of construction in Church Street.

While his five slaves, including one bricklayer, labored on the structure of the edifice, Waite claimed, he had engaged in the more skilled work of carving the wood-paneled interiors. To this end, Waite alleged that he had "finished the architecture and conducted the execution thereof, viz. In the joiner's way, all tabernacle [door] frames, that in the dining room excepted, and raised all the said work in the four principal rooms; also calculated and adjusted, and drew at large for the joiners to work by the Ionick entablature, and raised the same in front and round the eaves of Miles Brewton's."[26]

These claims demonstrate just how much the image of the wealthy merchant or planter lay in the hands of the craftsman. According to Waite, he had designed and realized the "look" of those rooms in Brewton's house that were most likely to be used to entertain guests. Recent research by architectural historians seems to support Ezra Waite's authorship. Comparison of the design of Brewton's interiors to designs featured in the British pattern books and guides listed in Waite's inventory, and to those in the contemporary Charleston Library Society, reveals numerous similarities in both form and motif. What is more, the design of Brewton's interiors seems to have heavily influenced other wealthy Charlestonians who were raising city houses in the same period. Planter William Burrows, Colonel John Stuart, and planter Peter Boucquet all commissioned residences with similar interiors in the immediate pre-Revolutionary decades.[27]

The firm that had undertaken Brewton's project was a sizeable enterprise, capable of marshaling a workforce that was large and diverse enough to successfully complete the construction of a three-story detached mansion. This complexity signals the final area in which the act of creating Charleston's landscape was ushering the Low Country into the embrace of an urban British Atlantic of economic dynamism; individual construction companies were beginning to achieve the size and stature of their transatlantic counterparts. At the Revolution, one-man enterprises still existed, but contracts were increasingly completed by those who could offer a larger workforce. Bricklayer Thomas Gordon, for example, was able to deploy five hands on a contract for Charleston attorney Othoniel Beale in 1757. His contemporary, James Cook, a carpenter, had at least four slave employees at work during the 1770s. A detailed 1783 bill for building a new store and wharf for merchants Jervey & Walter shows master carpenter Thomas Harrison laboring alongside his seven white apprentices, his journeymen, and his three slaves for the entire seven months that it took to complete the building. Only at the end of the contract did Harrison spend six days working alone, presumably putting the finishing touches to the edifice while his workforce went on to a new job.[28]

Harrison's enterprise, like those of nearly all his fellow contractors, included a number of unfree tradesmen. Indeed, many free white builders depended largely on South Carolina's character as a slave society as they expanded their businesses. The relationship between those black and white skilled workers who worked alongside one another was often a fraught one in the Low Country, and the conflicts between white artisans and their black counterparts are well documented, leading historians to conclude that slave labor was rarely conducive to the creation of an innovative skilled enterprise.[29] Yet, for the most part, whites were extraordinarily successful at forcing slaves to conform to their European work practices, a success no doubt encouraged by the dire alternatives that blacks faced on the rice plantation. Builders used their existing apprenticeship arrangements to train slaves in their trades, and blacks' quick absorption into skilled work structures was already reflected in the 1740 Fire Act. There, the metropolitan idea of implementing fixed rates for labor and materials, to prevent unscrupulous artisans from taking advantage of desperate and homeless victims, was transposed to the Low Country. But in addition to rates for white masters, journeymen and apprentices, the act also specified lower fixed sums for slave bricklayers and carpenters, thus incorporating this new kind of labor into existing ideas about the regulation of work.[30]

Soon, slaves had been embraced by the building sector and had become integral to its day-to-day operation, a state of affairs reflected in the slave Boston King's unhappy experiences as an apprentice in Charleston to a group of carpenters who were building houses in the city.[31] Up to 1800, Charleston building artisans owned at least 250 slave carpenters, bricklayers, painters, and plasterers.[32] The carpentry firm of Wyatt and Richardson—one of the few artisan enterprises for which detailed records survive—drew a quarter of its

workforce from among Charleston's black population.[33] Slave labor was crucial to Charleston's building industry, to the extent that if artisans and other
Low Country slave owners had not encouraged blacks to work as builders, the
emergence of such a sophisticated industry could well have been stymied.

In a much broader sense, the success of "modern" stylistic ideas about
building in the Low Country also rested on the ability to accommodate the
needs of a slave society situated in a subtropical climate. Importantly, the
new type of uniform, terraced, brick property being raised in towns throughout Britain by the middle of the eighteenth century had a footprint that also
answered the needs of a city with a large slave population. New developments
in the metropole were often laid out on long, narrow plots, with a kitchen
at the rear and a selection of outbuildings at the foot of a garden. Such an
arrangement perfectly suited the Charleston household, as outbuildings and
kitchens could simply be detached and adapted to accommodate a family's
slaves. And as extant urban plats show, such rearrangements of this model
were indeed made by Low Country house owners. Architecturally and economically speaking, the innovations transforming the British building industry
had proven themselves remarkably fitting for a slave society, facilitating their
speedy transmission to Charleston in the course of the eighteenth century.[34]

From the late 1730s onward, Charleston builders merged legal and architectural innovation with local circumstance to forge a Low Country construction industry that was truly transatlantic in its character and its reach. In creating such an entity, moreover, the town's builders had introduced important
processes of economic and cultural change to South Carolina—forces that
would have had little impact had it not been for the growth of Charleston.
To a greater extent than in its the founding years, the town had given rise to
unique processes. As the settlers involved in the propagation of these trends
set about building homes and warehouses, they elaborated a lived connection
between Charleston and other towns in the English-speaking world, forging
an urban British Atlantic as they went.

## Money

As host to particular economic and cultural processes, the English-speaking
townscape of 1750 was beginning to display a range of common characteristics,
and Charleston was no exception. Greater regulation of private buildings, the
favoring of brick houses, a concern among the wealthy for permanent, prestige

dwellings, and the development of professionalized construction concerns in answer to the new requirements of these trends, were all visible processes in larger British Atlantic towns. Every one of these developments signaled a level of economic dynamism inherent in the townscape that had previously lain untapped. Thus far, though, we have only touched on these universal developments in the realm of the law and the workplace. Equally important to South Carolinians—and tangible to them on a day-to-day basis—was the income and capital that their development of urban land brought to their households and to the region's economy.

Rural land purchase and speculation is universally recognized as a central force in the economic and social development of colonial America. Buying, selling, and cultivating "empty" tracts made many a fortune in the Southern and Middle Colonies, while strictures on the availability of agricultural land strongly influenced patterns of settlement in New England. With a few exceptions, America's urban land markets are not thought to have made such an important contribution to pre-Revolutionary development, which was mostly a staple-led affair. Instead, the great era of city property booms arrived after 1783, arm-in-arm with the emergence of the American metropolis.[35] Yet, as the dramatic physical expansion of Charleston, and the legal and economic innovations that accompanied it, would suggest, the market for urban land in the Low Country was vibrant and full of potential as a generator of income and capital in its own right. Without the possibility of agricultural cultivation for the market, how did it generate those funds? And, more to the point, just how much money could urban land create in comparison to the rural lands surrounding it?

With the Office of Mesne Conveyance based in Charleston, many hundreds of land transactions were registered with the colonial authorities, making it possible to provide answers to such questions in some detail. These conveyances reveal that from the 1740s onward, urban property was indeed a crucial foundation of wealth among South Carolinians. Charleston became an independent generator of income and capital that not only funded the expansion of the plantation economy, but also made fortunes all of its own. When they invested in town lots, Charlestonians again articulated their membership in a transatlantic culture of urban land development; moreover, the process reveals how early America's cityscapes were becoming autonomous sources of economic growth even before the Revolution.

Our exploration of urban property speculation must begin with the building artisans. With their skills and knowledge, the purchase and development of urban lands presented them with an obvious opportunity for profit—one that British builders had already seized upon in the wake of London's Great Fire. As English general contractors streamlined their costs and working practices in a quest for greater efficiency, it became more common for them to broaden their income-seeking activities. In 1763, for example, the modest middling tradesman Henry Gough, a bricklayer in Liverpool, made £840 sterling from a small project in which he raised sixteen tenements on a downtown plot. The response of Charleston's builders to the Low Country's need for homes proved remarkably similar. Altogether, half of all white carpenters who were recorded as working or living in Charleston in the eighteenth century were involved in the buying and selling of land.[36] In some cases, they were encouraged in their activities by the building lease, which supported speculative construction by allowing a builder to pay for its cost through rents and sale to the plot owner. With their access to "free" slave labor, white Low Country bricklayers and carpenters also found it easier to buy and develop land, as they could undertake projects without having to hire and pay additional employees. As they speculated in land, developed it, and sold or rented houses, carpenters and bricklayers facilitated the continuing growth of the urban population and carved out novel modes of making money, inaccessible to settlers in more rural parts of the colonial South.

Building artisans adopted a number of strategies when investing in town lands. Their chosen path depended on how much capital they had, how much they were willing to borrow, and for how long they wished to tie up their initial outlay. Probably the most common type of investor was the carpenter or bricklayer who, like Gough, developed just a handful of town lots. The carpenter and sometime speculator in the coastwise trade James Verree was one such builder, who bought a small plot of land in the center of Charleston and sought to recoup his initial investment by building houses and selling them on as speedily as possible. Verree built his three houses on part of a Tradd Street lot purchased in 1764; by moving his family into one and selling the remaining two, he likely covered his costs for the construction of his own home. This small-time activity continued at the edge of the town after the Revolution. The modest lot on the outskirts of town purchased by the house carpenter Gilbert Chalmers for SC£2,800 in May 1796 realized SC£4,200 a few months later, when grocer John Gennerick bought it complete with its new wooden buildings.[37]

Even if they only had a few hundred pounds available to purchase half an acre and develop it, Charleston's builders were adept at using their skills to turn empty lots into income. However, many were willing to take much bigger risks in the hope of more substantial gains. Other builders, who were more entrepreneurial than Verree, turned to the security offered by equity of redemption to take out large mortgages to sponsor house construction on a more perilous—but ultimately very rewarding—scale. One such speculator was Robert Deans, a house carpenter and general contractor who immigrated to Charleston from Scotland in about 1750. Deans started out by buying an acre of land on Queen Street. To pay for the land, he took out a mortgage for SC£1,400 with the seller Thomas Boone. In 1763, once the original sum had been paid off, Deans remortgaged the property to merchant Thomas Buckle, this time for SC£5,000. This second loan was almost certainly sought by the carpenter to fund the development of his property, because, when silversmith Alexander Petrie took over the management of the lots for Deans (who was visiting Scotland) in late 1764, they were known as "Deans' Square." Petrie was commanded to "view and examine the condition of all real estate including houses, messuages, tenements, and hereditaments and to make necessary repairs . . . [and] collect due rents." During his management, Petrie was also allowed to sell the property if a profitable opportunity arose. Within the year, the silversmith had managed to dispose of the development for a total of SC£10,100.[38]

Deans's strategy had demonstrated how, by holding onto land and improving it, the developer was ultimately rewarded with a significant sum of money. Another builder who viewed town development as a major, longer-term, investment was bricklayer Anthony Toomer, who, shortly before his death, had engaged to develop a similarly substantial set of town holdings. In his will, Toomer instructed his executors to sell off undeveloped country lands straight away. However, they were to keep his city property and "compleat [the] buildings in Hazell Street according to the plan that is known to my family," as well as improving "the lands which I purchased of Mr. Cannon to the best of their judgment."[39] The Hazell Street property of Toomer is detailed in the plat drawn up shortly before the bricklayer's death; quite possibly this was the plan with which the deceased's family was familiar. The plat illustrates a 27,000-square-foot holding situated on the edge of Charleston as it stood in the last quarter of the eighteenth century, divided into seven developed lots. Descriptions of the buildings to be laid out on these lots suggest that

Toomer was planning a substantial development. Each piece of land bore a "house three stories with cellars of brick and covered with slate roof, kitchen and washroom two stories with cellars of brick, covered with slate, stable and carriage house one story with lofts of brick covered with tiles." These properties were clearly destined for occupants of some wealth, who would be willing either to rent or to buy for a handsome sum—enough to presumably support Toomer's widow and the couple's sons well into the future.[40]

Although it was easiest for builders to buy and develop Charleston lots for profit, the potential rewards and the continuing demand for homes meant that urbanites in other trades and professions soon became proficient speculators as well. Two such developers were the blockmaker Barnard Beekman and the blacksmith Tunis Tebout, who in 1761 laid out SC£5,010 for a prime lot on the East Bay. A few months later, the two craftsmen were able to sell the estate, complete with the "now erected long brick building containing many shops and stores" to merchant Benjamin Smith for SC£10,000.[41]

However, Tebout and Beekman's venture was small in scale compared to those of other, wealthier, Charlestonians who gained a firm foothold in the market for land, house construction, and rentals. The successful silversmith John Paul Grimke purchased a Tradd Street lot for SC£2,105 in 1762; by 1766, it had a brick house on it substantial enough to attract the planter Arthur Middleton as its tenant. In February 1768 Grimke purchased another town lot on the corner of Queen and Meeting Streets for SC£2,600. He then mortgaged his Tradd Street assets for SC£3,000 the following October, almost certainly using the money as capital to finance the development of his second lot, as by September 1769 he had a "new finished house" for rent on it, with two additional three-story brick houses to be ready for rent in the new year. In 1778, with the Charleston land market at its pre-Revolutionary zenith, Grimke took his chance and sold both lots with their houses for the grand sum of SC£16,500.[42]

Equally successful was Thomas Elfe, one of Charleston's best-known cabinetmakers. Elfe operated on a grand scale. At the opening of accounts in 1768, he was in possession of five town properties: two grander houses and lots on Friend and Broad Streets; a pair of tenements, also on Broad Street; a lot with his shop on it, on King Street; and an empty lot situated on Queen Street. For the entirety of this period, Elfe rented his own town home from the merchant and planter Othoniel Beale. Both the houses and tenements were rented out, and constant occupancy of all three properties meant that in the space of eight years, they brought in a total of SC£8,720. Of course, this sum did not amount to a straight profit, as Elfe was frequently making repairs and improvements to his holdings. He spent small sums, usually under SC£40, on installing pumps, drains, and wells, putting up fences, painting and glazing windows, and maintaining the brickwork. The cabinetmaker also undertook some larger improvement projects: he spent SC£551 on a new kitchen for the Broad Street tenements, and SC£50 on a coach house adjacent to his workshop in King Street.

However, Elfe was also interested in further increasing his holdings and, if possible, acquiring more rental properties. In 1773, after having made SC£3,750 from selling off a portion of his Queen Street lot, Elfe embarked on the construction of another house. The house, built by the local carpenter and contractor Benjamin Baker, cost SC£1,979 and was completed at the beginning of 1774; by 1775, Elfe was renting it out for SC£330 a year. In April 1774, the cabinetmaker made his last major investment of this period; he purchased a fifth rental property in the suburbs of Charleston and let it for SC£330. At the end of his accounts, in late 1775, Elfe was receiving SC£660 more in rent a year, and despite substantial expenditures on his holdings, was SC£6,224 better off.[43]

For many urbanites, then, property served as income-generating capital, producing a surplus that could then be invested in yet more property or in other business ventures. As these examples demonstrate, entering the rental market proved to be one of the more popular routes to profits. Demand for homes and rooms to rent in the British Atlantic city rose considerably over the course of the eighteenth century, for a wide variety of reasons. Flourishing towns had become highly attractive to economic migrants searching for work. Many such people either found it hard to accumulate the wealth needed to buy urban land, or did not view their long-term future as being in the city so chose not to make a purchase. At the other end of the social scale, rural gentry increasingly sought to spend leisure time in the town while maintaining their country residence. And, as towns grew ever faster, new arrivals seeking accommodation might find it hard to immediately find properties for sale.[44]

All such men and women—and their slaves—proved to be a ready market in the Low Country for the urban property owner seeking to make his or her assets pay dividends, and Charleston's rental properties attracted a broad range of tenants. In 1750, Governor James Glen's assessment of East Bay property was done on the basis of rents paid, as opposed to the value of a building at sale. Prime buildings close to the center rented for up to SC£900 per annum, with cheaper ones at the less developed western end of the bay going for SC£100.[45] These larger sums were garnered by landlords from wealthy planters, such as Arthur Middleton, who paid handsomely to lease a town residence. Many such rental properties could be quite luxurious. The Scottish settler Dr. William Murray rented a house that he described as "not small when I tell you that the doctor . . . Annie and I have each of us a good room . . . we have a good parlour and a dining room besides."[46] The large merchant firm of Faesch and Guerard rented a town house from building contractor Richard Moncrieff, and a tenement owned by the carpenter Henry Gray was let out to the Reverend Mr. Martyn. Indeed, by the end of third quarter of the eighteenth century, renting had become so customary that some house sale advertisements included a note about the sum that they usually rented for. The merchant Barnard Elliott's holdings brought in an estimated SC£1,570 per annum in rent. And the silversmith Jonathan Sarrazin's house "usually let at SC£350 year," and his corner tenement on Broad Street, "if it was to let, would no doubt command a very great rent." The bricklayer Anthony Toomer was also keen to inform the public that his Archdale Street tenements, up for sale in 1773, "can be let for SC£350 per annum."[47]

The liveliness of the rental market encouraged some Charlestonians to develop property portfolios even more impressive than those of the likes of Thomas Elfe and John Paul Grimke. Barnard Elliott appears to have owned a house on the bay that was occupied by the businesses of a wine merchant and a printer; a large residential property on Queen Street; a smaller house on the same thoroughfare; a lot on which the town fire station stood; a retail shop; a barber's shop; a gunsmith's shop; and an inn. And shipwright John Rose's holdings almost matched those of Elliot; in 1782 Rose owned a three-story brick house, two tenements, a wooden house, a brick house, and a wharf and store, all situated in town.[48]

Such widespread purchasing and renting of town properties took place not merely because it was a good route to a steady income, but also because it could even represent a better choice than investment in rural land. A lack of data makes sustained comparisons between the rural and urban land markets difficult, but it is clear that annual returns on urban lots could be substantial, especially in comparison to actual and potential returns gained from improvement of a rural tract. Thomas Elfe, for example, regularly received a greater than 20 percent annual return on his town holdings. In contrast, the cabinetmaker's suburban plantation on Daniel's Island vacillated between an 8.6 percent loss and a 7.3 percent return over the same years.[49]

Elfe's experience was not unique. With the average price paid for a lot on Queen Street in the 1750s and 1760s at SC£1,124, Barnard Elliott's charging of SC£500 a year for the rent of his brick house on this street would furnish him with an impressive 44 percent return had he paid a current price. In the same decades, the average price paid for a lot on Archdale Street was SC£3,850; Anthony Toomer's tenement on that street rented out for SC£250, yielding a 9 percent return, even from this more modestly situated house. Similar profits are suggested by Governor Glen's 1750 figures, as the average price of an East Bay lot between 1753 and 1767 was SC£4,745 and Glen's rental estimates averaged out at £404 per annum—again, a return of 8.5 percent. This was in the same region as the figure Alexander Petrie was receiving from his East Bay property, which had been purchased for SC£7,025 in 1758, and in 1768 was renting out for SC£840 a year—a return of 12 percent on his original purchase price. Without being able to calculate the outlays associated with the majority of these properties, such estimates must remain approximate, but they nevertheless suggest an impressive return that was at least on a par with—and often outstripped—the 10 percent projected by contemporaries who discussed investment returns on South Carolina's rural lands.[50]

For landowning Charlestonians, urban property undoubtedly made a notable contribution to their status as financially comfortable men who had found success in the Low Country. Collectively, however, their personal urban assets also generated income for South Carolina as a whole. The 1767 General Tax accounting put the total value of Charleston lots at SC£2,881,600, when all other rural and urban lands in the colony totaled SC£2,956,910. Clearly, most of this sum was capital tied up in property and so cannot be considered under the same auspices as the income brought to the region through the export of rice, indigo, and other agricultural products. However, in the period 1767–73, urban property sales witnessed £82,967 sterling changing hands in the colony, meaning that the average transaction value of Charleston's land market in this period almost equaled the value each of livestock, grains, and sundry produce exported from the colony during the same period. The town had become a not inconsiderable generator of income in South Carolina.[51]

Without any tax records in existence for Charleston, and with real property absent from inventories, it is easy to miss the noteworthy fortunes created by those who invested in the town. But to leave out the fertility of the urban landscape in the Low Country is to miss a major part of the story in South Carolina's ascent as one of the richest colonies in colonial British America. For those urbanites with money to invest, building on their land, and then renting or selling off the finished product, had proved a very rewarding course of action, and it is unsurprising that so many of Charleston's wealthier merchants and tradesmen chose this option. As they speculated, such settlers also became crucial in the introduction of the latest financial innovations of building leases and mortgages. In short, these groups of Low Country society had adopted an urban mentality that enabled them to view Charleston lands as an investment equal to any rural tract that might be on offer. Sometimes, this mentality had roots in an investor's trade but more often than not, the lure of urban land and the rents it could yield were enough to persuade a potential buyer to take the plunge.

At the Revolution, Charleston had itself become an asset to the Low Country. Settlers had discovered that by buying, selling, and developing town lots, they could provide for their families, set aside funds for the future, and generate more capital, that they could either lend out at interest to other South Carolinians or simply plough back into the expansion of their own property portfolios. By exploiting the unique possibilities of urban land with tools that were proving themselves across Britain, the owners of Charleston's lots were not only active in forging a transatlantic culture of town speculation, but had also bestowed the town with a role in the generation of income in the Low Country. With the success of the staple economy as its launch pad, Charleston in the years after 1740 began to play its own part in the creation of Low Country fortunes.

## Whose Money?

Raising a town clearly brought profits to some in the Low Country. But a critical question about the character of Charleston's expansion remains. Whose profits were these? The success of the town's land market was not simply about its ability to introduce specific income-generating mechanisms that complemented the plantation as a route to success. It was also about who rose up in this new society and whom they rose above. In the English-speaking town, urban property development had provided a new opportunity for commercial middling sorts to increase their income and to rise to prominence. British property impresarios like Nicholas Barbon and John Wood had made their reputations and their fortunes through speculative construction on a massive scale. This success had been so visible that both men had attracted a large number of critics, ready to label them as flashy arrivistes whose property wealth challenged the existing social order and the moral economy. No such figures emerged to monopolize the Charleston property scene, which was, after all, a relatively provincial affair in relation to that of London and Bath. However, some groups of settlers clearly began to dominate property ownership in the town, giving them superiority over their landless counterparts.[52]

In Charleston, the most obvious impact of urban development was to separate those white settlers who could legally own land from the large number of enslaved residents who could not. By closing off the promise of land ownership in an urban setting, whites excluded blacks from one of the best routes to riches and kept them forever as their tenants. For most slaves, this legal barrier was a moot point, as it was unlikely that they would ever manage to accumulate enough money to purchase their own freedom, let alone their own land. However, the implications were especially pertinent for Charleston's small community of free blacks, as it was also extremely difficult for them to acquire town lands. Recorded city land transactions yield only three instances in which free black Charlestonians owned or purchased land: in 1764, the free black butcher Matthew Webb laid out SC£900 for part of a King Street lot, and the free black woman Judith West put her six acres of Charleston Neck land in the trust of a fellow free black, John Mitchell, in 1756. At the 1790 census, there were 106 free black households in Charleston—and it is likely that among those, all but one or two paid rent to a white property owner.[53]

In contrast, no particular social or legal restrictions applied to the white ownership of city land. However, there were economic barriers for those whites who could not afford to purchase a home or lot, and this put them in the pay of those whites like Deans and Elfe who had become landlords. What is more, the rents that these property owners charged had become so high by the second half of the eighteenth century that poorer tenants were often forced into penury. One such victim was the baker Claudius Guillaud, who announced "to public and former customers that he is moved from Union to King Street opposite Mr. Peter Valtons, where he will carry on the baking business nb. it has generally acknowledged by his customers that his bread is better and sweeter than any other bakers in the province, the reason why he before left off baking was because house rent was too high for him and his profits would not allow him to pay 350l per annum."[54]

Others might not have suffered as Guillaud and his family did, but many poorer Charlestonians were never able to afford their own home or shop, and owning multiple houses remained a distant dream as they were barely able to find the money for their monthly rent. Some tenants were left in a very precarious position indeed. When blacksmith William Carruthers died in 1775, SC£9 of his already meager possessions had to be sold to pay for rent owed. Fellow metalworker William Randall, however, found himself in an even more desperate situation. After merchant Barnard Elliott had seized the SC£1,485 that Randall owed for shop and house rent, the blacksmith's heirs found that there was only SC£50 of goods left over.[55] The circumstances of these two men, who struggled to fulfill even their obligations to their landlord, were plainly quite different from those of wealthy property owners.

While being reduced to poverty by high rents, poor townspeople were also forced to live in less than pleasant conditions, as landlords often aimed to maximize profits by squeezing as many tenants as they could into the cheapest building they were able to raise. Records show that well-off men, such as the planter Benjamin Huger, put up rows of tenements that were rented out to shopkeepers and artisans who could not afford their own homes. Charleston's major churches also owned similar properties, with the St. Philip's vestry and the Congregationalists both building blocks of tenements to rent out to poorer citizens. Despite earlier fire regulations, these tenements tended to be entirely built of wood and of an insubstantial nature. With some land leases requiring such buildings to be cleared away at the end of the lease period, there was little encouragement to raising a sturdy home.[56] A rare surviving sketch of lesser eighteenth-century houses in Charleston probably depicts the average tenement, which was a long way from the grandeur of still-standing edifices such as the Miles Brewton house (see fig. 3.2).

Ownership of town land, much like the ownership of plantation land, evidently had the potential to create groups of townspeople who had economic control over property and homes within Charleston. Acknowledging the emergence of such a group is, on its own, important to our perceptions

Fig. 3.2. A plat with houses bordering King Street and "adjoining the allee," plus two other properties. (Courtesy of South Carolina Department of Archives and History)

of the town's ability to influence the structure of Low Country society. But in order to better assess that influence, we must also comprehend how this cadre of urban property owners intersected with the emergence of a South Carolina elite. Were Charleston property owners also plantation owners, or did they represent a discrete group in the colony? Fortunately, surviving eighteenth-century land records can provide the answer, as they allow a detailed exami-

nation of who bought, sold, and owned land in Charleston during its years of
expansion.

These surviving land deeds show that between 1680 and 1783 pieces of
land in Charleston changed hands hundreds, and perhaps even a thousand, times. Individual Grand Modell lots, covering roughly two acres apiece,
were often divided up and sold in parcels, increasing the number of units of
land for sale even further. By 1790, there were probably only a few places in
which an entire numbered plot remained in the hands of one owner. This process meant that many lots ended up with complicated ownership histories.
Lot 166, a piece of land next to the place occupied by the present-day Circular
Congregational Church on Meeting Street, was sold to the tailor James Ackles,
the shipwright James Brown, and the attorney Peter Manigault between 1750
and 1760 alone. Likewise, lot 103 on King Street had originally been granted in
1694 to a Huguenot gunsmith, Anthony Boureau, but had then passed to the
baker Anthony Portall, who left it to his daughter Elizabeth at his death. Elizabeth subsequently married merchant James Poyas, who then sold it to blacksmith Michael Muckinfuss in 1761.[57] At the same time as original lots were
being divided and sold on, private citizens and the colonial authorities were
also laying out new lots. Marshland on the south side of the Charleston peninsula was reclaimed and put up for sale. Development also extended west from
the original center, making the area known as Charleston Neck suburban in
character by the time of the Revolution. In a short time, ownership of town
land had therefore become extremely complicated and ever more expansive,
and it is evident that the aforementioned property speculators were but the
lead actors in a much larger cast.

Within this vibrant urban land market, clear trends emerged among the
buyers and sellers of Charleston's lots. Artisans formed the largest group of
traders throughout the third quarter of the eighteenth century (see table 3.1).
What is more, these craftsmen significantly increased their stake in the town
as the century progressed. Merchants were also a very important group of
property traders, maintaining a quarter share of the market throughout the
period. Together, planters and men who did not list a profession but styled
themselves as gentlemen, also made up a notable proportion of buyers. However, numbers suggest that these elites gradually withdrew from the urban
land market as the number of tradesmen buying and selling increased. Likewise, as the town matured, women became less involved in the purchase of
urban land. Overall, merchants and tradesmen consolidated their share of

Table 3.1
**Occupations of land conveyancers in Charleston, 1756–1773**
(as % of all buyers or all sellers)

| Occupation | Sellers 1756–67 (N = 249) | Sellers 1768–73 (N = 189) | Buyers 1756–67 (N = 249) | Buyers 1768–73 (N = 189) |
|---|---|---|---|---|
| Artisans/service workers | 25 | 37 | 37 | 44 |
| Merchants | 19 | 24 | 20 | 23 |
| Planters | 17 | 16 | 9 | 12 |
| Gentlemen | 13 | 8 | 13 | 8 |
| Widows/spinsters/wives | 11 | 4 | 8 | 5 |
| Professionals | 5 | 9 | 9 | 7 |
| No status listed | 10 | 2 | 4 | 1 |

*Source:* Langley, *South Carolina Deed Abstracts.*

urban lands at the expense of planters and gentlemen, who, in the five years between 1768 and 1773, represented only a fifth of all buyers, but almost a quarter of sellers.

The Low Country's plantation and merchant elite did have a notable stake in urban property—property that further augmented their wealth and their status as the leading members of South Carolina society. Without doubt, merchants like Henry Laurens, who owned town land and a plantation, used rents and profits from their urban land deals to bolster their fortunes and social position. However, it is equally clear that urban growth also supported the wealth of an urban "middling sort," made up of tradesmen grown rich on the town. Many of the merchants engaged in the purchase of land were not of the highest rank, and never truly became "planter-merchants" of Laurens's ilk.[58] This tendency to concentrate wealth in the city was also reflected in the habits of Charleston's artisans, only 7.4 percent of whom bought a rural tract, whereas 80 percent traded in town lots. The result of such an investment strategy was a convergence of the quantity of land owned by individual middling town dwellers throughout the British Atlantic town of the eighteenth century. In Britain's provinces, about 65 percent of the metalworking craftsmen owned city real estate, and among property owners a holding of circa 1.5 properties was the average. In Charleston, there was an identical level of real estate ownership among artisans, with 66 percent of testators mentioning town property in their bequests. What is more, since these colonial crafts-men held an average of 2.2 urban properties each, they had actually become more successful than their metropolitan counterparts in their domination of the town's land market.[59]

However, in order to confirm the importance of these groups in urban property ownership, it is essential to discover what proportion of urban lands were changing hands. If such land deals were simply taking place on the mar-gins of the town, with certain men holding firmly on to large, central tracts of the town and bequeathing them to family members at their death, these sales statistics become meaningless. All the activity of merchants and tradesmen in the land market would amount to nothing more than a sideshow to the con-trolling interest of the select few. But this was not the case.[60] Even though vague descriptions of property in the land deeds mean that is only pos-sible to trace half of all transactions to a particular lot, figure 3.3 shows that a large proportion of town land was bought and sold. Furthermore, lots in all areas of the original town plan changed ownership, with expensive areas like the East Bay enjoying just as much trading activity as the cheaper dis-tricts of Charleston. The trading of lands outside of the original Grand Modell lots, in newer suburbs like Ansonborough, Charleston Neck, and Hampstead, was also feverish. Overall, 71 percent of lots mapped out in the Grand Modell changed hands in this third quarter of the eighteenth century.

The rising share of lands purchased by artisans, merchants, and profes-sionals did, then, indeed represent an overall increase in the proportion of the town that they owned. Significantly, the same groups of people who were increasingly interested in purchasing town lands in the British town, were showing a similar eagerness to do so in the New World town. Even if plant-ers maintained a notable presence as urban landowners, it is not possible to claim that they exercised absolute control over town property in the years of Charleston's fastest expansion.

The ultimate upshot of urban growth in the Low Country was, therefore, the complication of its socioeconomic structure. While planters rose to the top of colonial society on the back of rice and indigo, some artisans, shop-keepers, and merchants also carved out a superior position for themselves through urban property speculation. Often, this meant that Charleston prop-erty holders not only gained the edge over their poor and black urban coun-terparts, it also led to them becoming the landlords of the plantation owner who wished to build or rent a city property for himself. Charleston had pro-

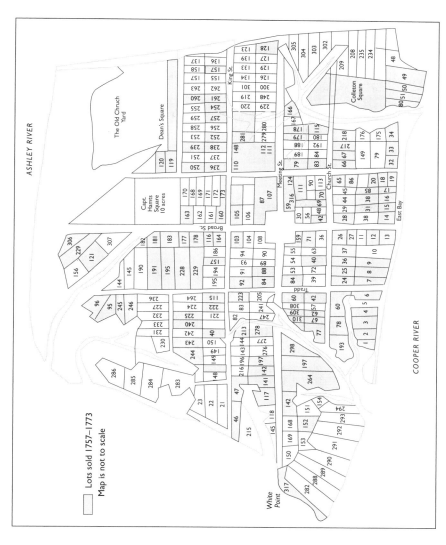

Fig. 3.3. Charleston town lots sold between 1757 and 1773. (Map by Bill Nelson)

vided an alternative route to wealth and status that, although it did not quite have the prestige associated with rural lands, nevertheless bestowed enough social and economic standing to make it a popular option. Because increasing numbers of settlers chose this route, urban and rural began to fall into contrasting economic spheres—between those who viewed their economic futures in terms of the city, and those who turned to the country.

Charleston's growing dynamism within the Low Country came in the first instance from the most obvious, but easily overlooked, source: the process of raising the town itself. Without charting the economic activities of the vast majority of Charlestonians—and without even straying into their cultural and political lives—we can trace the ways in which the presence of such a major town shaped the development of the Low Country. From 1740 onward, against a background of sustained success in the staple economy, disaster intervened to ensure that the English law in its Carolinian guise responded to the most innovative elements relating to the development and trading of urban real estate. As a result, lawmakers and land buyers alike picked up the tools that would facilitate the construction of a classical townscape, ripe for cultivation by entrepreneurs seeking to make money from its development. Building artisans also looked to the same tools when they began to arrive in the Low Country, and by partnering innovation with a steady demand for new houses, they transposed a dynamic metropolitan construction industry into a New World setting. Consequently, elements of South Carolina's economy joined a British Atlantic path of development, bringing the region into processes greater than itself.

With these industrial and economic innovations came the commoditization of urban land in Charleston. Builders and other tradespeople began to view the townscape as an investment opportunity equal to the vast tracts of rural land that were on offer. As developers seized this opportunity, they widened the modes through which Low Country settlers might accumulate wealth; where other Southerners' fortunes might have begun to founder once established planters had engrossed the best rural land, closing off the most promising possibilities of property ownership, the development of Charleston through the 1740s, 1750s, 1760s, and 1770s opened up new possibilities for new arrivals and existing landless residents with cash to spare. Soon, the purchase, mortgage, improvement, and rental of Charleston's lots became commonplace generators of capital, credit, and wealth. This process not only made for a culture of risk-taking and speculation, it also encouraged an urban property boom. As prices and rents in Charleston rose, the town became an ever greater source of wealth for successful landowners, making Low Country fortunes that were not directly associated with rice and indigo production. What is more, urban property ownership affected the social stratification of the region, as it underpinned the emergence of a group of settlers who had found wealth on the basis of their urban landholdings. This group—although intertwined with the planting elite at some points—was nevertheless discernible from it, and within Charleston its members claimed power over poor whites and free blacks who constituted an important sector of the market for rental properties. The group's profile was also closely allied to that of similar groups in growing towns throughout the English-speaking world. As the Low Country developed, then, its population became characterized by contrasting types of settlers, who had secured their futures either through rural tracts or through urban lots.

The growth of the town therefore embodied the most important ways in which Charlestonians were beginning to forge a living urban, British Atlantic. First, they were bringing the region into processes of economic and cultural change that were simultaneously affecting British urban society. This parity with other British Atlantic towns meant that any adaptations to local conditions were not adjustments of long-established customs, but represented instead the meeting of new trends with New World circumstance. Second, the town was emerging as an important alternative source of wealth creation and economic development that complemented the plantation economy in the Low Country. This distinguished the Low Country from other staple societies, yet united it with the British Atlantic's urbanizing regions. Finally, Charleston had a part to play in shaping the social organization of the Low Country as it fostered distinctive urban and rural loci of power and wealth. Along with a growing domestic market, urban construction offered up a new set of economic opportunities in South Carolina, distinct from those already inherent in plantation agriculture. What needs to be investigated more broadly, therefore, is the impact of these opportunities on the socioeconomic structures of the region. After 1740, South Carolina was no longer a society and an economy solely shaped by plantation agriculture. Now, the urban scene intruded to introduce new forces for change and development.

# 4

❧

# Urban Households, Economic Opportunity, and Social Structure

I N 1770 John Wyatt, an English house carpenter, disembarked at Charleston after the long journey from the Old World to the New. Despite his unfamiliar surroundings, and an apparent lack of family or friends, he quickly established himself on the urban scene. Marrying the daughter of a successful town blacksmith, he inherited a plantation and a number of slaves, but sold the rural land and put his slaves to work in his shop. Like the other building artisans in Charleston in this period, Wyatt used this labor to capitalize on the demand for his services in the growing town. By raising houses for town dwellers who contracted his services, and engaging in some speculative building, the carpenter made a comfortable living for his family.[1] But although Charleston's construction boom played an important part in Wyatt's ascent, these activities only represented one facet of his family's diverse business portfolio. Soon, the carpenter extended his interests by setting up a carting business and reexporting exotic woods from the Caribbean. At the same time, his wife, Violetta, contributed to the household's income by hiring out skilled slaves, lending money at interest, and taking in boarders. Together, the Wyatts managed to make a good life for themselves by exploiting the many commercial possibilities on offer in Charleston.

So plentiful were the opportunities of this growing town that the Wyatts had shown little interest in "turning planter." Instead, they had explored Charleston's potential to build a household economy that extended into every corner of the urban economy and far beyond the principal trade of John Wyatt as a carpenter. The Wyatts' economic choices united them with a growing group of Charlestonians. Indeed, such people were so abundant that visitor Josiah Quincy noted their presence on his visit to Charleston in 1773, when he proclaimed that the town's "middling order" were "odious characters," quite distinct from South Carolina's "yeomanry and husbandmen."[2] This "middling sort" was marked out by its members level of prosperity. Where the richest decile of the colony's white population owned over half of all wealth, and the poorest quarter just 1 percent, there were 65 percent of whites in-between, with 45 percent of assets distributed among them.[3]

Although historians have fully acknowledged that early America's cities developed a unique socioeconomic structure during the eighteenth century, existing works have given little space to families like the Wyatts, especially in the southern colonies. In Boston, Philadelphia, and New York, war eventually brought about rising poverty and a narrowing of opportunities. Those city dwellers that were in the "middle," as the Wyatts were, began to experience increased economic insecurity as urban society adopted a binary structure of haves and have-nots. Additional groupings among the population of the colonial town centered on occupation, not socioeconomic status, and a powerful artisan or merchant identity often cut across any emerging strata. In Charleston, historians have argued, such cleavages between rich and poor in white society also appeared, but were superseded in importance by the racial divides of the region.[4]

However, the Wyatts' experience clearly suggests that social differentiation came about not because of economic disadvantage, but because of urban opportunity. Whereas war took away possibilities for some, burgeoning markets in domestic goods, imports, and land opened up new horizons for others. What is more, the socioeconomic group born of this opportunity was not broken apart by strong professional identities, but was united by the lack of loyalty among its members to any particular trade.

Not unique to Charleston, such trends were common in many provincial towns on the British side of the British Atlantic. Expanding rapidly, their flourishing commercial societies proffered new opportunities, supported entrepreneurship, and rewarded those who were willing to cast off "the choking blanket of corporation and fraternalism that [had] smothered . . . business lives" in earlier times. Thus, those who attained greater financial security and a place in the middle did so not because they had been prevented from rising to the wealthiest ranks of society by urban depression, but because they had been successful in reducing economic uncertainty by taking advantage of urban growth.[5]

After 1740, Charleston's white population experienced shifts in its socioeconomic structure that resembled those taking shape in other English-speaking towns. Now that the plantation economy was not the only source of economic gain in this young society, urban growth proved a powerful imperative that, despite the particularities of the town's location, sponsored the appearance of an entrepreneurial middling sort. Moving beyond the restrictions of their particular occupation in new and intrepid ways, and implementing innovations in their workplaces, householders carved out a new position for themselves in South Carolina society. For these middling sorts, investment in town land and rental property was only one element in a larger strategy of diversification within the urban economy. The choices made by this emerging group in the spheres of business and family distinguished them both from those whites (and, of course, blacks) below them, and from the local planter-merchant elite above. What is more, their socioeconomic strategies make it abundantly clear that most did not harbor a frustrated ambition to join the merchant-planter elite, but instead owed most allegiance to a town-centered middling sort, whose particular outlook was informed by their close ties to the urban environment. Charleston's growth had sponsored a notable shift in South Carolina's social structure, a shift that moved the colony out of purely "southern" patterns and into the mainstream of British Atlantic processes.

## Independent Trading Householders

The early American household was an extensive affair and, as such, was the foundation of everyday life for the vast majority of colonial settlers. The precise structure of that household was often determined by the region in which it was situated. New England's rural households contained older children still awaiting some land of their own to work, some white servants, and few enslaved Africans. In contrast, southern rural households were more complex, comprising masters, mistresses, slaves, semi-separate black households, and perhaps even white overseers. Depending on the location and the social status of a household, the function of its members within the economy also varied greatly. Where the wealthiest wives and spinsters managed a household through delegation to slaves or servants, less well-off women frequently labored hard as "deputy husbands," or even as sole traders. Servants, apprentices, and slaves all worked at the command of the master with whom they shared a house, yet the balance of skilled and unskilled labor, and the amount of work undertaken outside the home, was rarely constant. Although households across early America were the principal unit of production and consumption, economic activity did not follow any set template.[6]

Householders' economic roles did not just vary across space, however; they also varied across time. Within the wider British Atlantic the arrangement of economic functions and roles within certain urban households underwent significant change during the seventeenth and eighteenth centuries. The "independent trading household" was the result of these shifts. Characterized by its ability to respond to the growing urban economy, householders eagerly seized the opportunities on offer in the growing town. Both male and female householders alike looked beyond their primary occupations and economic roles to achieve greater income and prosperity. Although male householders innovated in their main business and branched out into related areas of the economy, women also became crucial figures in the pursuit of a family's financial security, working with their husbands or on their own accounts. Rather than being a place where wives were domestic helpmates and husbands pursued a single trade, the urban household became a headquarters from which productive members oversaw an array of business interests. Working after this fashion, the independent trading household promoted an "industrious revolution" and achieved a measure of financial security in a world otherwise characterized by profound uncertainty.[7]

As the urban economy acquired a momentum of its own after 1740, the activities of settlers like John and Violetta Wyatt prompted just such changes in Charleston's households. Innovations made by these families were first of all visible in the head of household's business, which more often than not was part of the town's manufacturing or service sector. The largest single group of household heads at the 1790 census, tradesmen had maintained a significant presence in the town from the 1730s onward. In 1770, when Governor William

Table 4.1

**Requests placed by Charleston artisans in newspapers for slave and free white labor**

| Decade | Black labor | White labor |
|--------|-------------|-------------|
| 1730–39 | 4 | 17 |
| 1740–49 | 10 | 9 |
| 1750–59 | 5 | 7 |
| 1760–69 | 15 | 30 |
| 1770–79 | 52 | 28 |
| 1780–89 | 49 | 14 |
| 1790–99 | 61 | 38 |

*Source:* Index of Artisans, Museum of Early Southern Decorative Arts.

Bull estimated that Charleston had 1,292 dwelling houses and a population totaling around 12,000, craftsmen and their dependents made up roughly a quarter of both households and urban inhabitants overall.[8]

In other British Atlantic towns, these artisans participated in an increasingly dynamic preindustrial workshop economy in which a discernible pattern of development emerged within individual concerns. Throughout large and small towns, craftsmen had begun taking on more employees, and it became rare for a craftsman to work alone and in isolation. Simultaneously, working roles within artisan shops also became more specialized. Sometimes, the masters would coordinate their workforces so as to create production lines capable of turning out considerable quantities of a semi-standardized product. In the pursuit of greater output and efficiency, it also became customary for artisans to pool their resources and form partnerships. And, in certain industries, vertical integration occurred as tradesmen strove to smooth the path between supply and demand for their product.[9]

A look at the profile of Charleston's larger manufacturing enterprises between 1730 and 1780 suggests that artisans did not leave this dynamism behind when they left the Old World, but brought it across the Atlantic with them and used it to exploit the possibilities of the urban economy in the Low Country. In the first instance, master tradesmen revealed themselves to be flexible and innovative workers, as they quickly embraced the potential of slave labor. Indeed, the availability of enslaved hands was critical to the growth of Charleston's workshop economy (see table 4.1). Those white artisans who

Table 4.2

**Percentage of Charleston artisan probate records mentioning slaves**

| Number of slaves | Inventories 1730–49 (N = 30) | Inventories 1750–69 (N = 48) | Inventories 1770–89 (N = 62) | Inventories 1790–99 (N = 60) | Census 1790 (N = 491) |
|---|---|---|---|---|---|
| 0 | 36.6 | 13.0 | 27.7 | 35.6 | 37.5 |
| 1–4 | 31.7 | 29.6 | 33.7 | 33.9 | 38.9 |
| 5–9 | 24.4 | 38.9 | 18.1 | 16.9 | 13.6 |
| 10+ | 7.3 | 18.5 | 20.5 | 13.6 | 10.0 |

*Sources:* Charleston County Inventories, 1730–1800, Charleston County Public Library; U.S. Bureau of the Census, *Heads of Families at the First Census of the United States, Taken in the Year 1790. South Carolina.*

had enough money wasted little time in purchasing their own slaves, and within a matter of decades a majority had access to a chattel worker, leading Governor Bull to note in 1770 that Charleston's residents included 5,831 blacks who were mostly "employed as domestic servants and mechanics."[10]

Slave ownership among craftsmen then remained at high levels throughout the eighteenth century, with probate records suggesting that between 1750 and 1779 no less than 73 percent of artisans owned slaves at the time of their death, with about a third of these masters having five or more bondsmen (see table 4.2). Fairly quickly, a majority of artisans in Charleston were working and cooperating with slaves on a daily basis, as blacks and whites learned their trades together. As a result, advertisements, such as that placed by carpenter Thomas Bennett announcing that he "wanted immediately a handy white lad and two negro boys as apprentices to carpenter's trade," became commonplace in Low Country newspapers.[11]

Yet the availability of slave labor did not simply allow the most successful tradesmen to replicate the capacity of the workshops in Britain's growing provincial towns; it also permitted them to import innovative structures of production, as well as more specialized working roles, to the Low Country. Surviving records of master craftsmen working in Charleston's economy show how, from the late 1750s on, their working methods grew ever more sophisticated, eventually becoming typical of men plying the same trades across the British Atlantic. One of the best examples of this growing complexity comes from the workshop of the cabinetmaker Thomas Elfe—a man well known as the maker of some of Charleston's most elegant furniture.[12]

The innovations implemented by Elfe in his workshop were almost as striking as the craftsmanship of his tea tables, bookcases, and dining chairs. In the seven years covered by Elfe's surviving daybook, his business flourished, as Charleston's cabinetmaking sector experienced its first economic peak. Elfe alone took over one thousand orders for all types of furniture, and also undertook to repair pieces already owned by wealthy South Carolinians. The workshop making these items comprised the master, his business partner Thomas Hutchinson, and about eight slaves. Since Elfe was a long-established master, one or two apprentices could well have joined this nucleus. The workforce specialized in a range of cabinetry tasks, namely the frame and panel construction of casegoods and seating furniture, furniture repair, the assembly and disassembly of beds, the construction of tables, and the manufacture of other small wooden objects such as tea trays and coffeepot handles. The activity within Elfe's own workshop, however, was supplemented by the labor of some twenty-three other white craftsmen whom the cabinetmaker had employed to perform additional jobs essential to the making of a complete piece of furniture. Of these men, three-fourths remained in the cabinetmaker's service throughout the seven years covered by the records, receiving payments for work on an almost monthly basis. The stability of this wider workforce suggests that Elfe had created what amounted to a small factory, where as many as thirty-five workers were united in furniture production.

What is more, the members of this extended enterprise were divided into five groups according to their role in the manufacturing process. The cabinetmaker had assembled a production line. This production line started with the mahogany sawyer Jeremiah Sharp, who cut the lengths of wood that Elfe purchased from local merchants. At the same time, a second group of carpenters prepared the cypress that would be used for the carcass of the furniture. Presumably, this was work in which Elfe's slaves and apprentices would also have been engaged. The major part of the construction process would then take place in the shop itself, with all of the work for smaller items probably completed there. Elfe's workforce, however, was obviously lacking in carvers. These were the craftsmen that he employed most frequently to provide embellishment for items such as chair backs, bookcases, and table legs. The last stage of production was the completion of the upholstery, another task that was always done outside of the main shop. Significantly, by using this method of subcontracting to complete work, Elfe was re-creating workshop network structures deployed by some of London's most prominent cabinetmakers of the same period. Famous furniture craftsmen such as Thomas Chippendale and Samuel Norman achieved higher output by forming alliances with neighboring carvers, gilders, and upholsterers to finish their product. These workshop networks were also becoming common among the metalworkers of Birmingham and Sheffield, who used them to produce toys and buttons for the foreign and domestic markets.[13] Elfe further mirrored these English urban craftsmen with his aforementioned habit of investing his profits in urban property, a large proportion of which he then rented to practitioners of his own or allied trades, who then became part of his production network.[14]

From 1750 through 1770 Charleston artisans in other manufacturing trades were also making efforts to organize their labor so as to smooth out production processes and raise efficiency. Increasingly popular among the town's master tailors and perukemakers was the custom of employing "foremen"—a strikingly industrial position—in their workshops. The foreman was usually a white journeymanlike figure who, as the term suggests, undertook to organize and lead the labor of apprentices, slaves, and other journeymen in the enterprise. As early as 1758, John Boomer advertised that "he has for sometime lived with Mr. Moses Audebert, perukemaker . . . in the character of foreman." Setting up on their own, the tailors Logan & Williams noted that they were "late foreman to Mr. Walter Mansell, and . . . have work'd with him several years."[15] The possibility that these tailors' workshops might have become sizable is confirmed by the 1773 inventory of the master tailor Alexander McCormack. In McCormack's "cutting room" were twelve adult slaves, and his estate executors noted that many of the firm's white workmen had yet to be paid off.[16]

While increased professionalization meant that Charleston's largest manufacturers ranked alongside their British contemporaries, it also made them stand out from their local compatriots. Craftsmen who owned ten or more slaves never comprised more than 20 percent of white masters in Charleston, while those who had between one and nine slaves made up half of the skilled working population. But many lesser tradesmen also participated in this culture of innovation, not least when they too embraced slave labor to expand their business. The painter John Stevenson, for example, worked alongside his five slaves in order to complete his contract at St. Michael's Church, and the house carpenter John Williams did the same when engaged to build a tenement for Charles Pinckney.[17]

What is more, these smaller employers still often formed more modest workshop networks to produce innovative products. Already, at the relatively early date of 1756, the cabinetmaker James Kirkwood and the painter Robert Cochran cooperated to produce decorated fire screens for Low Country customers. Likewise, John Ruger and his slave were contracted to complete the painting and gilding work on the coaches that were built and renovated in the chairmaking shop of Benjamin Hawes and Uz Rogers. And Thomas Ralph, a master carpenter who worked for Thomas Elfe, was simultaneously engaged with Edward Bullard, a town woodworker who already had sixteen slaves in his employ, and with Thomas Bee, another city tradesman.[18] Indeed, masters in smaller shops were quite capable of participating in many working networks at once, forging complex connections across Charleston's skilled economy. The painters and glaziers Crawford and Wallace, along with their journeyman and three slaves, contributed to the products of the cabinetmakers William Jones and John Marshall, of the scientific instrument maker Alexander McCleish, and of the carver William Gardner. Of course, the company also glazed furniture and picture frames, cut magnifying glasses, and decorated homes throughout the Low Country on their own account at the same time.[19]

Eventually, tradesmen's willingness to use slave labor in innovative ways in their workshops, and a lively demand for goods in the Low Country, created the economies of scale that satisfied the needs of South Carolina's consumers. Even medium-sized firms—such as that run by tinsmith Robert Beard— organized themselves so as to be capable of considerable output of a standardized product. Putting in a claim for financial losses suffered because he had remained loyal to the British during the Revolution, Beard estimated that his tinsmithing business "for many years past ha[d] brought in near £300 sterling per annum." A schedule of property provided by Beard revealed that his workshop included two slaves, Joe and Tom, who between them possessed twenty-four years of tinsmithing skill. A last-minute estate sale before he fled to Scotland shows that Beard had also owned seven other slaves in his employ. Furthermore, shortly before departing South Carolina, Beard had advertised for the services of a white journeyman tinsmith. Altogether then, Beard most likely had eleven pairs of hands (including his own) to deploy in his workshop. Even though he headed up a workshop of quite modest proportions in comparison to some of his fellow townsmen, he was nevertheless able to achieve a considerable output. Shortly before the outbreak of the Revolution, and the hasty exit necessitated by his Loyalist sympathies, Beard had accepted a commission from the merchant William Ancrum for two thousand tin canisters, with both parties agreeing that the contract would be fulfilled within three months. As the deadline for delivery drew near, Beard admitted to his customer that he had only managed to complete five hundred canisters. Ancrum noted in a disgruntled tone that Beard's failure to come through on his word could not be put down to a lack of workshop capacity, but had probably been the result of his taking on too many orders at once.[20]

From the late 1750s onward, Charleston's most successful tradesmen established workshops capable of larger-scale production of a standardized product. What is more, they had achieved this position through their willingness to purchase and train slaves as workers in their enterprises. Their businesses stood a long way from being "factories," but were nevertheless representative of the ever increasing capacity of manufacturing that could easily be encountered in many a provincial town across the metropole. Artisans in Charleston from a wide range of trades had embraced such innovations as the division of labor and the creation of production networks. Far from being lone producers engaged in the careful crafting of bespoke goods for select clients, these master artisans had taken advantage of slave labor and a strong demand for their services to build large, dynamic workshops.

Increasingly, however, tradesmen's exploitation of economic possibilities did not stop at the limits of their particular skill. Growing provincial towns such as Charleston were ripe with opportunities to extend business beyond the workshop, and, appreciating this fact, South Carolina's urban craftsmen quickly branched out into other areas in order to secure their family's future. As they met and mingled with the retail and service sectors of Charleston's economy, these craftsmen joined the ranks of the town's "independent traders."[21]

Exploration of the full range of economic opportunities on offer in the town was so common as to be customary among the leading figures in the town's craft sector. When placing an advertisement in the local newspapers, almost 80 percent of artisans proclaimed that, in addition to their specialist skills, they were offering further goods or services.[22] Without doubt, one of the most common points of overlap in the Charleston economy was between retailers and manufacturers, and many successful artisans entered the retail trade while still keeping up their workshops. Clockmaker Joshua Lockwood announced that he had "glassware, as good as were ever imported into this province . . . directly from the manufacturer" for sale in his Charleston store. Later, Lockwood even went so far as to employ journeymen in a related trade, so as to offer a wider variety of repairs and custom-made items under one roof. Jewelers, clockmakers, silversmiths, coachmakers, gunsmiths, gardeners, upholsterers, and paperhangers became regular importers and advertisers of British goods. William Rigby Naylor, carpenter, surveyor, and architect of the Charleston Exchange, advertised in 1771 that he had "a large and complete . . . assortment" of carpenter's tools, bigger then any "as ever was imported into this province." He hinted at the quality of planes and saws that a buyer might expect by noting that they "were picked out . . . by one of the trade, and may be depended on to be some of the best exported from London."[23]

In addition to retail imports, many Charleston tradesmen also participated in the wholesale purchase of raw materials and components essential to manufacturing in the Low Country. Cabinetmakers appear to have been especially fond of this diversification, and more than one was involved in the mahogany trade between Charleston, the West Indies and Europe.[24] Trading in wrought metal components for furniture also proved an attractive sideline, and Thomas Elfe pursued this opportunity on a considerable scale. Between 1768 and 1775, Elfe had an ongoing relationship with the London merchant firm of Alexander Shrimpton & Co., from whom he purchased hundreds of pounds sterling worth of lockplates, handles, escutcheons, brass screws, and nails. Although he used some of these fittings on the furniture that he produced in his own workshop, his records show that he regularly sold such items to other local craftsmen, along with imported panes of glass for bookcases.[25]

A popular sideline among the more successful town traders, however, was accounting. As Margaret Hunt has highlighted, accounting skills were a particular feature of the trading household, which, juggling many business interests in an economic environment often plagued by uncertainty, had to keep a firm handle on income and expenditures.[26] Low Country upholsterer John Blott advertised that he was willing to take on "the care of one or two sets of books, of principal houses [of] merchants." While Blott looked for a book-keeping position, other tradesmen were already at work in this capacity, and a 1769 court dispute about debts reveals that the Charleston coachmakers Laughton and Bookless had been paid by the merchant William Whiting for "bringing up and settling" the latter's books. Wives were also expected to be skilled in this arena. Violetta Wyatt apologized after her husband's death for not being able to understand his books, excusing herself on the grounds that "she was always much occupied at home in the duties of managing." The wife of the Loyalist shipwright Daniel Manson, however, was fully cognizant of her husband's financial situation when, after his flight from Charleston, he fell into a deep depression and could not bear to confront the "low state" of his fortunes.[27]

As these cases highlight, a woman's work and skills within the urban economy were critical to the trading household's ability to take advantage of the opportunities within the town. The dawn of the nineteenth century may have heralded a doctrine of "separate spheres" in which women stayed at home and men ventured out into the world of work, but such a dichotomy is difficult to locate in this earlier period. As teachers, coffeehouse owners, tavernkeepers, artisans, money lenders, and shopkeepers, wives,widows, and spinsters pursued a range of trades that saw them making a substantial contribution to a household's livelihood. Far from being assistants to their husbands or performers of incidental and occasional work, these women were in charge of stable businesses that were a permanent fixture on the urban scene. Even though the law prevented all but those with *feme sole* status from being equal partners, such business women were vitally important to the financial success of their household.[28]

Women made their contribution in a variety of ways. A typical trading household was the one headed up by John Stevens and his wife. The couple, who had five children, had managed to cling to their middling circumstance through a lifetime of fluctuating fortunes. At the start of their marriage, Mr. Stevens had had a "genteel fortune" and had entered the merchant's trade in London, but his business failed and he was forced to take his family to St. Kitts, where he was fortunate enough to achieve success. With his finances restored, Stevens moved his brood again, this time to Georgia, where he purchased a small plantation and a few slaves. Disaster struck once more, however, as Stevens's venture was burned to the ground by his slaves, who had joined with others in an unsuccessful rebellion. At the age of fifty, though, the Stevens's at last found solace in Charleston; he as the postmaster and the organist of St. Michael's Church, and his wife as a sole trader and the proprietor of a "genteel coffeehouse . . . frequented by the officers of His M. Navy & Army & the first people of the Town only." Renting a town house, the family could afford two enslaved servants—a cook and a housekeeper. Whereas Stevens poured opprobrium on his Georgia experiences, he praised the opportunities and the people of Charleston, a place that, "with great prudence," could "keep us Genteel" into old age.[29]

By looking to all corners of the urban economy in order to maintain a respectable status, the Stevens shared much with other families, such as the Linds, the Ramadges, and the Crosses—merchants, milliners, tavernkeepers, schoolmistresses, and coffeehouse owners—whose comfortable but modest lifestyles were underpinned by the running of successful businesses in a flourishing town.[30] Women's work was vital in all cases, making the laboring woman quite visible within the Charleston economy. Roughly half of all liquor licenses granted in the town were given to town wives like the baker's spouse Anne Bodell and the shipwright's wife Susannah Pritchard, both of whom took on a tavern or dram shop to bring in extra money to the household.[31] Rachel Lawrence, wife of the woodcarver William Lawrence, also announced that, "having obtained credit from some merchants in Charlestowne in order to carry on business on her own proper accounts, as sole dealer and separate trader, exclusive and free from any concern with her husband . . . she . . . makes this declaration . . . and gives notice that she has opened a house of entertainment near the Beef Market where Mr. Doughty formerly, Mr. Cannon after, and Mr. Prince Lately have lived."[32]

The men and the women in these families, however, possessed a final instrument with which to achieve their independence as trading householders. In most British Atlantic towns, the "family economy" incorporated a productive husband and wife and perhaps some older children. Servants and apprentices, although bringing in some income, usually incurred much expenditure. But, using the skills and labor of their slaves, Charleston's trading households shifted the meaning and the parameters of the urban "family economy." Despite official legislation designed to prevent the ownership of slaves with a wide variety of skills, urbanites persisted in exploiting chattel labor to their advantage. Depending on the gender and skill set of a slave, householders were able to deploy unfree labor in a number of settings—all of which had the benefit of increasing the financial security of the free part of the household.

In the first instance, slaves supported the stability of the male head's principal trade. The flexibility of slave labor allowed firms to weather difficult economic times and continue their development, where those in an entirely free labor system may have failed. With not enough work to go around among Charleston's shipwrights in the 1740s, those men who had been able to invest in slave labor were able to charge cheaper rates and complete work more quickly, meaning that they garnered most of the contracts on offer. Those without slaves could not find work and had to resort to charging much higher rates than their larger competitors.[33]

Slave labor could also be hired out to other artisans to produce a steady income, even if contracts were sparse in one's own workshop. Thomas Elfe's accounts reveal that he hired out seven different slaves in seven years, with their work earning him a total of SC£2,021. Overall, Elfe was achieving a handsome return on his investment in slaves, as illustrated by his experience with Cyphan, a man whom he had bought from the merchant Edward Shrewsbury in June 1772. Elfe paid SC£700 for Cyphan, a sum substantial enough to suggest that the slave already had some skills. One month later, Elfe hired out Cyphan at a rate of SC£20 a month, and in January 1773 he received a total of SC£108 (a rate of 18 shillings per month) for another six months' work. Had Elfe continued hiring his slave out, he would have amortized his initial investment within only three years.[34] Indeed, the benefits for a white master created by "permanent employees" even meant that John Wyatt could continue his carpentry business in St. Augustine while in exile in 1783; by recruiting two of his slave carpenters to go with him, he simply relocated his workshop and went into the production of ready-made, exportable components such as doors and window frames.[35]

By putting slaves to work outside of their principal occupation, however, trading households made the income brought in by chattel laborers *central* to their economic strategy. Charleston families bought slaves who could work separately from the family's main concern, hiring them out for regular income in the private or the public sector. Carpenter James Cook's slaves included the carpenters Frank and Jack, Frank's wife and daughter, Hagar and Molly (a laundress and a seamstress, respectively), a sawyer, a gardener, "Hattie an excellent cook and house servant and her son Plato a working boy," and finally a "complete seamstress," Arabella, and her four-year-old son Bob. Between them, therefore, the carpenter's slave force of ten practiced six different trades, with only two young boys (aged four and eight) not listed with a skill. Other Charlestonians in possession of for-hire slaves included the clockmaker Francis Gottier, whose two bricklayers, Billy and Abraham, were surely not helping him in his workshop; the carpenter Esaie Brunet, who owned barber Jack; and the silversmith Alexander Petrie, who had no less than three slave carpenters, a barber, a tailor, and a cook.[36]

The economic security provided by slavery was, however, a family affair. When two urban trading families united through marriage, their individual slaveholdings could be amalgamated to the benefit of the entire household. At the time that John Wyatt had married blacksmith's daughter Violetta Lingard at the beginning of the 1770s, he had no slaves and (according to his acquaintances) was in possession of a moderately, but not overly, successful workshop. With Violetta's inheritance of slaves from her father, however, Wyatt's business went from strength to strength, and he quickly became one of Charleston's most prominent post-Revolutionary master carpenters. Indeed, fellow townsmen openly acknowledged the role that Wyatt's marriage had played in his rise, noting that the match had "fixed him very happily in his worldly circumstances."[37] Even after a tradesman passed away, his skilled slaves then continued to contribute to the security of his family. As they brought in earnings for widows, slaves ensured that white townswomen would maintain the status to which they had become accustomed. Artisan wives and widows, like Rachel Blott and Violetta Wyatt, could keep up their finances by hiring out their husband's slaves when the latter stopped earning; Blott hired out a slave painter trained by her husband by the year, and Wyatt received a steady income from the labor of her slave carpenters who had worked for her husband John.[38]

Apparently not yet troubled by the issues of control that hindered the success of slavery as an urban institution in the antebellum period, Charleston's traders eagerly embraced chattel labor to make it a vital tool in their quest for financial stability.[39] In the Low Country town, slave labor allowed white urbanites to exploit business opportunities to their fullest extent, creating a stable household economy. Slave ownership, moreover, was part of a strategy that called on each productive family member to move beyond his or her primary economic role and to explore the possibilities inherent in the larger urban economy. In doing so, these Charleston families had become "independent trading households," joining a group of similar individuals who had advanced their situation by taking advantage of the new opportunities on offer in growing provincial towns across the British Atlantic world.

## Countryside in Service of the Town

For the planter-merchants who marshaled slaves and resources at far-flung rice plantations from their town mansions, the city was truly in the service of the countryside. Their homes were clearing houses for country produce and stages for conspicuous displays of wealth and mastery for the benefit of their black and white inferiors. Indeed, the colony's rural aspect appeared so dominant that historians have frequently assumed that the rice economy drew people out of the town, setting up a "natural" progression from city merchant or artisan to plantation gentleman for the successful settler.[40]

With the superiority of rural opportunities a given—and the status associated with plantation ownership an added bonus—who would not want to make the leap from urban trader to rural master of one's own world? Such a question was easy to answer for clock and watch retailer Stephen Cater, who announced about five years after his 1753 arrival in Charleston that he was "removed to his plantation near Dorchester, lately possessed by George Sommers Esq." Like Cater, cabinetmaker Abraham Roulain severed his city connections in favor of the countryside. Later, wealthy shipwright John Rose was keen to inform the Loyalist commission that he "was King's shipbuilder at Charleston, he retired from this business . . . having made a considerable fortune. He then purchased lands . . . and was worth more than SC£40,000." These men were all more successful than the unfortunate John Stevens, who believed that he had negotiated all hurdles and turned plantation squire in Georgia, but whose misfortunes saw him return to town business after just a few short years.[41]

For a few who had started out their economic lives in the city, then, plantation ownership remained the logical reward of hard work in commerce or manufacturing. Yet it is clear that Charleston's success as an urban economy in its own right—and the investment made in that success by certain households—also began to alter the balance of the relationship between urban and rural economies. After 1740, the preoccupation of the independent trading household with the urban scene contributed to rural developments that saw plantations close to Charleston focusing more on provisioning, leaving those farther-flung enterprises to underwrite the staple economy. Looking for further money-making opportunities, urban households put their sights beyond the town's limits, but did so in a way that incorporated rural enterprise into their urban businesses. Now, the countryside was servicing the purposes of the town and had been recruited into underpinning the latter's ever-increasing dynamism. These town dwellers thus helped to shape the function of a Low Country plantation, and as well as being a country seat or a slave labor camp, the plantation also became an extension of the entrepreneurial trading household.

At the same time, it is clear that the status that went with rural landownership became less important to those urban householders who moved into agriculture. Such changing attitudes toward the function of land ownership placed those who took this route within a larger trend; they joined urbanites elsewhere in the British Atlantic world who viewed their primary socioeconomic locus as being the city, even when they had accumulated sufficient wealth to give up urban life in favor of the character of a country gent.[42]

Incorporating a plantation into an urban household economy was no easy matter. Even if financial resources were not an issue, getting the hang of running a plantation and tending to an urban business often proved to be a difficult tightrope to walk. This was particularly so if the two pursuits proved difficult to integrate and in need of equally close attention. William Murray, a doctor who immigrated to Charleston from the Scottish border town of Dumfries during the 1740s, attempted to juggle the establishment of an indigo plantation with the continued running of a successful medical practice. Only two years after his arrival, Murray's success as a physician led him to pronounce medicine as "the best travelling profession," with Charleston being an especially "fine place to be a surgeon." But he wanted more, and in 1757 Murray's brother John duly reported to their mother:

We are now building a little commodious house and as severall Scots tradesmen came out by the Leith ships we have indented two carpenters, who will build our house and our negroe houses which are already done, and make our indigo vats. All this they will do if they keep their health and our having two tradesmen of our own for these purposes will save us 80£ or 100£ sterling for they seem to be carefull and sober lads and are engaged for a year. . . . My brother and cousin still continue in the practice of physick and will at least remain so for a twelve month.[43]

For a time, William was tempted to leave the city for the life of a planter. Indeed, his purchase of the tract near Port Royal had come after an earlier declaration that he was "now resolved to quit physick and turn planter as I now see that the only way of making an estate quickly is by planting." However, with the plantation some sixty miles from Charleston, William found the situation to be too remote for his liking. According to his brother John, William's change of heart, and his subsequent decision to stay in Charleston—and in the business of doctoring—was aided by the fact that "the small pox is now in town and the Doctor has a great share of the beneficial article of inoculation in which he has been remarkably successful." Early the next year, William's cousin and medical partner reported that, "the town encreases every day and the Practitioners decrease. Dr Moultrie is become very infirm, Dr Oliphant has done very little business lately; he is either very valetudinary or much at Santee. Dr Milligan loves ease and repose, Dr Chalmers is assiduous but often goutified: Last Fall and Winter the business was chiefly in Dr Garden's hands and since he gained upwards of £1000 and I above £800 sterling in less than a year." Ultimately, the opportunity opened to Murray by the laziness or illness of his competitors in a time of epidemic proved too attractive, and in 1764 the working plantation and its crop were sold at a profit, with the doctor preferring to pocket the proceeds and continue the urban lifestyle that he had enjoyed since his arrival in Charleston some twenty years earlier. Tending to town business and giving due attention to the indigo trade had proved too much.[44]

Other Charlestonians also discovered that increasingly successful urban businesses tested their commitment to a separate plantation enterprise and forced them to choose between the two. Like Murray, the carpenter and shipwright Gilbert Chalmers also plumped for town. Chalmers assured the readers of the *Charleston Gazette* in his advertisement of sale that "the only reason that the plantation is now offered for sale is that the present owner's business requiring his constant attention in town prevents him from having it in his power to give the requisite and necessary attendance to the business in the country." Chalmers's description of his country property indicates that he was not simply returning to his Charleston pursuits on a whim. His six-hundred-acre Wadmalaw Island plantation, some distance from Charleston, was cleared and equipped with a river landing, a six-room house with "kitchen, barn, negro, and other necessary outbuildings," tools, a stock of poultry and hogs, peas, potatoes, a schooner, and some "negroes now on the place." Also deciding to "decline the plantation business" were the brick-layers Timothy Crosby and Peter Horlbeck, who both returned to Charleston and to their building firms; and the carpenter Stephen Shrewsbury, who gave notice in 1775 that "he has returned from the country, where he has been at work upwards of two years past and intends carrying on the HOUSE CARPEN-TER'S BUSINESS . . . as formerly." The demands of urban businesses uncon-nected to these separate and distant plantation enterprises had proved too much for these Charlestonians, who ultimately viewed their proper place as being in the city.[45]

This was not the experience of all urbanites, however, and a growing cadre of Charlestonians mastered the art of running a plantation and a town con-cern at the same time (see table 4.3). It appears that they achieved this feat where others had failed by ensuring that their plantation became a suburban, or hinterland, extension of their Charleston household enterprise. Often using slave labor or white hired hands, these city dwellers located their farms on a site easily accessible from town and grew crops, or exploited natural reserves, that were needed for sale in Charleston's marketplaces. Not designed to be the beginnings of a plantation empire in the vein of those extensive operations under the command of South Carolina's richest men, these "farms" were des-tined from the outset to fulfill the needs of the urban market. As such, they were much closer in character to the "truck gardens" commonly found in the hinterlands of early America's other cities.[46]

From their very foundation, townspeople's plantations were oriented according to the owner's knowledge and the needs of their urban businesses. Newly acquired land in South Carolina was often heavily wooded, meaning that there was much work to be done if the land was eventually to be deployed in the production of crops or in the raising of livestock. Even at these prelimi-nary stages, however, townspeople were acutely aware of the uses for these timber supplies in Charleston, showing a willingness to exploit them as inten-sively as possible in order to take full advantage of urban demand. To get his suburban plot cleared, cabinetmaker Eleazer Phillips advertised "a quantity of oak and pine wood, not three miles and an half from the city, very near a landing" to anyone who was willing to take the timber away. Gunsmith John Milner was also appealing to the needs of urbanites in order to get his land cleared when he rented twenty acres for a nominal sum of SC£20 to ship-wright John Imrie so that Imrie might fell and process the timber reserves.

Table 4.3
**Suggested and actual use of plantations owned by Charleston tradesmen,
and of all plantations**

| Suggested or actual use | Tradesman-owned plantations (N = 38) | | All plantations (N = 1,827) |
| --- | --- | --- | --- |
| | *Number of incidences* | *Percentage* | *Percentage* |
| Cattle | 23 | 61% | 26% |
| Corn/Provisions | 19 | 50 | 48 |
| Lumber | 13 | 34 | 25 |
| Rice | 10 | 26 | 69 |
| Other | 9 | 23 | 3 |
| Indigo | 5 | 13 | 12 |
| Manufacturing | 5 | 13 | 6 |

*Sources: South Carolina Gazette; City Gazette and Daily Advertiser; South Carolina Gazette and Country Journal;* Charleston County Inventories; Daybook of Thomas Elfe, Charleston Library Society; Edelson, "Planting the Low Country," 157 (table 2.8).

In total, Milner made SC£1,059 from the white pine, oak, and hickory that he sold to Imrie—wood that the shipwright presumably used in his trade or sold on to other willing buyers. Milner had exploited his plantation's timber reserves much more intensively than a full-time planter. Whereas Henry Laurens took seven years to make SC£456 from timber sales off of his five plantations, Milner made over twice as much in just twelve months.[47]

Making money from the clearing of virgin lands and the subsequent sale of timber in Charleston was a finite activity. When the forests were razed, settlers could then get on with the task of establishing a functioning farm. By the 1760s, many townspeople had had an opportunity to buy rural land and get their farming efforts well underway. The next stage in the creation of the trading household's rural outpost had begun. A notice placed by shipwright John Rose in the newspaper, advertising the sale of his fellow shipwright John Daniel's plantation, illustrates especially well the strategy followed by townspeople when they developed their rural property. Daniel was recently deceased, and his land was being sold off according to his will. Rose described the property:

A plantation in Christ Church Parish, containing eight hundred and thirty seven acres, formerly belonging to John Daniel; it is exceeding good land, and well-timbered, has several thousand cords of oak & hickory firewood on it; not more than six miles from Charles-Town, and is very convenient to several good landings:—The market might be attended to great advantage; a handy boat, with proper management, may with ease, make a trip everyday to town with wood:—There is very good clay for brick-making on it, and a brick yard already settled with a reservoir of water for swimming the cattle that tread the clay; a great quantity of wood for burning bricks and lime very near the brick-field; also a small dwelling-house, kitchen, and other out houses, a good barn and corn-house, and every convenient building needful on a plantation.[48]

The features noted and described by Rose centered on the production of goods for the domestic market, as well as on the convenience of the plantation's location for supplying that market. Rose perceived that the property's chief assets were its still-plentiful timber resources, a burgeoning brickmaking factory, and the potential for shipping these products to the Charleston market on a daily basis. Both the deceased artisan who had developed the land, and its seller, understood its promise in terms clearly oriented toward the service of the domestic, urban, market, rather than its transatlantic counterpart.

Indeed, throughout the descriptions of plantations put up for sale by Charleston tradesmen, their suitability for rice-growing came up rarely, with the emphasis instead more likely to follow the path laid out by Daniel. The bricklayer Timothy Crosby suggested that his plantation might eventually be useful for corn and indigo, but noted that it already had a stock of "fine fruit trees . . . horses, cattle, and hogs." And the merchant Richard Beresford sought "a man well-acquainted with the management of grass grounds both meadow and pasture as they are kept in England upon grassing and dairy farms, for the making of hay, fatting of cattle, and making of butter and cheese" to manage his suburban smallholding. As the British vacated Charleston, Captain Thomas Wallace's executors sold off a lease on his Daniel's Island plantation, which was "in a most delightful situation . . . only 6 miles from Charles-Town, and very convenient for the market, on it are a very good dwelling house . . . a good stock of cattle, and a great number of Seville and China orange trees, with quinch, apple, peach and other fruit trees." And, after the Revolution, the merchant Thomas Eveleigh put a plantation twelve miles from Charleston up

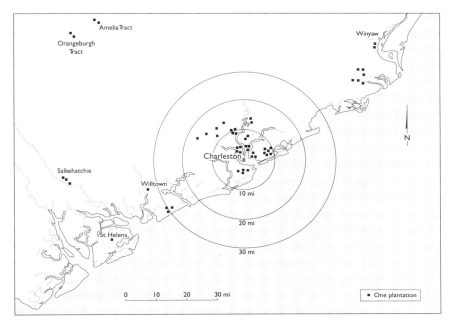

Fig. 4.1. Location of plantations owned by Charleston tradespeople. (Map by Bill Nelson)

for sale, noting that a dairy farm and tanning business formed the core of the enterprise.[49]

Commensurate with their urban-centric outlook, the Charleston owners of these hinterland farms also valued highly their convenience to the town's produce markets, and they often took care to note this attribute. George Milner described his father John's plantation, up for sale after the latter's death, as "well calculated as profitable farms for supplying the Charleston market." Daniel Cannon, advertising for a manager for his plantation, mentioned that he specifically needed someone "capable of tending the market."[50] Plotting the locations of a sample of farms also shows that the vast majority of them were indeed positioned as close to the urban market as possible (see fig. 4.1). Some 70 percent of Charleston tradesmen's plantations fell within a thirty-mile radius of the town, and 50 percent within a ten-mile radius; Daniel's Island, a peninsula across the Cooper River and about a mile from town, was home to four "farms" owned by urban traders.

In seeking managers to run their suburban enterprises, both Beresford and Cannon also revealed that these farms were not country seats in the mode of many Low Country hinterland operations, but were purely commercial concerns. Such was the mentality with which Thomas Elfe approached the development of his, similar, Daniel's Island enterprise—a place that from its very foundation was intended primarily as a profitable extension to his urban operations. Elfe purchased the 250-acre tract on Daniel's Island in 1765. By 1768, the cabinetmaker's new plantation comprised "buildings, cattle, horses ... [and] five working negroes and three children," to the value of SC£2,500. At this stage, however, the property was still in the process of being developed into a full working plantation, as Elfe spent a further SC£1,325 on it during the seven years for which we have records. Monies disbursed went toward enlarging Elfe's stock of sheep, hogs, and cows; buying ploughs, seeds, and hoes to plant food crops; and in appointing an overseer (and later an indentured laborer) to supervise the work of his small slave force. Elfe also purchased and refitted a small sailboat, presumably for transporting goods across the Cooper River to the town. By 1770, the plantation was starting to yield the provisions that it had been shaped to supply and, after five years, it had brought the cabinetmaker and his family SC£1,174 from the sale of calves, fruit, beef, and other foodstuffs in the Charleston marketplace.[51]

Devoid of such symbols as a lavish country house, the suburban farm was a more utilitarian affair and—much like the speculation in urban properties—was another method for Charleston's commercial sector to extract a living from the town economy. Thus, while there were those who abandoned city business for countryside pursuits, there were many others who did not view their rural holdings in these terms. Thomas Elfe died a city dweller, not showing any interest in retiring to his rural property. Likewise, right up until his death, Charleston bricklayer Cato Ash managed his town brickyard alongside the rural concerns that he had developed to service the urban market. Ash was in possession of not one, but two farms, both of which raised a variety of livestock and produce; on his Edisto farm six slaves staffed a concern that produced poultry, pork, corn, peas, and potatoes, and at his James Island plantation the bricklayer kept eight slaves who tended a second stock of poultry and further crops of peas and corn, along with cattle and a modest honey-producing enterprise.[52]

In the fifty years or so before the Declaration of Independence, the relationship of many white urbanites to South Carolina's plantation economy had undergone a substantial shift. As Charleston businesses became successful in their own right, townspeople's perspective on the possibilities and the uses of rural South Carolina evolved. For some, the town did remain a base from which they could manage distant plantations, channel staple goods and slaves through the market, and eventually dream of retirement to their nearby estate. However, this was not the only outlook. For many other trading households, the potential of the countryside became wholly subordinate to the promise of the town. As a result, these households developed rural farms that could be incorporated into their economic strategy as urbanites—places that were easily managed from a town base, and would cater to an urban marketplace the needs of which were simple to assess for those so embroiled in it already. And because the town remained the main locus of the household, moving to the countryside became less of a priority. Like other trading households enmeshed in the town economies of the British Atlantic world, townspeople could no longer envisage themselves that far from the urban milieu they knew so well.

## Independent Trading Households; Middling Households

With the growth of Charleston came a species of South Carolinian who was comparatively detached from the colony's chief crops. In their quest to take full advantage of the opportunities inherent in the urban economy, settlers deployed slaves' labor and developed their business interests in novel and innovative ways. Introducing new strategies and variety to the family economy as it developed in South Carolina, urban householders adapted the colony's principal labor system and broke down occupational divides among the free workforce. So abundant were the possibilities of the urban economy that Charlestonians did not necessarily look in on the town from the perspective of the staple economy, but rather looked out toward the countryside through the lens of the city. This was a fresh outlook within the Low Country, but these urban family economies were far from unique in the British Atlantic world as whole. Indeed, their appearance united South Carolina's urbanites with their counterparts in other fast-growing English provincial towns, all of whom shared similar attitudes toward urban and rural opportunity.

In these other provincial towns, however, not every household had the capital, the man and woman power, the skills, or the good fortune, to be able to build on the opportunities on offer. And as certain individuals among the growing urban population became more successful at exploiting an opening than others, new socioeconomic divides began to open up among inhabitants. Those urban households who enjoyed ownership of their own businesses and had access to the resources needed to explore multiple opportunities drifted away from those who stood at the bottom of the social and economic order. At the same time, with their hard-working women and their center of gravity firmly in the town, this middle group remained distinct from the local gentry who did not need (or wish) to have female business-owners working in distinct professions in their family economies. At the very least, this group was an urban middling sort whose economic strategies and social networks set them apart from others. The growth of the provincial town had encouraged the emergence of a more complex, tripartite social structure.[53]

What was the impact of these independent trading households on the social structure of South Carolina? In their rural parts, the southern colonies were rapidly becoming a society of elites, slaves and plain folk. Planter-merchant patriarchs had used slave labor to maneuver themselves to the top of these societies' economic structures, and in doing so were able to regard below them a laboring "lower sort" that was generally an amorphous group (though it was clear that some were lower than others). At various points, plain folk came into close contact with slaves, not as their masters but as fellow workers—a situation that elites found so worrying that they were careful to create a mantra of white solidarity in the face of black danger from an early stage. Yet, however universal this social and economic dynamic was in rural South Carolina, the growth of the colony's urban population after 1740 quickly introduced a new—and much more British Atlantic—structure to the region. The presence of successful independent trading households in Charleston meant that there was little chance that white society would remain a simple division between elites and "plain folk." As it reduced the importance of occupation as a social marker, the emergence of an urban middling sort in the Low Country after 1740 also redrew socioeconomic boundaries.[54]

Initially, it was economic circumstance, credit, and the kinship networks of middling town dwellers that bound them together into the distinctive group that Josiah Quincy had observed during his Charleston sojourn. As already noted, there were approximately three layers of wealth-holders in

South Carolina. Such patterns of wealth distribution mirrored those in colonial America's other cities, where independent trading households stood
between merchant elites and a laboring poor. In Boston in 1760, relief for
losses sustained in the large fire of that year was distributed according to
whether a claimant was rich, middling, or poor; 59 percent were poor, 28 percent in the middle, and 13 percent rich. In Philadelphia and in Albany, New
York, the middling stratum of urban society was populated by a mixture of
successful shopkeepers and artisans. Alice Hanson Jones's measurement of
colonial wealth in 1774 across the thirteen mainland colonies also revealed
esquires, gentlemen, and merchants to be wealthier than professionals, shopkeepers, innkeepers, and artisans, who themselves were richer at death than
mariners, laborers, single women, and those men who were listed with no
occupation at all.[55]

Heading up Charleston's middling group of wealth-holders were very successful tradesmen, like the bricklayer Anthony Toomer, whose $13,000 estate
and thirty slaves were the legacy of a lifetime's toil in the town's building industry. Next came those of more modest—but still notable—wealth. These were
individuals like Francis Morand, a shopkeeper whose trade in dry goods and
ownership of a fishing boat and three slave fishermen kept his family comfortable until his death, or the tailor William Williams, whose town business
and suburban farm totaled £587 sterling in wealth. Slightly poorer was Robert
Fairweather, a perukemaker and hairdresser, who died in 1763 with a fortune
of £310 sterling, and the building contractor William Rigby Naylor, designer
of the Exchange, who left possessions worth £387 sterling.[56] In addition to
the personal property listed in inventories, many middling decedents also
owned real estate. Anthony Toomer left undeveloped rural land, city rental
properties, and a new housing development under construction. Artist Jeremiah Theus left two town lots and a 200-acre country tract; cabinetmaker
John Prue left two lots, a yard, and a farm on Charleston Neck; and carpenter Thomas Weaver left two undeveloped tracts in the backcountry, a farm on
Charleston Neck, and a large town lot.

Land ownership, however, was not a feature of all middling estates. Many
families, like the Stevens's, had no real property, but still occupied a separate
socioeconomic stratum from the town's "lower sorts." Martin Pfenninger, a
renowned cabinetmaker, also had no land to his name when he died, but he
did leave three slaves and an estate worth £22 sterling after debts.[57] Compared

to the vast fortunes left by the greatest merchant-planters, these estates were modest, but they were enough to keep a family off the breadline. Indeed, they were sufficient to provide households with many of the comforts of life that the poorest members of society lacked. The shipwright Samuel Lacey enjoyed luxuries such as a tea table, looking glass, and a few silver teaspoons. Robert Landall's £150 sterling estate was mostly made up of two slaves, but he still ate from china bowls with silver spoons.[58]

However sparse the luxuries owned by these poorest middling families, such families were still divided quite clearly from those free white town dwellers who had no slaves, no assets, few skills, and a meager income. As the body charged with looking after Charleston's poor, the St. Philip's vestry increasingly found that it was inundated with requests for relief, and the amount of Poor Tax it needed to levy rose steadily from the 1740s onward. Whereas the white population of Charleston doubled between 1750 and 1770, the amount of tax requested by the vestry more than tripled, from SC£1,500 to around SC£6,000. As Revolutionary troubles loomed, the numbers of "transient and resident" poor continued to rise, to the point where the vestry noted that it would need SC£25,000 to look after them for three years. Some who benefited from this charity were families, like George Lee and his wife, who were allowed SC£7.10.0 per month in 1775. But life as a propertyless and slaveless white Charlestonian proved to be especially hard for widows and spinsters, who, without a slave's earnings to live on, were more prone to falling into destitution. Single women and orphaned minors, such as "Mrs. Roche and her three children," were granted "immediate relief; and cloathing . . . at the discretion of the Church Wardens." The poor school received a substantial number of new pupils soon after its establishment, and a corrupt overseer of the poor was instructed to confine his family to just two rooms in the workhouse, in order to provide more space for its increasing number of occupants. It was especially apparent that some slaveless white women suffered long-term destitution: for instance, Janet Eden, being granted "her allowance as usual" by the vestry, and Elizabeth Toussiger, receiving monthly payments of SC£3.[59]

Middling townspeople were also firmly removed from their destitute inferiors by their superior position within South Carolina's credit networks. The wealthiest could claim enough credit with the colony's elites to enter into financial agreements with them, as well as with their fellow tradesmen. Thomas Elfe lent money to other Charleston master craftsmen, but he also had long-standing commitments with the planter Robert Cochran. The cabinetmaker's casting up of his and Cochran's dealings in 1772 shows that each had stood in the other's security for sums of over SC£4,500, which had been advanced in a series of bonds and notes over the course of the previous four years. Furthermore, Elfe had received SC£200 as a fee for his "trouble in transacting the several business with Ben Smith," implying that the cabinetmaker had been entrusted with the care of some of the planter's town business affairs. Many other prominent merchants and planters, among them William Bampfield, Miles Brewton, and William Henry Drayton, also extended loans to Elfe. Other wealthy craftsmen held a similar credit in the Low Country; at his death, silversmith John Paul Grimke was owed bonds by the planter Stephen Bull and the merchant Jacob Valk, and bricklayer Anthony Toomer had lent sums to Charles Pinckney, the eminent doctor David Ramsey, and the planter Daniel DeSaussure.[60]

Although Charleston's wealthiest traders were in good financial standing with Low Country elites, they were nevertheless entangled with others in credit networks that united the urban middling sort. Elfe appeared on the margins of the planter-merchant elite's systems of credit and debit, but he had more connections with other city traders of his own standing, having SC£12,478 tied up in bonds with, among others, seven woodworkers, three widows, two "sugarbakers," a ship's captain, and a coachmaker.

Such a pattern of lending and borrowing was replicated among middling people who entered Charleston's mortgage market. Russell Menard has shown how, before 1740, the majority of mortgage capital flowed from Charleston to the countryside and to those planters setting up new enterprises on the frontier. However, it is also striking how, from the 1730s onward, middling traders with sufficient real and personal property turned to each other in a mortgage market that was principally confined to the town, and to others of their ilk. In mortgages where one party was a Charleston-based tradesperson, the other party was another town tradesperson in 42 percent of cases, a merchant in 28 percent, and a planter or gentleman in only 21 percent. What is more, lesser merchants, rather than very wealthy elite traders, such as Austin & Laurens or Smith & Brewton, formed the vast majority of lenders and borrowers.[61]

If financial matters brought Charleston's middling traders together into networks of credit and obligation, social ties reinforced these connections. As we have seen, the family was of immense importance to the success of middling traders in the workplace, making it critical to perpetuate that family in such a way as to ensure its continued security. The best way to achieve stability was to marry one's children off to the sons and daughters of other town traders who had assets useful to ongoing involvement in the urban economy, and this was exactly what the majority of middling traders chose to do. From 1720 through 1780, just 17 percent of traceable marriages occurred between Charleston merchants and artisans (or their daughters) and the offspring of a planter. Marriage partners from the families of full-time town dwellers were clearly favored. And when the nuptials were between townspeople, they often cut across occupation, creating a white middling sort bound together by a common interest in the urban scene rather than driven apart by profession or trade. Clockmakers married the daughters of shipwrights, silversmiths the daughters of merchants, milliners wed shopkeepers, and carpenters tied the knot with the offspring of their business partners. One such marriage was that between the carpenter Benjamin Wish and Anne Poe, who was the daughter of his business partner. Likewise, Isham Williams married Elizabeth, the daughter of fellow shipwright Edward Shrewsbury, and in 1784 the cabinetmaker Charles Desel took Polly Muckinfuss, the daughter of a contemporary cabinetmaker, for his wife. Shipwright and blockmaker Nathaniel Lebby successfully found husbands for his daughters, Eliza and Mary, who married a painter and a carpenter, and carpenter William Lee's daughter and son were respectively wed to a clockmaker and to the daughter of an artist.[62]

This marriage strategy contrasted sharply with that of non-middling South Carolinians. At the very top of South Carolina society—where country and town interests overlapped in the creation of a colonial elite—merchant-planters married freely into each other's families. Thomas Corbett took the daughter of John Harleston, the St. John's Parish planter, as his wife in 1769. Country-dwelling men also married the daughters of the most successful merchants, as did James Postell of Ashepoo when he took the hand of Catherine Douxsaint, the daughter of merchant Paul Douxsaint, as his wife in 1764. Almost all unions between townsmen and planters' daughters involved well-established merchants, like that of Miles Brewton, whose 1759 match with Polly Izard ensured the perpetuation of two great fortunes.[63]

Among Charleston's middling sorts, bonds forged at the time of a marriage were then strengthened when new relatives, and best friends, were kept close in business matters. Although these ties are often difficult to uncover, they were always thrown into relief when townspeople confronted their own mortality, and the wills and inventories of Charleston's independent traders yield multiple connections to others from their socioeconomic group. Thomas Nightingale, a saddler and racecourse owner, was typical. In 1767, Nightingale appointed son-in-law and blacksmith William Johnson as his executor, with carpenter John Remington and merchant William Wayne bearing witness to his last testament. Gardener John Watson similarly surrounded himself with his Charleston friends and relatives; his will was witnessed by a son who was to continue his gardening business, two merchants, and a doctor, and his inventory drawn up by sons who had trained in the town as upholsterers and a tailor. Overwhelmingly, assessors and executors of the wills of town dwellers came from the town themselves, to the extent that the connections laid bare at death give the impression of an urban community almost hermetically sealed against the rural aspect of South Carolina. Quite often, town and country communities had grown to occupy two contrasting spheres—a state of affairs reflected in the administration of the estates left by Charleston County residents who died as the United States was born. Assessors and executors of rural property never overlapped with those engaged to settle the estates of their Charleston brethren; while planters relied on their fellow plantation owners, townspeople resorted to the traders and manufacturers who had populated their social networks.[64]

Given the strictures experienced by whites with no skills and no slaves of their own, and the relative stability enjoyed by those who could access chattel labor, it is unsurprising that poorer Charlestonians were willing to risk everything for the opportunity to improve their social and economic standing through purchasing a slave. One artisan who took such a chance was the shoemaker Patrick Hinds. In 1757 Hinds sank all of his savings into the purchase of a newly imported slave, whom he soon discovered to be grievously ill with sores that would not heal despite expensive treatments from the physician. The shoemaker appealed for compensation from the seller, hinting that his family would be destitute if he came out of the bargain with lost savings and no additional labor to help him in his workshop. Although Hinds's purchase seems to have been a rather ill-advised one, within the context of the urban South Carolinian economy it was considered a worthwhile risk. Subsequently, Hinds's gamble paid off, and by 1790 he had fifteen African Americans working in his boot and shoe warehouse. Hinds was now the head of an "independent trading household"—a manufacturer, retailer, and landlord. Furthermore, he had secured his comfortable position through his successful purchase of slaves.[65]

South Carolinians like Patrick Hinds, often overlooked in the unrelenting focus on the region's planters and merchants, and its staple economy, played a critical role in shaping the socioeconomic structures of the colony during the eighteenth century. As a numerous and easily identifiable group, Hinds and his fellow townspeople were influential in three respects. First, as they pursued multiple urban business opportunities they established complex workshops and forged a tangle of working relationships with each other, moving away from the classic "pre-industrial" model of the tradesman who worked alone in a small enterprise. These tradesmen introduced dynamism to the economy of South Carolina that was a mirror of the kind of small, but nevertheless significant, shifts taking place in preindustrial workplaces across other towns in the British Atlantic world. In the Low Country, moreover, this transformation was achieved when urban tradesmen adapted South Carolina's labor system to suit their requirements.

Slavery also sponsored the emergence of a new type of household economy in Charleston. As members of urban households, slaves were commandeered into white town dwellers' family economies, enabling these free whites to diversify outside of their particular profession or trade and achieve the kind of broad economic base found in other British Atlantic towns. Using the family economy as a springboard for the pursuit of trading, farming, and manufacturing activities, urbanites even marshaled the countryside into the service of their productive units, and far from being a conduit for the Atlantic trade and a base from which planters might coordinate their rural empires, or even merely the center of new patterns of domestic markets, Charleston became the headquarters of urban households that sought to remake the rural economy into an extension of their town pursuits.

Influencing the trajectory of economic development in South Carolina, and pushing elements of it toward larger currents of British Atlantic change, Charleston's trading households made their mark on the colony; and with economic change came new social strata. Those Charleston households with the resources and the entrepreneurial skills to develop multiple, and often complex, business interests soon formed a distinctive group. Just as their urban-centric economic strategies and their concept of a family economy distinguished them from South Carolina's planter and merchant elites, so their status as business owners and slave owners set them apart from their poor white counterparts in the town. Like middling sorts elsewhere in the urban British Atlantic world, Charleston's middling sorts—highly visible to the town's visitors and to South Carolina's governor—were marked out by their particular levels of wealth, their multiple interests in the urban economy, and by the close social connections forged between and among families in the name of maintaining their position. Neither plain folk nor patriarchs, their distinct status rested to a large degree on the ownership and deployment of slave labor. Charleston's trading householders thus found themselves equally distinguished by their location at the center of the white social structure and by their reliance on black chattel laborers to maintain that position. The growth of Charleston nurtured a new socioeconomic category that, although novel to South Carolina, was increasingly common in English-speaking cities of its ilk—a middling sort of people. This distinct identity, however, was not something that came from socioeconomic status alone. Class identities were also forged in cultural and political arenas. Since Charleston harbored a middling sort, we must therefore inquire as to how the town and this middling group affected these other facets of colonial South Carolina society.

# 5

*

# Criminal Pleasures and Charitable Deeds:
# Town and Culture

I NTERTWINED with Charleston's rise as a city was the arrival on
American shores of new cultural trends that profoundly changed the style
of life in the colonies. Across colonial America elites set about acquiring
the British manufactures and locally-made goods and services required for
the enjoyment of a genteel lifestyle. Selecting wares from the influx of British
goods—books on conduct, issues of *The Spectator*, tea, fabric, and chinaware,
for example—settlers surrounded themselves with such objects. Using these
material purchases, along with newly learned codes of manners, they strove
for elegance, virtue, refinement, and a polite society. In taverns, gardens,
drawing rooms and assembly rooms, planters and merchants then endeavored to show off their newly acquired good taste. By incorporating this genteel element into their self-fashioning as a traditional aristocracy, southern
elites maintained a special identity, while also participating in a wider cultural
movement. So, while South Carolina's planter-merchants stood out from their
counterparts in the northern colonies, both groups nevertheless spoke the
new language of British Atlantic gentility.[1]

Indeed, the tale of how colonial elites sought to emulate an English example persists as a dominant narrative of cultural development in British
America. In the Low Country, where South Carolina's elites appear to have

promoted Charleston's growth with a carefully nurtured "fervent adherence to English values," this storyline seems especially fitting.[2] As a concept, *emulation* has also been critical to historians' understanding of cultural shifts among the larger swath of early America's free white population. Following closely in the wake of elite Anglophiles were numerous less-wealthy colonists seeking to ape the style of life among their betters. Middling sorts across early America made attempts to acquire the equipage and manners of polite society. Sometimes their efforts were mocked—famously by Alexander Hamilton during his encounter with Morison, a man whose coarse eating habits and poor attempts at polite conversation clashed with his stylish possessions and a genteel, tea-drinking wife. At the same time, however, such endeavors were often welcomed by southern gentry keen to unify white society in the face of a black majority. Overall, the quest of elites to be as genteel as their metropolitan cousins, and of lesser colonists to attain the manners of their superiors, appears to have formed the foundation of a binary society of the refined and the unrefined, the elite and the "others."[3]

But, as recent historians have noted, this model of colonial cultural development seems to oversimplify the situation. Colonial elites looked to metropolitan manners in their search for identity, but they also nurtured values that sprung from their local situation. South Carolina's planters, for example, made their ideal of *plantership* a core element in their identity as a New World provincial elite. At the same time, middling emulators did not mindlessly copy the gentility of their superiors—they began to adapt genteel codes of behavior to their own requirements as independent traders. In particular, the emphasis on body control that the literature of conduct stressed struck a chord with a social group who owed its success to hard work and self-discipline.[4]

Across the Atlantic, in Britain, historians have also questioned whether the emphasis on emulation was a sufficient model of cultural evolution. In the metropole, the rise of urban societies complicated cultural development. Towns nurtured provincial, urbane, cultures that made vital contributions to the composite character of gentility and refinement; mapping a cultural center and periphery no longer fully revealed the dynamic at work in this system. Bath, Edinburgh (and Boston) were all involved in the fashioning of a British Atlantic culture. Even smaller provincial centers like Chester and Colchester had a part to play as they grew into genteel spaces that did not merely emulate a London paradigm, but also created new versions of a national culture. At the same time, some among the middling sorts who rose to prominence in these towns began to reject emulation of the genteel standard, eventually developing a separate culture that stressed a range of values linked to their particular socioeconomic status. In sum, expanding towns and their populations fostered a process of differentiation, creating cultural modes that went beyond simpler ideas of genteel and un-genteel, elites and lower sorts, blacks and whites. Urban growth confused and challenged traditional boundaries, undermining the cultural hegemony of the elite.[5] With a large town containing a substantial trading population, South Carolina proved no exception.

Consequently, to focus exclusively on the Low Country elite's use of Charleston as a site for the emulation of metropolitan gentility is insufficient for understanding cultural development among the colony's free white population. As we have seen, one of the primary spurs of growth in Charleston after 1740 was the involvement of its traders in the provision of goods and services to elite consumers in an "economy of gentility." As this native service sector grew, tradesmen and shopkeepers colluded with customers to create a provincial genteel culture—not a direct replication of the English model, but one that was distinct in its own right, and recognized as such by its practitioners. Many traders bought into the genteel style that they were selling, reinforcing its development. But, since the economy of gentility also underwrote the success of many independent trading householders, it encouraged the creation of a separate identity by those town dwellers who no longer found emulation of genteel models to be so attractive. Already pursuing their own economic strategies, some extended their emerging philosophy of hard work into the cultural arena, setting themselves apart both from the elites above them and the plain folk and slaves below them. Like its socioeconomic counterpart, the cultural landscape that emerged was not easily divided into the world of elites and lower sorts.

## Creating a Provincial Gentility

The English-speaking provincial town of the eighteenth century came into its own because it was vital to the production and the pursuit of genteel appearances and behaviors. As we have already seen, the urban landscape was essential to the purchase of the clothing, trinkets, and accoutrements that underpinned the genteel style of life. Towns then acquired even greater importance, because they provided the public spaces where such possessions could be put on display. At assemblies, concerts, promenades, gardens, tea rooms, and theaters, men and women set about the task of constructing the genteel and urbane persona that would showcase their newfound qualities to one another and to their social inferiors. The provincial town thus became the mediator of cultural forces that arrived from elsewhere—principally, London, the cultural center of the elite British Atlantic world. However, the town also evolved in such a way as to become an active promoter of cultural change—as a vital player in the dissemination of British Atlantic cultures, and as the creator of provincial variants on this culture. Rather than simply emulating the center, the provincial town entered into a cultural dialogue with it.[6]

As it grew into an urban center of note, Charleston came to play just such a role in the fashioning of elite culture, becoming an intermediary for metropolitan trends and an advocate of provincial variations. This role was clearly visible in the pages of the colony's premier newspaper, the *South Carolina Gazette*. Commonly found in just about every British Atlantic town by 1750, the local newspaper was the bearer of information from across the empire and an arena for the parallel emergence of local identity. Reporting metropolitan and local social events, publishing poetry, literature, and opinion pieces, and advertising consumer goods and services to its readers, newspaper content ranged across all aspects of genteel culture. Although readers drew on other sources too, the newspaper was the most convenient and regular piece of print available and thus became a vital tool for those who wished to develop their "polite" identities—it was a filter, assisting its readers to make the "right" cultural decisions. In the Low Country, the *Gazette* was an envoy of culture from afar—a medium that brought metropolitan styles into South Carolina homes. However, it was also an organ for the promotion of a provincial gentility, created by South Carolinians for South Carolinians.[7]

It is not always easy to detect where emulation of metropolitan genteel culture ended and the adaptation for provincial consumption began. In many situations—for example, in an item about the staging of a play first seen in London—the interplay between center and periphery remained invisible. However, in the *South Carolina Gazette*, that interplay was quite obvious in the advertising section, where local tradesmen peddled the material culture of gentility. The gentility that they sold was one that respected the metropole as a guiding light, but it also sought to devise a unique niche for the potential consumer and owner of their product.[8] On the one hand, artisans in the luxury trades strenuously emphasized their knowledge of recent metropolitan styles. The carver William Lawrence boasted that he had "seen the newest taste in London" and could replicate it for customers who chose to patronize him. The upholsterer Richard Bird explained that he could provide curtains, carpets, and furniture covers "in the genteelest taste now in vogue" to his clientele. Countless other manufacturers described their Charleston-made goods as being "in the most new and approved taste," "in the newest taste now in London," or of the "politest taste," or in the "neatest and genteelest taste."[9]

Advertisements also stressed how Charleston tradesmen could act as direct and living links to the distant metropole, emphasizing that their special skills could keep consumers in touch with what was happening at the headquarters of gentility—London. Philip Tidyman promised that his customers would find the "newest fashions . . . as soon as invented" in his Charleston silversmith's shop; Mary Baker and Eleanor Dryden, both milliners, informed the public that they had gotten their hands on some "new fashioned pinking irons made in London," which could be used to cut novel effects into ladies dresses; and Mary Cranmer, another milliner, had "lately imported from London . . . a beautifying wash for the face, which will in a few times using, entirely eradicate all manner of spots, freckles, tan etc." If the tradesman had a direct contact with the metropole, all the better. The tailor Walter Mansell used the *Gazette* to announce his 1756 trip to London, promising that he would "take orders for your suits, and bring them out with him on reasonable terms." The gardener John Watson claimed that his seeds were superior to anyone else's because he had had them sent by his brother in London, who had a direct connection with the Royal Gardens at Chelsea. Likewise, perukemaker Richard Herbert advertised his repeated trips to the British capital for the purpose of selecting the "choicest hair" for his Charleston-made wigs of the "newest and best fashion."[10]

On the other hand, advertisements for goods and services also revealed how South Carolina, rather than being a mere disciple of the metropole, was becoming a member of a British Atlantic world that was the sum of its provincial parts. Thus, it became increasingly common for tradesmen to build their credentials by referring not to London, but to other, provincial, places in the British Atlantic world with a reputation worth advertising. The dyer

John Brown boasted that he had "engaged one of the best Manchester silk dyers, who will soon arrive from Liverpool," and others stressed their roots in Newcastle-Upon-Tyne, Philadelphia, Bristol, or Edinburgh. To be salable, the equipage of gentility no longer needed to come directly from the British capital, it could now originate elsewhere.[11]

Charleston too was beginning to make its mark as a legitimate provincial hub—a place in which consumers could purchase items that not only reflected their connections to London, but were also suggestive of a particular version of this larger genteel culture. The clockmaker Joshua Lockwood, for example, strenuously highlighted the novel modifications that he made to imported British clock mechanisms in order to "please his friends" in the Low Country. Usually, larger grandfather and bracket clocks were adorned with generic hunting scenes, depictions of the phases of the moon, or pastoral idylls; Lockwood's movements, however, depicted "high water at the bar" in Charleston, and were equipped with "spring alarums to call an overseer at what hour a gentleman pleases." The clockmaker also identified additional complex motifs of local interest that were incorporated into his wares. Consequently, some timepieces displayed "a representation of Sir Edward Hawke in the Royal George, pursuing the French fleet," and others, "privateers in chase of merchant men." Other clocks showed "a slave planting in the arch and the motto Success to the Planters," and still others had "the representation of a Cherokee Flight in the arch, where a drummer seems to hear the several tunes that are played." Lockwood's pièce de résistance, though, was a mechanical picture "of a negro beating rice, which he seems to do very naturally." One can imagine that the last contraption in particular would have prompted both admiration and amusement as the wealthy planter and his guests sipped claret in the drawing room of the great house.[12]

With Charleston's flourishing luxury and service sector, the Low Country's elite consumers had access to a world of goods that did not merely emulate metropolitan gentility, but also carved out a provincial genteel identity. As already noted, however, the town was also essential as a local stage on which elites could act out their gentility, its amenities being far superior to those of the countryside. Charleston's cityscapes thus promoted the creation of a provincial gentility in the Low Country—one which united the plantation gentry with their urban counterparts across the British Atlantic world.[13]

Such provincial genteel identities were first of all fashioned in the shops of the advertisers whom we have just encountered. Across the British Atlantic, consumers and manufacturers were making the purchase, and not just the ownership, of luxuries into a component of the genteel lifestyle. To this end, the *London Tradesman* (a guide for parents wishing to find a trade for their offspring) advised that young men wishing to make a living in the lacemaking business would need to "entertain the ladies; and be master of a handsome bow and cringe; should be able to hand a lady politely to and from her coach, without being seized by a palpitation of the heart at the touch of a delicate hand." The act of consuming had now become a refined behavior that both embodied and created gentility.[14]

Charleston's retailers provided the arena in which wealthy consumers could browse, promenade, and socialize. In the years after 1740, the town's shop spaces gradually became more sophisticated, with wares laid out in such a way as to encourage customers to peruse them at their leisure. By the 1780s, Charleston grocers, McCawley & Co., had fitted out their storefront with large windows that invited passers-by to stop, look and, maybe, enter the shop. Inside, McCawley equipped the store with a full range of drawers, canisters, and bowls, inscribed with the name of their contents and designed to allow customers to cast their eye over what was on offer. Retailers of luxury goods were especially likely to create an alluring shop space, all the better to cater to an elite clientele. Charleston's jewelers installed glass "show cabinets," merchants commissioned the building of "shoe cases," and watchmakers installed the bow windows closely associated with the best shops in Georgian London.[15] Town tradesmen did their utmost to make the purchasing process genteel once they had lured a customer into the store. By the late 1760s, some of the leading Charleston shops were giving customers slips of paper with the company's monikers and logos printed on them—a keepsake of their visit to a particular store that the customer could take home. These business owners also hired professional shopkeepers who could chat with the kind of polite clientele that they hoped to attract; the musician and musical retailer Thomas Bradford announced, for example, that he wished to engage "a genteel lad to attend store, a capacity for a musical education will have the preference."[16]

Indeed, the experience of Eliza Wilkinson, an elite woman from Yonge's Island, demonstrates just how entrenched genteel shopping was by the time of the British occupation of Charleston in 1780. Despite the presence of an occupying army, Wilkinson visited the city seeking relief from the twin stresses of the Revolutionary conflict and life on her plantation. While in the town, she and her friend Kitty (both of them wearing their "silk gowns") went "to take a walk on the Bay," punctuating their promenade with some browsing in the town's shops. Using one shop as a social space, the women engaged in banter with the storekeeper about a roll of ribbon they had spied on a shelf and that appeared to have thirteen stripes on it; their audience was a group of British officers, who "sat on the counter kicking their heels." The anecdote illustrates that, although the gentlemen of Charleston's Meddler's Club had kindly requested that women end their frequenting of the dusty, busy Bay and relocate to the "many fine greens near the town much better accommodated for air," the thoroughfare was far too well established in the leisure habits of the region's elites to abandon, even in a time of war.[17]

Wilkinson's activities, moreover, placed her closer to British provincials, who had access to a town, than it did to her rural Chesapeake neighbors, who did not. Many women among the Tidewater elite were excluded from genteel shopping activities by virtue of their bucolic situation—a state of affairs that was apparent in the letters written by Maryland barrister Charles Carroll. In sending a clothing order to London, Carroll intimated that his wife had been consulted about the size of the shoes to be purchased, but the barrister then asked for a ladies gown made of rich silk flowered brocades, explaining, "I have seen . . . they were in fashion when I was in England." In the same year, 1763, Carroll also ordered ladies' cloaks, shoes, gloves, ribbons, stomachers, hats, and necklaces, and a china tea set. By taking charge of these purchases, he had become the ultimate buying authority for his wife as well as himself. A similar situation was manifested in the correspondence between another Marylander, Samuel Galloway, and his London contacts, with the requests of his daughter for fabric and millinery going through her father's letters.[18]

Sophisticated shops and stores may have been numerous in Charleston, but they were far from the only genteel leisure sites specific to the urban environment. Theaters appeared to accommodate the traveling companies of actors who staged plays fresh from London's West End, and Charlestonians created designated spaces in the town's numerous taverns for assemblies and balls—the "long room," the "court room," or the "assembly room." These rooms were familiar locations in many provincial towns of the era, and in England represented the reshaping of traditional sites of urban social activity for new leisure pursuits.[19] At least four of Charleston's major inns had such a room, and some of the more prominent dancing masters established their own premises in which to hold balls and assemblies. Just a mile from the town center, Charleston's other main leisure site was the Newmarket racecourse. Growing from a single annual race in the 1750s, the meets at this suburban location went on to become very elaborate by the third quarter of the eighteenth century. Extensive newspaper reports of the day's races, with detailed descriptions of the contenders, conditions, and odds, suggest a widespread interest in the event. At the same time, it became customary for city merchants and shopkeepers to travel out to the racecourse, set up booths, and hold sales and public auctions.[20]

Hosting a range of events that eventually formed an annual social timetable, this ensemble of urban spaces worked together to carve out a place for Charleston as a provincial center of genteel sociability. Gradually, a "season" of events taking place at a particular time every year developed in the town. The "season" was a novelty taking shape in many English-speaking towns of the period, but not every town shared the same season. According to the town's location, its season generally took place at complementary times in the year, thereby permitting attendance at a number of seasons in succession by the professional socializers who might be found among the metropolitan elites. Thus, one could while away the year by attending the Bath spa season in the summer, the London season in the autumn and early winter, and the provincial town season in the months between Christmas and Easter. The provincial season often reached its height at the time of more-traditional annual events, such as the county assizes or the parish elections. As such, it represented a local variant on a larger trend, making a particular contribution to the cultural life of the metropole.[21]

In both its time frame and its character, the Charleston season shared much with the spring social calendars of Britain's provincial towns, meaning that it occupied a similar position in the fashioning of a larger genteel culture. The period between Christmas and Easter contained an increasingly coherent and wide-ranging set of leisure activities in the town. At the same time, events became more sophisticated as they grew in size and scale, and were ever more likely to occur reliably on an annual basis. In the 1730s, social gatherings were sporadic, scattered, and did not take place at any particular time of year; a ball and the occasional one-off theatre performances might be supplemented by a fireworks displays on the king's birthday, and some lectures on philosophy.

However, events were staged with much greater frequency from the 1740s onward, with July 1748 even witnessing the opening of Charleston's first bowling green. Shortly afterward, especially with the founding of the Newmarket race course in 1754, the calendar of social events formed a coherent season. A typical course of annual events resembled those that helped to make up the 1766 season: concerts, balls, theater performances, scientific lectures, and a week of races at the Newmarket course in early February. One could either hear "a lecture on HEADS . . . delivered . . . at the theatre in Queen Street," or enjoy a less-educational evening at a performance of "The Mock Doctor, or the Dumb Lady Cured." By 1785, Charleston's assembly was organized enough to have appointed a master of ceremonies. This position was first created and made famous by Bath's Beau Nash, and the managers of the Charleston dancing assembly invested their own version with "the full authority to conduct the etiquette" of the event.[22]

By the second half of the century, Charleston's program of social events had become known among its participants as "the season," with managers of one of the town's assemblies announcing that it would take place in Dillon's Assembly Room "fortnightly during the season" and a theater performance also billed as being "positively the last night of the season." As it provided social opportunities for the Low Country elite, the Charleston season drew the town into a social system that now spanned colonial as well as provincial British towns.[23]

Charleston's spaces, retailers, and service providers had become essential to the Low Country elite's gentility. Through the town and all it had to offer, wealthy planters and merchants achieved the many and various attributes required for admission into a British Atlantic world of fashionable countenance and engaging conversation. Although South Carolina's elites existed in reference to a metropolitan cultural center, this did not mean that they were blind disciples of London's example. By the second half of the eighteenth century, events such as a concert of Charleston's St. Cecilia's Society embodied the flourishing of a more autonomous provincial gentility that had emerged with the growth of the town. Held in specially built premises, with a "loft for fiddlers," the musical highlight of the concert was the performance by "one Abbercrombie, a Frenchman," who was retained by the society with a generous 500-guinea salary. Two hundred and fifty ladies turned out for the event, their "richness of dress" surpassing their counterparts in the northern colonies. The gentlemen were also dressed with great elegance, but all were put in the shade by the "two Macaronis . . . just arrived from London," who attracted a flurry of comments about their extravagant attire and manners.[24] Because of Charleston, Low Country elites were able to build the hall, purchase the fashions, and employ the musicians required to stage an event that could attract premier members of metropolitan high society in search of a genteel fix in the provinces.

Such was Charleston's reputation as a provincial center of genteel culture that many contemporaries commented at length on the town's success in this respect. Indeed, rather than being looked down on as a backwater populated by an elite pathologically emulating London high society, many writers saved their appreciative notes for their experiences of Charleston as a place of sophistication and gentility in its own right. There was, in fact, universal agreement that the town's social scene elevated the region and its better sorts onto the same level as similar urban provincial places in the metropole. Peletiah Webster waxed lyrical about the London harpsichord player he had heard, and the fine collections at the Library Society, concluding that Charleston was "an agreable and polite place in which I was used very genteelly and contracted much acquaintance for the time I staid there. . . . Tis a flourishing place, capable of vast improvement." Thomas Griffiths, Josiah Wedgwood's agent on a mission to find new clay reserves, could not wait to leave the backcountry for "dear, and long wish'd for Charles town," which he esteemed to be "a very gay and compact town." Hewitt's history also picked out the city's cultural offerings as one of the highlights of early South Carolina, admitting that social events were "attended by companies almost equally brilliant as those of any town in Europe of the same size."[25]

Even among those in the metropole who had not visited Charleston in person, the city garnered a refined image and was frequently singled out as a superior, urbane society. Before the Seven Years War focused British eyes on their colonial possessions, Charleston held its own in the polite discourse that filled the pages of the *Gentleman's Magazine,* with men like Charles Lining receiving praise for their learned contributions to science and the arts, and engravings devoted to the fashionable architecture in the town. As the threat of losing the colonies to the French grew, increased interest in their character prompted more detailed accounts. In one such article, Charleston remained the only city whose inhabitants were described as "very genteel and polite," a character said to stem from sophisticated urban institutions such as public libraries. Maryland and Virginia, on the other hand, were dismissed in a few brief sentences, precisely because of their lack of any significant towns.[26]

With its season, its star-studded concerts, and its extensive opportunities for the leisurely purchase of luxury goods, Charleston had become the facilitator of gentility among the Low Country elite. Recognized in both America and Britain as a provincial cultural hub, Charleston alone in the region offered the amenities that made achievable the style of life to which wealthy South Carolinians were accustomed. With the help of those who worked to produce the goods and services requisite for a genteel life, elites had become provincial contributors to a British Atlantic urbane gentility. United to an ideal of plantership that stressed the virtues of life as a staple producer, this provincial gentility helped to create an elite environment that spent less and less time seeking acceptance on the metropolitan stage, but that was increasingly accepted by those at the center as one of many provinces contributing to the cultural development of the British Atlantic world as a whole.

## Gentility and the Middling Sorts

To a significant extent, better-off middling sorts in the British Atlantic town had a cultural agenda that overlapped with that of their social superiors. As tradesmen and merchants, many were *au fait* with the latest material trappings of gentility, their homes as well as their shops often full of the consumer goods they peddled to eager elite consumers. Contemporaries were quick to note this cultural overlap, and not always because they approved. Permitting the mixing of elites and middling sorts to an extent not imaginable before the eighteenth century, spa towns and urban pleasure gardens received the special attention of such commentators. Bath, for example, attracted a diverse enough crowd for Smollett to satirize its clientele as being made up of "the wives and daughters of low tradesmen, who, like shovel-nosed sharks, prey upon the blubber of those uncouth whales of fortune."[27]

Social boundaries were, of course, especially blurred in colonial America, where the absence of a titled aristocracy inevitably fudged the line between those who made their money as landed gents and those who found wealth through trade, manufacturing, or the professions. In the New World's northerly cities, most who laid claim to the sort of urbane gentility adopted by

South Carolina's gentry were merchants who had achieved their premier position through trade.[28] In the Low Country, mixing also occurred, as Charleston
provided an arena in which the wealthiest merchants, planters, and lawyers
who formed the core of the region's elite socialized with lesser professionals, traders, and master artisans. William Murray, the doctor from the Scottish Borders who made a life for himself in Charleston during the 1750s, was
just such a man who knocked on the door of elite status but could more comfortably be described as an "upper-middling sort." Murray never retired from
business to lead a life of leisure, nor did he take up public office of any sort.
Yet, from the position of a man with secure but modest means, the doctor
noticed the ease with which he was accepted into Charleston society, com-
menting that the town had "all the eleganceys and conveniency of life in great
variety and plenty, and people here seem to make the most of life. They are
gay and extremely sociable and polite and are quite unacquainted with our
European stiffness, in short I am much better recommended to it than I was."
Honing in on the question of the relationship between landed elites and other
wealthy settlers, Murray further noted that the "gentry is not taken notice of
hear every one is . . . upon a levell the knights with the private gentlemen and
them with the one a nest pheasant if there [sic] circumstances are alike."[29]

Murray's observations were corroborated by the experience of one of his
fellow Charleston physicians, Thomas Dale, whose rise from relatively humble
(and even questionable) origins into the top rank of South Carolina society
was in part the result of his warm embrace by elite families such as the Brew-
tons and the Pinckneys. Dale's admission to exclusive social circles was signaled by his presence at the dinner parties, the assemblies, and the club meetings that constituted elite sociability in Charleston; his eagerness to take
advantage of the favors of his social superiors as much a mark of the desire of
this middling man to ascend the ladder as a manifestation of his acceptance
into an inner circle.[30]

Especially instructive of the power that gentility might exercise over lesser
Charlestonians was the experience of those who tried to access elite circles but
fell short. Such was the situation of postmaster, church organist, and sometime merchant, John Stevens, and his wife, the sole proprietor of a coffeehouse. The Stevenses perpetually strove to be included in the "genteel" social
circles inhabited by their superiors, with Mr. Stevens displaying an unhealthy
obsession with gentility in his correspondence. Stevens, however, was often

snubbed or ignored by those among the upper echelons of Low Country society, who clearly considered him worthy but nevertheless inferior.[31]

However, assuming that a version of gentility was the sole raison d'être of every British Atlantic citizen oversimplifies the cultural process, especially within the complex environment of the growing provincial town. As we have seen, urban expansion in the Low Country underwrote the emergence of a middling layer, distinguished from their superiors by their particular strategies in household and workplace. Elsewhere in the urban British Atlantic, a differing middling outlook often influenced the cultural pursuits of the men and women who occupied this stratum of society, encouraging them to pursue social activities that were commensurate with their values of prudence and hard work. The Reformation of Manners movement, active in England from the late seventeenth century onward, was overwhelmingly staffed by middling sorts, as were the more popular Religious Societies, where membership dues sponsored sermons for the associated schools and hospitals for the poor, and where upstanding behavior in private and in public was integral to continued participation. Middling tradesmen also tended to be in the majority when it came to targeted, private acts of benevolence, such as the founding of orphanages and infirmaries. Without exception, middling sorts constituted the bulk of membership if a society had altruistic aims, making the urban organization that promulgated morality and charity over gentility and pleasure a clear expression of an independent and new cultural move.[32]

From the 1740s on, this middling charitable associational strand became a British Atlantic phenomenon. Gradually, a body of middling people emerged in colonial America who did not wish to be "nest pheasants" with a leisured gentry, but instead wanted to see their own values expressed in their extracurricular pursuits. Boston's Episcopal Charitable Society, and the aptly named Charitable Society, met to hear sermons and dole out assistance to the needy. In Philadelphia, the Sons of King Tammany declared their purpose as a "society . . . of great Utility to the Distressed; as this Meeting [is] more for the Purpose of promoting Charity and benevolence than for Mirth and Frivolity."[33]

This middling cultural strand was also most clearly expressed in Charleston through the town's associational life. From the 1730s on, certain among the less exclusive of the town's clubs clearly became important sites of middling cultural activity. The earliest of these societies to be founded was the South Carolina Society, about which Alexander Hewitt noted that, "at first, it

Fig. 5.1. Banner of the Fellowship Society, attributed to Thomas Coram. (Courtesy of The Fellowship Society)

consisted not of the most opulent citizens, though many of these thereafter joined it, but of persons in modest stations, who held it an essential duty to relieve one another in such a manner as their circumstances would admit."[34] This charitable remit also applied to the Fellowship Society, a club that was founded in 1766 by Charleston upholsterer Edward Weyman with the motto "Posteri mea dona laudabunt," or "Prosperity will commend my beneficence" (see fig. 5.1). A similar founding imperative also lay behind the establishment of the German Friendly Society, which, although distinguished from other organizations by its ethnic imperative, was also intended to provide financial support for its members. The participants in all of these clubs were overwhelmingly town-dwelling merchants, retailers, and craftsmen. The 1778 rolls of the Fellowship Society listed 159 "town members" and just 47 "country members," with a fair number of the latter identifiable as former urbanites who had clearly decided to keep up their links with the town through the Society. Although the South Carolina Society accommodated more-elite, rural members, its rolls continued to be filled with a substantial number of urban men absent from the rosters of the more-genteel organizations.[35]

There were, of course, convivial aspects to the activities of the Fellowship Society, German Friendly Society, and South Carolina Society. Like other associations, members met in the "long rooms" of Charleston's taverns and took advantage of the food and alcohol furnished by the landlord. However, minutes of the Fellowship Society show that the club's officers were anxious to uphold the moral and religious reputations of individuals in a way that was of little concern to the members of Charleston's more-elite organizations. Instead of attending star-studded concerts or eating sumptuous dinners, meetings were spent listening to sermons given by local Anglican and dissenting ministers. Leftovers from meals were donated to Charleston's poor house and gaol, and indulging in too much drink at such events could easily result in exclusion from the society. There was also a general concern that members should uphold the good name of the organization through their deportment on the wider urban stage. As a result, John Pooley was asked to "answer for his impudent conduct," on the basis that "he had made use of very unbecoming expressions reflecting on the conduct of the society and the secretary thereof in public company out of doors." And rather than spend membership dues on French violinists, monies were used to purchase town lots on which were built poor hospitals, charity schools, and low-rent tenements for needy Charleston families; the donations made by individuals for these causes were drafted into service as a pointed example to others through the publication of thanks in the local newspaper.[36]

As permanent town residents whose financial assets, businesses, and families were rooted in Charleston, the men of the Fellowship Society channeled their extra money and free time toward the improvement of their town and the lifting up of their fellow citizens. Such charitable and moral principles also went with some townsmen to the grave. Underlining how a rejection of the elite lifestyle could comfortably coexist with the institution of slavery, the cabinetmaker John Prue commanded in his will that his chattel laborer Jerry should be sold and the proceeds donated to the South Carolina Society for the education of poor white children. Prue also set up the first endowment for the foundation of a college at Charleston. In an expression of the British Atlantic dimension of such principles, dissenting merchant and shopkeeper Thomas Corker expressed a wish in his last testament of 1771 that a sum be sent back to the Congregational minister in his home town of Nantwich in Cheshire for the education of twenty poor boys of the parish. The associations increasingly favored by Charlestonians thus reflected their preoccupations as hard-working tradespeople and began to ally them with others of their sort in towns and cities throughout the British Atlantic world, where newly wealthy townsmen frequently carved out cultural identities through the improvement of their environment and the citizens therein.[37]

Being the cornerstones of middling urban culture, the Fellowship Society and the South Carolina Society stood as important examples to other groups of townspeople wishing to establish more specialized associations. As a charitable organization founded to help out with funeral costs and support needy families, the Brown Fellowship Society—the first club set up by Charleston's blacks in 1790—was closely modeled on its white predecessors. As townsmen, free blacks clearly identified with the associational structures predominant among their white counterparts. The charitable society also formed the basis of those clubs organized by Charleston's artisans. Although an application for incorporation by Charleston's tailors led the South Carolina assembly to suspect "that they designed to monopolize the business and discourage strangers from their occupation," the tailors themselves insisted that they were only acting to secure the monies raised to help out the families of their number in hard times. And indeed, the tailors' original ordinance of 1765 had stated that their society was "for . . . giving relief to such members and their families. As may at any time, through misfortunes, be reduced to indigence." Failing in their quest for special status, the tailors subsequently transferred their savings to the Fellowship Society. Two years later, in the establishment of their own society, Charleston's barbers and hairdressers chose to state explicitly the links between them and their urban brethren in the Old World, explaining that "from time immemorial it has been usual and accustomed in the different cities of Europe to Incorporate the several trades who had formed themselves into societies . . . to protect brothers against hardship from accidents, and widows and children, and prevent frauds and impositions." As late as 1798 the Mechanics' Society also explained that, "from the nature of their employments, and the smallness of their capital in general . . . more exposed than other classes of citizens to the inconveniences and distresses arising from sickness . . . they have united in a society for the purpose of rasing a fund . . . [to] afford relief of the unfortunate."[38]

Although charitable associations were the most prominent pillar of an emerging middling identity in Charleston, growing numbers of these towns-people also carved out a distinct cultural space for themselves when they embraced the dissenting Christian message. Dissent was not the exclusive preserve of middling urbanites, but it is nevertheless clear that it provided a rallying point for this portion of the urban population, who found its open emphasis on morality, charity and prudence, and its vocal rejection of the excesses of luxury and gentility, to be commensurate with their overall outlook. The Fellowship Society, for example, had strong and prominent ties to the town's Baptist Church. Church membership profiles within Charleston also reflected middling tradespeople's colonization of these dissenting congregations. While the initial list of pew subscribers for St Michael's Church in 1759 included ten tradesmen and fifty elite merchants and planters, 40 percent of donors to the Congregational Church's building fund during the 1770s were artisans, and many others were small merchants and shopkeepers. The early sponsors of the town's Irregular Baptists were also all urban tradesmen.[39]

For this growing cadre of urban, middling adherents who filled the pews of Charleston's Congregational and Baptist churches on a Sunday morning, their religious choice reflected a commitment to much more than a weekly appointment to hear a more radical Protestant message. In particular, activities like the fund-raising for, and construction of, a new church acted to create alternative middling, dissenting communities that rested on a broader base. Building of Charleston's second Congregational church, for example, was set in motion by an initial subscription, with large donations coming from town professionals, merchants, and artisans like Thomas Corbett, Jonathan Sarrazin, Hopkin Price, and William Williamson. However, fifteen or more town tradesmen provided their subscription to the new church "by discount," and bricklayers, painters, carpenters, and a turner all contributed with their own labor—or that of their slaves. Work was carried out on a piecemeal basis by various master artisans who took on contracts for jobs such as "framing and finishing the roof . . . cornice . . . gallery, breastwork, . . . and fixing columns." Hence, the congregation had devoted their labor, their money, and their spare time to the raising of a church in which they all had a stake.[40]

This middling dissenting culture was also distinguished by the roles of its female participants. In the course of building the Independent church, the wives among the congregation made an individual and visible contribution to the process when they raised monies for a "neat mahogany pulpit and stair-case." These wives—all spouses in trading households of Charleston—thus drew a sharp line between themselves and their elite sisters, who tended to promote piety within a domestic setting, retreating from activities as visible as fundraising for the religious community. There is also evidence that the efforts of the Congregationalist wives were part of a wider middling women's commitment to a family's values, stressing a transatlantic tendency for the eighteenth-century middling public sphere to be somewhat more open to women's independent contributions. Among the donors to the Fellowship Society was "a lady unknown," who gave a guinea for the building of the poor hospital; like the male benefactors, this lady was also rewarded with public thanks in the newspaper.[41]

For sure, there were junctures at which this middling culture overlapped with its genteel counterpart. Elite men, such as the merchant Henry Laurens and the planter-preacher Jonathan Bryan, demonstrated that charitableness and politeness were not mutually exclusive, nor was benevolence the preserve of the town-dwelling tradesman. Nevertheless, the emergence of new leisure opportunities in Charleston also prompted the creation of familiar alternative urban communities forged along distinctive lines. Across the urban British Atlantic, private pursuits of "domestick order and prudential morality" spilled over into the public arena, becoming a marker of middling tendencies to favor propriety over politeness. Increasingly, these values of industry, propriety, and morality were also carried forth into the social lives of Charleston's middling people. In the clubs and societies spawned by the urban environment, and the dissenting churches of the town, middling sorts had the opportunity to conduct their cultural lives according to their own wishes, rather than in complete emulation of the example of urbane gentility provided by the Low Country elite in those self-same spaces.

## Divisive Landscapes

The years after 1735 witnessed the emergence not only of a provincial gen-teel culture in Charleston, but also of a middling ideology that emphasized a different set of values. Rather than being purloined by a single group in the name of gentility, the varied and complex urban landscape of Charleston had been diverted toward the purposes of differing interests. Thus, the emergence of discrete free white socioeconomic groups that came with urban growth was reinforced in the cultural arena. Town dwellers who had turned away from the model of plantership proffered by elites in the economic sphere, now also showed indifference to the cultural lead of their superiors. In some respects, this dynamic mirrored shifts experienced elsewhere in the South's evolving societies—most notably in Virginia, where Anglican elites pitched up against newly evangelized lower sorts who were part of a "counterculture" that challenged and antagonized colonial rulers.[42]

But in South Carolina, the town fostered a much more complex pattern of conflict. Rather than creating a stand-off between two opposing groups, Charleston provided a space in which many contrasting cultural strands might evolve side-by-side. On their plantations, elite men enjoyed a superior position as powerful patriarchs and masters of all before them. But when they came into town, as they frequently did, they were confronted by a place in which the boundaries between classes and races were constantly challenged by the differing cultural pursuits of the people who inhabited this urban land-scape. Such was the nature of the eighteenth-century urban environment across the British Atlantic world, where growing towns became ever more likely to become the focal points for those who embraced, as well as those who were more ambivalent about, the benefits of the new "polite and com-mercial" society. What is more, clashes between these groups often occurred in a landscape that continued to be a major site for the leisure pursuits of the lower sorts, whose behavior was rarely endorsed by either elite or middling folk.[43]

Serene depictions of the largest social events of the era did tend to present a harmonious, carnival-like aspect to South Carolina culture, stressing how such events had the ability to unite everyone together in the joyful pursuit of fun and games. There is little doubt that, at times, such accounts were accu-rate representations of the region's cultural life. Commentators thus described how, "after course racing was established it was one of the most fashionable diversions and drew from all parts of the province and state to Charleston, a greater number of spectators than any other amusement or business what-soever. . . . For two or three hours before their commencement the road lead-ing to the course is so crowded that access to the city is very difficult."[44] A similar harmony was achieved during such annual events as the King's birth-day celebrations, when a "genteel entertainment" of "curious fireworks" was admired by the wealthy from the balconies of their houses, and by the general public from the street, the townscape providing the setting for South Caro-linians to come together in the mutual enjoyment of their status as subjects of a powerful and wealthy British empire.[45]

Problems arose, however, when elites did not wish to welcome all South Carolinians to their leisure pursuits, but sought to preserve an exclusive politeness in an urban landscape cluttered with white and black "lower sorts" also seeking the space in which to enjoy themselves. As in other British Atlan-tic provincial towns, conflict occurred when elites privatized arenas that others considered to be public. Elites clashed with lower sorts when, in 1765, it was announced that the "ORANGE GARDENS in Tradd Street will be opened, for that night only when a concert of vocal and instrumental musick will be performed by the GENTLEMEN of the place, for the entertainment of all lov-ers of harmony. Concertos on the French horn and bassoon by Mr. Pike . . . none but subscribers will be admitted . . . tickets from Mr. Pike of the same place." The issuing of tickets and the admission of subscribers was clearly a strategy designed to exclude undesirable elements from the entertainments, as Pike went on to express a hope that "no persons will be so indiscrete as to attempt climbing over the fences to the annoyance of the subscribers as I give this public notice that I will prosecute any person so offending to the utmost of the law." Just as the members of the dancing assembly in York, England, had installed iron bars to stop the common folk pressing their noses against the windows of their hall, so Charlestonians raised a fence in an attempt to main-tain a proper distance between genteel elite and impolite rabble.[46]

Yet the "rabble" could never be entirely ejected from Charleston's public spaces, and, as Philip Morgan has ably documented, Charleston also devel-oped into an important center of working-class culture in the Low Country. Among blacks and poor whites, urban space represented a site where they could escape the gaze of their superiors and begin to carve out their own worlds. For blacks who lived on plantations, Charleston was a place to escape the watchful eye of the overseer or master and be free of the close control exercised over daily movements and habits.[47] Although city-dwelling slaves, free blacks, and poor whites inevitably remained in closer proximity to their Charleston masters, the large urban population and the plethora of shared public spaces also gave room for maneuver.

On many occasions slave and free could be found in the same place, enjoying themselves through similar pursuits, and in this respect Charleston became the principal location in which black, white, and undoubtedly mulatto, South Carolinians could go some way towards forging a working people's culture. Rather than frequenting the tavern, licensed by the town authorities and offering genteel entertainments, the lower sorts frequented the dram shops and tippling houses. There, apprentices, sailors, young men, and slaves drank and gamed. Although Charleston's watchmen—recruited from among the town's working people—were employed to prevent both general disorder and blacks' consumption of alcohol, they more often than not encouraged the spread of lower-class sociability by supplying drink themselves. Such activities repeatedly raised the ire of elite and middling South Carolinians. Seeking to preserve their town's genteel air, elites resented the intrusion of this popular culture on their efforts to create a town that was a beacon of provincial politeness. At the same time, Charleston's middling sorts were equally upset at the leisure activities of their inferiors, which, since they often involved drinking and gambling on a Sunday, fundamentally contravened their vision of a morally upstanding and Christian society.[48]

Charleston's cultural conflicts, however, did not only occur between its wealthy and its poor citizenry. As is suggested by the differing motives for the protests lodged by elites and middling sorts against their social inferiors, the town also nurtured discord between its better-off residents. Specifically, the emergence of an urban middling sort with a divergent set of cultural values proved divisive, as tradesmen parted ways with their superiors on the question of overindulgence in leisure and luxury at the expense of hard work and frugality.

Disapproval of the elite's pursuit of a luxurious lifestyle in the town was expressed in South Carolina from the 1740s onward. Comment in newspapers, pamphlets, and sermons created a persistent undercurrent of disgust at the overindulgence of rich planter-merchants in the urbane pleasures of Charleston. Such condemnation was far from unique in a British Atlantic world where a deluge of literature railing against luxury reached its peak during the war-torn decades of the 1750s and 1760s. As the chief vice of an increasingly commercial society, "corrupting excess" became the principal charge leveled against many different social groups, and writers variously honed in on women, the poor, and the aristocracy as the debauched perpetrators of a crime that might undermine the health of the entire body politic. In a specifically colonial context, those who feared that their new societies had fallen away from an original simplicity or honest purpose found a convenient culprit in the tidal wave of luxury that seemed to accompany increased wealth and material comfort.[49]

In the Low Country, critiques of elite luxury also emanated from various quarters of white society. However, the most persistent complainers were those dissenting Christians who had first found their voice during George Whitefield's many visits to Charleston between 1738 and 1741. As in nearby Virginia, some strong supporters of Whitefield's anti-luxury message were drawn from the elite planter class itself.[50] Most notably, the Bryan family, planters on the Savannah River, were long-standing adherents to the evangelical cause, and were constantly critical of the lifestyle of their fellow elites.[51] However, it is also evident that the main body of Whitefield's devotees sprang from Charleston's dissenting churches and their middling congregations. On his missions to the town, Whitefield soon discovered that the most fertile ground for his message was within Charleston's Independent, Scots, and Congregational churches, where the itinerant was eagerly embraced by ministers and adherents alike. On his second visit to the town, the renowned preacher "drank tea with the Independent minister, and preached at four in the afternoon, to a large auditory in his meeting-house." Only the next day, Whitefield was forced into an open-air sermon in the yard of the Independent Church, since the building itself was not "capacious enough to hold the auditory." On these occasions, Whitefield's principal message, other than the importance of personal salvation, appears to have been the necessity of shunning luxury and overindulgence and instead embracing charity. Explaining after one of his final sermons in Charleston that he had been "more explicit than ever in exclaiming against balls and assemblies," Whitefield departed from the town satisfied that he had successfully persuaded many townspeople of the importance of his message.[52]

Whitefield's activities, however, were not at all to the liking of the more elite Anglican component of Charleston's religious community. The Bishop of London's commissary, Alexander Garden, led the campaign against White-field, harrying him with a flurry of pamphlets and newspaper articles, and also managing to get him briefly detained by magistrates on a minor charge. Garden had many theological disagreements with Whitefield, but it is clear that his principal objection stemmed from the potential for the itinerant's brand of evangelical Christianity to encourage non-elites into aspirations and actions above their station. The emphasis on personal salvation and the uneasiness of evangelicals with slavery seemed dangerous to Garden, who, as minister of St. Philip's Church, represented a Low Country elite fearsome of the disorder that might result from efforts to Christianize Africans and encourage middling and lower sorts to take charge of their own faith.[53]

Yet, while elite Anglicans sought to discredit Whitefield and his message, dissenting ministers and their middling flock strove to perpetuate the preacher's memory after his departure from the region. Josiah Smith, a Congregational minister and Whitefield supporter, preached a number of sermons that sought to keep the itinerant's message alive in the minds of his middling flock. Using Charleston's destructive fire of 1740 to continue the attack on elite luxury, Smith interpreted the disaster as retribution for overindulgence by "daughters nurs'd up to it by their mothers," and for the prevalence of the "modern beau," the pursuit of leisure on the Sabbath, and the tendency of "some among us" to think "of little else, but our Assemblies of Musick, Dancing and Feasting." In all, the local elites "were at ease and quiet on their couches . . . immers'd and plung'd in criminal pleasures."[54]

Even after Whitefield was long gone, such messages remained popular in Charleston's dissenting churches, and attacks on elite opulence surfaced again, in the form of Baptist minister Oliver Hart's sermon against dancing, published in 1778 but first delivered, according to the author, "at an evening lecture, upwards of nineteen years ago." Even though he would "incur the censure of the gay gentry . . . and forfeit all pretensions to polite breeding and good manners," Hart launched into a stinging critique of Charleston's many "balls, assemblies and the play-house, where they take the timbrel and harp, and such like instruments of musick, which they play." Explicitly reiterating the words of British Baptists like John Gill, Hart indicted Charleston's elite women as haughty "daughters of Zion" whose "taste for pleasure and dissipation" often brought on "the destruction of soul and body."[55]

Listening to these stern words against elite luxury during their Sunday sermons, middling Charlestonians then began to take the message beyond the walls of their church. By the 1760s, those outside of the clergy were also observing that "'tis now a common thing for our planters in general . . . [to have] increased pride with riches." In his will, Frederick Struebell, a Charleston merchant and bricklayer, stressed that if his son John "shall so badly behave himself, as to lead a dissolute, idle and debauched life," he would not receive access to any of his inheritance.[56] In the local newspaper, the entire value system of the gentry, and those who sought to access it, was mocked:

Every Tradesman is a Merchant, every Merchant is a Gentleman, and every Gentleman one of the Noblesse. We are a Country of Gentry, Populous generosorum: We have no such Thing as a common People among us: Between Vanity and Fashion, the Species is utterly destroyed. The Sons of our lowest Mechanics are sent to the Colleges of Philadelphia, England, or Scotland, and there acquire, with their Learning, the laudable Ambition of Becoming Gentle-Folkes, despite their paternal Occupations, and we are all solicitous for the more honourable Employments of Doctors, Lawyers, and Parsons; whilst the pretty little Misses at Home are Exercised in no Professions at all, except those of Music and Dancing, which . . . make them very agreeable Companions, but will render them very expensive Wives.[57]

Drawing together the various objections to the prevailing urbane and genteel culture of the Low Country, this barbed commentary on the cultural landscape of South Carolina also placed in plain sight the terms on which, by the 1770s, the differences between middling Charlestonians and their elite counterparts were now in the public arena. On one side stood the gentry and their lesser followers, scrabbling, through their vanity and their devotion to the shallow manners of politeness, to make it on the British Atlantic stage. Ornamental wives and useless learning characterized the genteel family, who were no longer capable of making a worthwhile contribution to the advancement of civilization and wealth in the Low Country. But what was the implied alternative proffered by the author? It was the hard-working, entrepreneurial, charitable middling townsman, and his equally diligent wife—the characters who now, more self-consciously than ever, occupied Charleston's middling orders.

To a degree, Charleston was a stage on which South Carolina's elites could parade their mastery of a black majority and their successful emulation of a metropolitan gentility. As a large urban space, however, the town also influenced the cultural development of the Low Country in a far more extensive, and complex, manner. Because of its status as a provincial town, with the retail and leisure amenities commensurate with that role, Charleston afforded Low Country elites the opportunity to become a provincial gentry with an identifiable place in a British Atlantic world that was increasingly the sum of its various parts. In the town's shops, taverns, assembly rooms, and green spaces, the plantation gentry and the tradesmen (and women) who served them created a strand of gentility that not only exhibited an allegiance to the metropole, but also reflected their own identity as provincial Britons and as South Carolinians.

The burgeoning urban environment, however, also sponsored the emergence of other autonomous cultural forms. Many among Charleston's middling sorts placed equal, if not greater, import on the cultural values that stemmed from their experiences as urban independent traders. Stressing principles of industry and morality, tradesmen's clubs and societies nurtured different goals from those of the institutions founded by their leisured superiors. At times, middling Charlestonians even condemned the luxurious lifestyles of South Carolina's gentry, questioning the right of elites to set the cultural tone of the town. Meanwhile, both groups of free whites faced the contravention of their particular ideals by a large population of slaves and laborers. Heeding neither the rules of genteel behavior, nor the strictures of morality and industry, lower sorts claimed Charleston's streets, dram shops, and wharves as their own leisure spaces, despite the perpetual objections of their social betters. Charleston's growth had not only challenged the cultural hegemony of the region's elites, it had also ensured that the challenges they faced to their supremacy emanated from multiple sources. Like their counterparts in the British provinces, South Carolina's planters discovered that having a large town in their midst was advantageous and troublesome in equal measure. What is more, they were rapidly realizing that the rise of an urban middling sort also raised a challenge to their dominance of the colony's political scene.

# 6

## "A very essential service to this community"
### The Politics of the Town

HEN *South Carolina Gazette* printer and Charlestonian Peter Timothy declared to Benjamin Franklin in 1767 that the "public works" were "carrying on with spirit" in his home town, both of these correspondents would most likely have recognized the importance of this assertion to the image of South Carolina. Timothy was recounting Charlestonians' activities not just as an interesting footnote, but was offering them to Franklin as evidence of the "flourishing state" of his town. Difficult to achieve without considerable effort, improvements reached into every corner of the Charleston landscape, and Timothy's account of activity took in the raising of everything from sewers to state houses. Building also required the skills and participation of many tradesmen, the toil of an army of laborers, and a serious and ongoing commitment by authorities to the betterment of all aspects of the urban environment. Public works were thus a reflection of a civilized and industrious society, and they were an accomplishment worthy of boasting about to one of colonial America's most conscientious and active citizens.[1]

Rather than monuments to the endeavors of worthy tradesmen, however, the raising of public buildings and the improvement of Charleston's urban environment have usually been viewed in a very different way by the colony's historians. The State House, the Exchange, and the Court House, among others, have been seen as the chief symbols of the enduring might of elite power in South Carolina, not as evidence of a broader-based civic imperative. Charleston's landscape was, historians have argued, part and parcel of a dynamic that placed colonial South Carolina at the epicenter of an exclusively southern political culture that "prized attributes of civility and gentility precisely for their usefulness in muting political conflict."[2] These finely conceived, exemplary classical buildings, raised with no expense spared at the behest of the gentry, were also symbolic of the elite's ability to ignore the pleas of those free white people who lived and worked in the city all year round, and who frequently berated their superiors about that class's uncaring attitude toward the maintenance of daily order outside of their chief loci of power—their plantations.[3]

The elite's dominance of Charleston's civic landscape thus became an extension of their overall superiority in government and politics. Smothered by the "harmony for which we were famous," the political set-up of South Carolina was not only peaceful, it was distinctive within early America. Especially by the time that Timothy was penning letters to Benjamin Franklin, other ruling elites across early America were confronting domestic disorder. In major cities and in rural areas, like Virginia, gentry assemblymen faced down the challenge of raucous and populous lower sorts who emerged as the most radical protestors against British taxation efforts and as a major threat to the authority of their native leaders. Thus, in the North's cities, "the mass disorders surrounding the Stamp Act revealed to many in the urban patriciate the ghastly logic of . . . political development." If they were to reunify free whites in their colony, Virginia's elites would be forced to appropriate the rhetoric of the evangelical preachers who had so successfully rallied the lower sorts. In contrast, although some among Charleston's artisans did mount a handful of radical protests, on the whole they appear to have demurred to the leadership of their betters, failing to threaten the overall harmony of South Carolina's political scene.[4]

But, reexamining this political landscape through the lens of the town's emerging middling sort renders this narrative of exceptional harmony much less convincing. In particular, an investigation of the politics of urban improvement, as touched upon by Peter Timothy, paints a different picture—not just of South Carolina's political experience within a colonial context, but also more broadly of the sources of, and the motivation behind, urban radicalism in late colonial and Revolutionary America. Although the merchant-planter elite appeared to have maintained a grip on the reins of political power in South Carolina, from the 1740s onward Charleston's middling sorts were successful in building an influential position through their involvement in public works and the regulation of the urban environment. Such activity was an extension of their values within the economic and cultural spheres, as it reflected the emphasis on morality, order, and improvement so visible elsewhere. By the 1760s, middling sorts were not keeping these ideals to themselves, but, to an even greater degree than they had done in the cultural realm, were bringing them to the attention of the elite, whom they felt were not adequately serving the needs of the town and its population.

Far from behaving with quiet deference to their betters, Charleston's middling sorts were therefore quite willing to make it known that they found elites to be sorely lacking as leaders. Although they did not manage to dislodge the dominance of wealthy rulers, the emergence of their political consciousness onto the public stage suggests that it is dangerous to read the consensus of the later South Carolina political scene back into the eighteenth century, as in this earlier period an undercurrent of discord frequently drowned out any harmony peddled by elites. What is more, it is critical to understand that this challenge to the colony's rulers did not emanate from working-class artisans or occupation-based interest groups resentful of their oppression and suffering increased poverty. Instead, disquiet arose when successful middling traders sought to extend their values from the private and cultural realm into the public, political one. In making this connection, Charleston's middle sorts joined contemporaries in provincial towns across the British Atlantic world, who protested not because they wished to topple over-powerful authorities in favor of truly popular rule by the mob (something they possibly feared just as much as their superiors), but because they believed that local government was not doing enough to maintain discipline and good morals among the urban populace. Quite simply, they thought that the urban middling sorts, rooted in the town, were the men for the job. Within the context of escalating imperial rivalry after 1764, the emergence of this middling political consciousness also eventually became intertwined with debates about the appropriate reaction to attempts by the British government to tax its colonial subjects.

## The Work of Improvement

For the elites who legislated in the South Carolina Commons House and appropriated funds for the improvement of Charleston, the resulting edifices were undoubtedly a manifestation of their status as a ruling provincial gentry. This was a gentry that showed great commitment to the raising of buildings that might better the urban landscape, and the extent of Charleston's public works was summed up by Henry Laurens, who noted that he had "been a slave in the House of Assembly & upon some committees for some weeks past. We are regulating our port & harbour, going to build a sumptious Exchange & Customs house, extending fine streets & laying out new ones, [and] building a new hospital."[5] Laurens's "enslavement" in the name of urban improvement, moreover, had come only at the culmination of decades of public works that, starting with the building of St. Philip's Church in the 1720s, resulted in the raising of such works as the town's fortifications, St. Michael's Church, a harbor lighthouse, a market, a schoolroom, barracks, drainage, public pumps, a statehouse and court, the laying of pavements, and the enacting of detailed legislation designed to keep these buildings and streets clean and orderly. By the time of America's Independence, Charleston's elites had created an urban environment that ably reflected their rapid ascent to wealth and success.

But to view these projects only in the light of the narrow confines of provincial elite power is to fail to understand their broader significance—a significance readily identified by contemporaries. For it was this program of urban works, along with Charleston's emergence as the hub of provincial gentility, that had bestowed it with membership in a larger British Atlantic movement of urban improvement, making it a participant in a transatlantic, enlightened drive for order, cleanliness, and modernity in the English-speaking town.[6] The designs of civic buildings, such as the statehouse, closely resembled those very recently executed in Britain's provincial towns. There, old guild halls destroyed by fire had been replaced with modern seats of government, built in stone and conceived within the new, classical style. Many dark, Gothic churches were likewise superseded by new buildings executed in a lighter, plainer, and more Protestant manner, and Charleston's St. Philip's Church was celebrated as just such a place of worship with a plate in the *Gentleman's Magazine* (see fig. 8). Shortly afterward, St. Michael's Church continued South Carolina's achieve-

Fig. 6.1. St. Philip's Church, Charleston, as printed in *The Gentlemen's Magazine, and Historical Chronicle,* June 1753. (Courtesy of the Trustees of the National Library of Scotland)

ments in the arena of ecclesiastical architecture. Charleston was therefore a full partner in the creation of an English-speaking urban form that, for the first time, outstripped its Continental counterparts, and placed the town at the cutting edge of new architectural trends.[7]

As such, this ensemble of improvements struck Charleston's visitors as being very much part of this larger movement for urban betterment, and praise came from colonials and British alike, who recognized the town as a civic achievement rather than an emblem of elite authority. John Murray, writing home to Scottish relatives, pronounced that although the countryside in South Carolina was strange to him, the town was very similar to those he had known in the British provinces, and much more substantial than he had expected. And an anonymous British traveler, arriving in Charleston in 1774, even thought that the East Bay and Broad Street bore comparison to London's Oxford Street and Cheapside. Rather than being a southern colonial oddity, the townscape ably reflected contemporary ideas about modernity and progress, and thus had the power to make Charleston into a "compact town, finely situated" with churches "among the best structures in America," an Exchange that was a "very substantial handsome large building of brick," and "handsome modern built brick houses" lining streets that ran "straight and intersect each other at right angles." Overall, visitors were struck by the way in which Charlestonians had used classical regularity, wide streets, and brick buildings to produce a complete, modern, urban place. With no winding, narrow, lanes, ramshackle timber houses, or crumbling "Gothick" churches, Charleston was far from the "sad old town[s]" that eighteenth-century British travelers scathingly described when declining places did not meet the new urban standard. To all who visited and left a record of their impressions, Charleston was a beacon of British Atlantic civic endeavor.[8]

Elsewhere in the British Atlantic world, these civic projects were not undertaken solely by elites aiming to shore up their power over the rest of the population. In fact, many improvement programs had been launched so successfully in English-speaking provincial towns because they also benefited an emerging social group—the urban middling sorts. For the independent trader always on the lookout for a new venture to secure his family's future, public works projects first of all represented yet another great business opportunity. At the same time, the planning and direction of improvements formed an entirely new aspect of urban governance open to the participation of middling people who had previously been excluded from local power structures by elite oligarchies. Charleston's middling tradesmen clearly viewed the town's improvement program in a similar light to their metropolitan contemporaries, and from the 1730s onwards they became deeply involved in almost every major project. Thus, at the same time as Charleston's Exchange, or its fortifications, reflected the wealth and power of elites, they also represented opportunities for profit and participation among a quite different group of Low Country society.

The preeminence of Charleston's middling sorts was visible in every area of urban improvement, with master tradesmen becoming deeply involved in all sorts of projects. Between 1759 and 1768, various citizens were paid almost SC£19,000 for work that they did in the upkeep of Charleston's public places, and this expenditure represented the vast majority of monies leaving the public purse in the cause of the town's betterment. Three-quarters of the funds disbursed by the Commission for Fortifications went to middling artisans heading up substantial construction businesses (see table 6.1), and the Assembly paid out to the carpenters, bricklayers, and blockmakers who made writing desks and benches for the free school, repaired barracks, supplied fire buckets, sunk wells, and installed water pumps on a daily basis.[9]

Middling tradesmen's involvement meant extra income for all involved. However, a select group of white male citizens quickly achieved considerable influence through the engrossing of many small jobs of civic improvement. Establishing themselves as stalwarts and principal players, it seems that these tradesmen sought and won influence through their employment in public works. This process began early when, between 1725 and 1728, the Assembly initiated the first round of urban improvements: it built a brick bridge, strengthened the fortifications, raised the first St Philip's church, and put up an Armory, a statehouse, and a free school. Overall, twenty-two artisans were employed in these works, but six were involved in more than one group of works, and the bricklayer James Withers, along with the carpenters Samuel Crawford and John Leay, managed to garner employment in building the armory, the new bridge, and the first statehouse. Subsequently, Withers went on to become a major contractor during the 1750s. By the 1760s, this cadre of civic employees had become yet more visible, with all but ten of the forty-seven men employed on public works projects performing multiple jobs. Some among these tradesmen used appointment to a government

### Table 6.1
### Expenditures on fortifications in Charleston, 1755–1764

| Expenditure | Amount |
| --- | --- |
| Unskilled white labor | SC£70,514 |
| Master artisans (including black and white labor) | 53,270 |
| Raw materials | 27,995 |
| Tools and equipment | 7,973 |
| Food | 3,361 |
| Slave labor | 2,819 |

*Source:* Journal of the Commissioner of Fortifications, South Carolina Department of Archives and History.

post as a means to securing a steady supply of contracts: bricklayer Withers won new work following election to the Commission for Fortification, for example, and others found the post of Messenger to the Commons House to be a lucrative position. Soon after winning the role of messenger, the cabinet-maker Jonathan Badger was put in charge of maintaining the meeting chamber of the Commons House, with further contracts to repair the woodwork in the state house following quickly on the heels of his first job. The upholsterer Edward Weyman's benefits, however, were much greater: between 1761 and 1768, he received SC£803 for various work he had done, including the lining of the legislators' and governor's pews at St. Philip's and St. Michael's churches, supplying a mirror for the Assembly room, and "making a curtain for the King's Picture."[10]

Seeing that there were profits to be made in the improvement of Charleston, other townspeople then began to undertake civic improvement projects on their own initiative, privately promoting schemes that contributed to the betterment of their home town, and no doubt their own financial security. Praised by early South Carolina chronicler David Ramsay, conscientious townsmen, like the bricklayer Anthony Toomer and the baker John Eberley, undertook to improve the "quagmire as a great part of Charleston originally was," a task that required "time [and] labour" but was nevertheless taken on, "at an expense." Likewise, the wharfinger Christopher Gadsden was commended in the *South Carolina Gazette* for the "stupendous works" that he had undertaken in the name of urban improvement during the 1760s. Carpenter John Clements seems to have been similarly civic-minded when, after four years' work and "great perseverance, labor, and expense," he advertised the opening of his suburban causeway, which would allow travelers to move "with perfect safety . . . in any weather and at any time of the tide." Meanwhile, petitions brought by private citizens to the assembly also requested improvements to Charleston's streets and thoroughfares. In 1769, the residents of Coming's Point in the northwest part of the town explained that since Charleston was "large and growing," they wished for the laying out of new streets in their district. The assembly approved their application, and Coming Street, Beaufain Street, and Montague Street were duly created.[11]

While some middling sorts quietly increased their investment in the job of urban improvement with many smaller contracts and private projects, others became more prominent partners in Charleston's enhancement when they maneuvered themselves into key positions on the town's "prestige projects"— namely the raising of costly and imposing buildings such as the State House. Soon, such men were indispensable to the mission of civic betterment. Without doubt, such projects were initiated at the behest of the Commons House of Assembly and, once underway, they remained under the supervision of its members. Assemblymen gathered as a "special commission" responsible for overseeing the execution of the Act for Building. In June 1766, for example, the house committee appointed to build the Exchange was ordered to "prepare a plan and estimate for the building . . . and also get the ground where they recommend the Exchange." Thus, elites had the power to select where the new building was to stand and also took the ultimate decision as to its design.[12]

However, this was about as far into a building project as assemblymen could go alone, as Charleston's movement into the mainstream of civic improvement also made for an increased reliance on those middling tradesmen who had become custodians of the specialist skills and knowledge required to see construction through to its finish. Indeed, without any practical architectural knowledge, few building skills, no idea of the precise materials needed, and none of the right tools, South Carolina's elites would have encountered severe difficulties in creating and executing major public works without the assistance of the colony's skilled townsmen. Had they been working a century earlier, the assemblymen would almost certainly have been able to exercise complete control over their project, but, as we have seen, the long eighteenth century witnessed the growing power of the professional architect and builder. Starting with Sir Christopher Wren and Robert Hooke, the age of the great architect whose vision shaped the public landscape began in earnest. By 1747, architecture was no longer a hobby, but a full-time job, and Robert Campbell explained in his *London Tradesman* that the architect "draws the design and plan of a palace, or other edifice where he describes, in profile, the whole building in all its proportional dimensions; every member of the building is exactly delineated; all its ornaments ranged in their proper order; and every part of the edifice appears to the eye in miniature in the same disposition as they are intended in the real work."[13]

Striving for a "modern" town thus required the employment of specialists who knew how to build the classical edifices that dotted the new urban landscape. This emerging breed alone had the literacy, numeracy, skill, and book knowledge to plan a properly proportioned classical building, and craftsmen with such skills were becoming ever more common by the 1750s, as practical manuals such as Batty Langley's *Builder's Jewel* were readily available to instruct them in the intricacies of design and planning.[14] Consequently, just as Charles II needed Sir Christopher Wren and Nicholas Hawksmoor to plan London, and Northampton's aldermen relied on architect Henry Bell to raise a post-fire town, South Carolina's elites would need to hand over their urban vision to a professional.

Between the construction of St. Michael's Church in 1751, and the completion of the Exchange in 1772, major projects of public works became ever more likely to be shaped by the participation of Charleston residents who possessed those abilities lacked by the "laymen" who made up the Low Country elite. Mostly, such townspeople were drawn from the ranks of white master tradesmen—architects, builders, and general contractors—who had started to arrive in Charleston in large numbers from the 1740s onward. Elites first began to rely more heavily on the talents of Charleston's most experienced tradesfolk during the raising of St. Michael's Church. At the outset of the project, they handed over management of construction to the builder and architect Samuel Cardy. As the designer of a harbor lighthouse, Cardy was already well-known to the assembly, and with his successful winning of the contract to finish the interiors and exteriors of St. Michael's, he sealed his reputation as a central figure in the creation of Charleston's classical townscape.

Cardy's responsibilities as contractor were considerable, as it was his duty to realize the plans, to find materials, to invent machinery for lifting and transporting timber, and to engage specialist subcontractors. At the height of the works, Cardy was directing the efforts of about forty slave and free workmen on the site.[15] Some of these workers were unskilled slave laborers, hired from local planters, but most were other white Charleston tradesmen and their skilled slaves. Thomas Elfe and his employees carved parts of the church's mahogany interior, painter John Stevenson and his five slaves painted the exterior, and groups of black and white journeymen carpenters (unnamed in the records) earned daily wages for their work in raising the church's impressive spire. Ultimately, it was the autonomously practiced skills of this collective of townsmen—and not the precise desires of the elites—that produced the church that still stands in Charleston today.

Indeed, even after the church itself was finished, the vestry continued to rely on the expertise of middling tradesmen when it decided to fit a church organ and build a new parsonage for the minister. Before requesting a subsidy for the works, the vestrymen stated that they needed to "have liberty to consult with some proper carpenters on the proper dimensions of a single three-story brick house, and get a bill of scantling." Likewise, their decision to purchase an organ from a London maker proved problematic when they realized that they would have no idea how to ensure that the instrument would fit into the church, nor did they know how they would assemble it once it had arrived by ship. Thus, the vestry sent carpenter Benjamin Baker to Britain, explaining in a letter that he carried that "he has been employed both in the building and making alterations in the church, [and] he has promised to give a plan of the organ loft and any other assistance in his power."[16]

In light of this growing reliance on professionals in their midst, it is unsurprising that, in addition to employing Samuel Cardy to direct the construction of St. Michael's Church, the South Carolina Assembly sought the assistance of such men to an even greater degree as they continued the improvement of their surroundings. On deciding to build an Exchange, elites relinquished control over both the design and the construction of the building, and in February 1767 the assemblymen noted that they had "sought for and procured from several builders and architects several plans for an Exchange and Customs House, which they have considered and examined and are of opinion that the plan hereunto annexed will best answer the situation and extent of the ground at the place proposed. That they have also procured an Estimate upon the said plan."[17]

This "said plan" was the work of William Rigby Naylor, an Anglo-Irish master architect who had established himself in Charleston. Naylor's design was to be realized with the know-how of John and Peter Horlbeck, two Charleston-based builders who had emigrated from the German-speaking lands. With many of the major decisions about materials and plans entirely in their hands, this team of professionals would determine the outcome of the Exchange project to an even greater extent than Cardy had influenced the construction of St. Michael's Church.

Right from the beginning of the work, it was clear that an ongoing discourse between Charleston tradesman and elite assemblyman was the key to a successful building process. Putting together the Horlbecks' specialist knowledge, the assembly's financial resources, and Assemblyman Henry Laurens's commercial connections, the decision was made to send John Horlbeck to Britain, accompanied by a letter of introduction from the merchant Laurens, to buy building materials. The letter in question stressed that Horlbeck carried the responsibility for selecting suitable materials, and to this end would "inspect each article [purchased] himself and . . . will be satisfied with his own acts." At the same time, Laurens assured his London contacts that Horlbeck was "a plain and honest man and will give you very little trouble," and that he should be supplied with materials "bought cheapest for ready money." Furthermore, when some of the selected cargo arrived in Charleston in a poor state, Horlbeck "made a great noise about the quantity of broken [pieces]" and asked that Laurens withhold payment, at the cost of good relations between the merchant and his British contacts. Without doubt, it was not entirely due to the ruling elite that the finished Exchange welcomed Charleston into the circle of the "modern" and improved English-speaking town. Instead, Naylor's original idea and the Horlbecks' power over the selection of materials had played an equal role in the raising of the building, and had thus transformed it into a collective expression of civic endeavor by middling master tradesmen and their merchant-planter compatriots.[18]

The deep involvement of so many townsmen in the improvement of Charleston means that there is more than one lens through which we must view the rash of public works that constantly transformed the South Carolina townscape between 1730 and 1780. These works not only represented the aspirations of provincial elites seeking to reinforce their power; their successful realization depended equally on the involvement of middling sorts in projects that promoted their interests as tradesmen and necessitated the use of their skills. Charleston was the result of the work and commitment of middling tradespeople to improvement, as much as it was the preserve of the merchant-planter rulers.

## The Politicization of the Town: Building a Political Culture out of Urban Space

As far back as the 1730s, the growth of Charleston's public spaces had, therefore, opened up avenues for non-elite South Carolinians to become important to the creation and maintenance of the physical aspect of the Low Country's principal public institutions. In their capacity as contractors, architects, and tradesmen, these successful independent householders had benefited greatly from a parade of improvement projects providing lucrative work and a role in the transformation of their home town, Charleston. Far from being awed by public buildings that were a monument to elite power, these middling townsmen found themselves at the heart of projects that demanded their skills, brought substantial financial rewards, and gave them some measure of influence within the urban landscape. Because they shared in the rewards of urban growth, people of the middling sort could not complain that the elite were branding their mark on the landscape at their expense.

At the same time, however, middling involvement in urban improvement did not necessarily mean that this group deferred to elite aspirations, and we cannot automatically assume that the middling sort were willing accomplices in the shoring-up of planter-merchant power. Indeed, given the diffidence toward elite cultural values and the planting lifestyle already documented among Charleston's more successful traders, it would be surprising to discover that they gave unquestioned support to their superiors' public shows of power. In the metropole, the improvement of the eighteenth-century town was undertaken by provincial gentry who wanted to broadcast their refinement and wealth to the larger nation. But, as previously noted, works were also prompted by a drive for order, modernity, and neatness—qualities inherent in many a town's broad streets, pavements, and classical architecture. In short, urban-betterment projects embodied principles already embraced by middling sorts in their cultural and family lives, and it was also as a result of this overlap that these people found the project of urban improvement especially attractive. As well as providing lucrative employment and a stake in their environment, public works furnished this group with an opportunity to further develop their distinct identity as industrious and upstanding town citizens. Ultimately, it was the articulation of this identity that brought middling sorts to blows with their elite counterparts—a conflict that had its roots not in increased poverty and marginalization, but one that instead represented the maturation of a separate ideology among a new and confident section of urban society.

Along with employment in projects of civic improvement came a certain measure of influence over the urban environment. However, if middling people were to make their opinions about their town heard, they also needed to increase their presence within the town's decision-making institutions. In Charleston, the arena that was most open for the independent participation of the middling sort was the town's assemblage of commissions. The commission system, set up in Charleston under the auspices of St. Philip's vestry, replicated innovations in the government of non-incorporated towns in the mother country—a similarity that had been carefully noted by Governor Glen as early as 1750. The twenty or more commission posts associated with these bodies were filled annually by elected officials, who were bestowed with the power to regulate and govern various areas of the urban environment: markets, streets, the harbor, the workhouse, and the wharves. No other southern colony relied so heavily on such institutions, and their ongoing deployment in South Carolina was in part a function of the special regulatory needs of a large urban environment. Far from being marginal, the commissions were viewed by contemporaries as important elements in the colony's governing structure. Indeed, their power was such that Governor Glen, in an effort to prevent encroachment on his authority, attempted to dissolve the commissions, because they were allowed to appropriate and spend money without authorization from the Royal Council and thus, he argued, had become "a sort of corporation having perpetual succession."[19] Glen's failure to abolish the commission system meant that subsequent governors would have to deal with a well-established infrastructure of urban regulation. Writing his "Representation of the Colony" in 1770, Governor William Bull wished his readers to "take notice of a turn which prevails more in this than any other province, which is a gratuitous execution of many branches of power under a desire of shewing a public spirit and easing the public expences." Bull continued his report by making reference to the "various commissioners" involved in town regulation, and the "laudable spirit" with which they generally undertook their responsibilities.[20]

Charleston's commissions, then, were an important site of formal, political, power outside of the Commons House of Assembly, and as such they had substantial duties, similar to those of the new public bodies springing up in British towns were often improved and maintained through special commissions, a practice that began in Salisbury, Wiltshire, in 1737, and subsequently became popular and widespread throughout the provinces. Since the new posts had no history of oligarchy and were wide open for the election of those who had previously stood outside urban government, middling men quickly formed the majority of the commission's members. With their role as custodians of the improved town, commissions also reflected the larger concerns of the middling townsman, who sought a well-ordered and modern environment in which to live and work. Hence, these bodies turned out to be the perfect arena for those who had already developed an interest in public works but who did not yet possess a stage on which to articulate their civic ideals.[21]

Charleston's commissions had a similar social profile to that of their transatlantic counterparts (see table 6.2). Between 1742 and 1779, few who identified themselves primarily with the countryside sought control through the mechanisms of urban government, leaving the task to those whose chief economic and social ties lay within the town. At the same time, those urban-dwelling merchants and planters who might have counted themselves as part of a colonial governing elite by virtue of their election to the Commons House of Assembly constituted only 30 percent of those who held a commission post. For those assemblymen who did also serve on Charleston's commissions, most were to be found among vestrymen or firemen, positions that enjoyed the most prestige, but that did not often require a day-to-day commitment of time. In short, it was the lesser merchant and tradesman with a close connection to Charleston, and no position in the colonial governing elite, who claimed the most authority over the town's spaces. This authority was frequently reinforced by a tendency to serve on the town's commissions year in, year out. Just as new forms of urban government had given new groups in society a voice in the metropole, so had they opened up such channels in the Low Country.[22]

Importantly, the type of townsman who was chosen as a commissioner was more often than not an individual who had already demonstrated a strong commitment to the improvement imperative, and there was a clear correlation between those Charlestonians who served on a civic body and the

Table 6.2

**Occupations of Charleston committeemen, 1742–1779**

| Commission | *Merchant* | *Professional* | *Artisan* | *Planter* |
|---|---|---|---|---|
| | | *Occupation* | | |
| Vestry of St. Philip's | 120 | 27 | 20 | 26 |
| Commissioners of markets and workhouse | 76 | 5 | 59 | 0 |
| Firemasters and commissioners of the streets | 109 | 0 | 36 | 18 |
| Packers | 1 | 0 | 172 | 0 |
| Wood and coal measurers | 22 | 1 | 62 | 0 |

*Source:* Vestry Minutes of the Parish of St. Philip's, Charleston, South Caroliniana Library.
*Note:* Post-holders were counted each time they were elected, and were counted on every committee on which they served, even if they held multiple positions simultaneously. Occupations for those persons listed in the available annual election results (1742–55 and 1763–79) were sought in the contemporary records.

most active participants in those Societies that were devoted to the enrichment of the town and its population. Increasingly, it was Fellowship Society and South Carolina Society members who took these posts, until they filled almost 60 percent of the available positions. Through their domination of these institutions, men like blockmaker Barnard Beekman, tailor Theodore Tresevant, merchant Darby Pendergrass, and bricklayer Timothy Crosby had, by the 1760s, firmly established themselves as a cornerstone of urban public life: . However, urban improvement, a civic political career, and charitable deeds united most clearly in the life of Daniel Cannon—a carpenter, contractor, and member of the Fellowship Society. Cannon could probably be described as Charleston's most civic-minded citizen and, as a by-product, one of its wealthiest tradesmen. At various times before 1776, Cannon had served as vestryman of St. Philip's Church, Commissioner of the Streets, and as a Commissioner for the building of the jail and workhouse. In every sense, Cannon was a middling tradesman who was fully invested in, and committed to, the civic cause, and he embodied the processes by which urban cultures were now becoming politicized by their intersection with the colony's apparatus of domestic government.[23]

Reaching out beyond involvement in public works, and in the process embracing merchants and shopkeepers, this civic faction had coalesced into a visible, proto-political group. Their coming together, moreover, had not occurred because of economic disadvantage and marginalization, but was instead the result of a shared interest in urban improvement, and a belief that ordering and modernizing Charleston would make it a better place. Furthermore, from the 1760s onward, rather than simply being separate from a colonial elite on paper, this new faction began publicly to construct its particular vision for Charleston. Civic leaders increasingly committed to a separate agenda that centered on their role and their identity as concerned and enlightened townspeople; they were now propagating an alternative political culture of civic responsibility, in plain view of South Carolina's elite rulers, whom they felt were not serving the best interests of the town.

The agenda of Charleston's civic lobby initially emerged with the publication of William Simpson's *Practical Justice of the Peace and Parish Officer of His Majesties Province of South Carolina* in 1761. Here the customary duties expected of the conscientious town commissioner (as this post had evolved over the previous quarter-century) were committed to paper for the first time. By including sections concerning Charleston's streets and markets, the handbook put on record the existence of a group who had a distinct civic mandate that included particular goals and responsibilities for the town's custodians. As such, Simpson's guide offered much more than practical advice; it made it abundantly clear that there were certain standards that needed to be achieved if an officeholder was to fulfill his civic duty properly. By adhering to these standards, the public servant would become the very model of a virtuous, concerned, and enlightened townsman.[24]

This printed articulation of a civic ideology was then reinforced through the proper execution by middling townsmen of the roles so clearly laid out on the page. Although a lot of work had been done in Charleston to build modernity, just as much time could be devoted to ordering the potentially disorderly elements that occupied this space, perpetually threatening to destroy civic aspirations. It was to this end that Simpson's *Practical Justice* explained to readers that, if they received an appointment as commissioner, it would be their responsibility to prevent Sunday trading and to ensure that all butter and meat sold in the Charleston market was the correct weight.[25] Through their imposition of expected norms of urban order, Charleston's governing citizens forged an urban ideal that brought them closer to each other, aligned them with their British cousins and, at the same time, distanced them from South Carolina's governing elites.

The emergence of this shared ideal of civic order was most evident, however, in the conspicuous steps taken by Charleston's commissioners in the name of executing the duties of their office. When necessary, town officeholders did not hesitate to reprint excerpts of the statutes relating to urban order in the *South Carolina Gazette,* parading them under the noses of elite assemblymen as a standard to which all conscientious South Carolinians should aspire. By 1774, ideas about urban order were becoming ever more coherent, and the newspaper pointedly reported:

The commissioners of the markets with two magistrates have spent a whole week in a very essential service to this community, which had been too long neglected. . . . They visited the butcher's slaughterhouse and pends, tried and adjusted the weights, beams, and scales, and fined them for killing on Sunday contrary to the law. They next tried and adjusted the weights . . . at every wharf, and some other places. And concluded, with trying the baker's bread, so much of it was found deficient . . . that they were obliged to seize near 900 half crown loaves which they distributed to the poor of their own hands.[26]

Making an event out of the execution of their duties, commissioners reinforced a collective civic ideal and advertised its desirability to those outside of their immediate group. In addition, they strenuously highlighted the fact that they had seized the opportunity to help out the town's less fortunate residents with the giving out of free bread. Officials used the medium of print to point out to all readers of the *South Carolina Gazette* what they believed to be the civilized and morally just principles by which Charleston should function, and the noble activities that they were prepared to undertake in the name of enforcing standards.

Increasingly, these pointed newspaper reports were accompanied by demands for more action from colonial elites with regard to urban order, mostly taking the form of calls for incorporation. Such pleas began to appear in the *South Carolina Gazette* from 1763 onward, and in 1765, "A Tradesman" suggested that the only solution to the woe of a poorly regulated town was to "directly instruct our REPRESENTATIVES; petition the GENERAL ASSEMBLY FOR A PROPER LAW; APPLY FOR AN ACT TO INCORPORATE THE TOWN."[27]

In possession of a coherent identity and a clear ideology, Charleston's civic faction now sought to gain control over the town so that they might see the principles they promoted in their charitable societies, and in the course of their own service in the name of civic government, spread among the wider urban populace.

This middling civic group also sought to impose their principles on their governing superiors through their choice of assemblyman; from the 1750s onward, they elected representatives for the parishes of St. Philip's and St. Michael's who aligned as closely as possible to their own interests. Although the men who served them in the Commons House were drawn from the elites, they did not adhere to the typical profile of the South Carolina grandee. In the first instance, their economic interests were more urban than was the norm, and representatives tended to be merchants or attorneys based firmly in the town; if they owned rural land, it was either undeveloped, or farmed for the domestic produce market. As full-time Charleston residents, the representatives were also well-known to its middling electorate as they often sat alongside them on town commissions. Men such as Hopkin Price, a tanner turned merchant, Benjamin Smith, and Thomas Savage all had long histories of service on the town's regulatory bodies, demonstrating a firm commitment to the civic ideals of their middling compatriots. At the same time, many town representatives had shown themselves to be of a like mind in their cultural activities too—not a few were Congregationalists, prominent town militiamen, and paid-up members of charitable clubs such as the South Carolina Society. Finally, many were disposed to individual acts of generosity to their inferiors; assemblyman Benjamin Smith, for example, was a staunch supporter of Alexander Garden's negro school, and a donor of over £2,500 sterling in his will to causes such as Charleston's poor and the South Carolina Society.[28]

Since the middling townsmen's chosen representatives were only in a minority in the larger Commons House of Assembly, the call of "a Tradesman" for incorporation was not answered, but the founding of a Charleston District Grand Jury in 1770 staunched the flow of letters to the newspaper, as it inadvertently provided an important new arena in which civic leaders could press home their separate agenda.[29] Unrest in the backcountry and the rise of the Regulator movement had prompted the assembly to draw up the Circuit Court Act of 1769, supplying the instruments of local government demanded by protestors. As a result, the grand jury that met in Charleston no longer needed to concern itself with matters connected to the rural parts of South Carolina. Although men from the adjacent countryside qualified for service on this new body, magistrates were more likely to be drawn from the town itself.

Immediately, the urban middling sorts who had become so prominent on other regulatory bodies exploited the possibilities inherent in an institution charged with policing the urban environment. Charlestonians turned out in much greater strength at grand jury meetings than did the representatives from the surrounding country, meaning that they consistently outnumbered their suburban and rural compatriots. What is more, those townspeople enthusiastically reporting for duty were also the most active in other areas of civic affairs—among them, tanner John Berwick, shipwright Paul Townsend, carpenter Joseph Verree, shoemaker John Matthewes, bricklayer Cato Ash, carpenter James Brown, bricklayer Timothy Crosby, and, of course, Daniel Cannon. They were aided in their efforts by the information of other active townsmen not actually serving on the jury: Patrick Hinds, John Ernst Poyas, and Thomas Elfe, for example, provided information of undesirable behavior by townspeople. At the same time, as the decade progressed, elite urban merchants, like Miles Brewton and Theodore Gaillard, who had been nominated for jury service, increasingly failed to show up at meetings at all.[30]

With middling tradesmen dominating the Charleston Grand Jury, the periodic protests concerning urban order grew into a torrent of complaints against elite inertia. The jury's thrice-yearly presentments, now regularly printed in Timothy's *South Carolina Gazette,* became the premier method for eminent townsmen to articulate publicly (and in great detail) their particular standards for government in Charleston. From 1770 onward, the contents of the presentments began to more clearly converge with the middling faction's leading principles, and a firm program for urban reform emerged. Thus, the presentments were an arena where morally upstanding citizens brought instances of un-Christian, immoral, and disorderly behavior to the attention of a self-interested and negligent governing elite. Complaints were ever more likely to be peppered with an ardent religiosity uncharacteristic of a genteel southern Anglicanism that had commonly placed reform of the beliefs and morals of the population-at-large a long way down its list of priorities. Calls for the incorporation of Charleston became routine.

Overall, the grand jury's grievances revealed how middling magistrates had fused their cultural, economic, and political values, into a single civic agenda that they now broadcast to newspaper readers on a regular basis. This was an agenda that placed great weight on the importance of moral and Christian behavior among both blacks and whites in Charleston, with the magistrates frequently despairing at the "great increase of irreligion, vice & imorality" among the urban population. As a group who were thought to be particularly susceptible to downfall, slaves were often singled out as the source of bad morals and the practitioners of many dubious pursuits, such as drinking, gaming, and Sabbath-breaking. However, whites were not protected from condemnation if they too fell into idle and immoral ways—on more than one occasion the Jurors lobbied in favor of the erection of public stocks in the marketplace so that those free Charlestonians who had indulged in dissolute activities might be made an example of in front of their fellow citizens—black and white. Also keen to promote a culture of hard work among the town's inhabitants, the magistrates attempted to bar blacks from the marketplace on the grounds that their presence prevented "poor and industrious families from obtaining an honest livelihood."[31] With an ordered population and an ordered townscape entirely complementary in the forging of an upstanding citizenry, jurors also stressed the responsibility of the town's officials to uphold order and promote good behavior. As a result, there were frequent complaints about the under-performance of constables, patrols, and militia officers who had turned a blind eye to market regulations, indulged in drink with poor whites and blacks, and ignored disorderly and dirty streets.

In the course of their involvement in urban government and renewal, Charleston's middling sorts had gradually established a power base for themselves within the town, developed a common outlook and ideal, and carved out a number of channels through which they might articulate this ideal to a wider audience. In doing so, this civic faction had also managed to separate themselves clearly from the concerns and agendas of those elite South Carolinians with whom they did not agree, both in the political and the cultural arenas. At the same time, this agenda distanced middling sorts from the town's poor whites and blacks, who were most often the targets of reforming efforts. The dissent faced by Low Country elites had not emerged from the ranks of plain folk, but was instead the result of the coalescing of middling power, principles, and aspirations within an urban context.

## Civic Conflict and Imperial Conflict

The creation of this middling civic agenda, however, was taking place during a decade of turbulent relations between colonists and their imperial masters. So how does this reading of civic politics in South Carolina relate to the first phases of Revolutionary conflict? It is very important that we answer this question as it has been widely argued that civic conflicts between emerging classes were often an important motivation behind Revolutionary protest.

Dissatisfied with their worsening economic situation, and resentful of their exclusion from the instruments of political power, the urban "lower sort" in Boston, New York, and Philadelphia—usually artisans—saw the imperial crisis that unfolded between 1764 and 1776 as an opportunity not only to protest against British taxes that might exacerbate existing post-war poverty, but also as a chance to voice their displeasure to native leaders who had done so little to help them through economic hardship. The Revolution thus forced the hand of colonial leaders, as popular pressure "from below" made them widen political representation and note the grievances of their inferiors. In Charleston's case, Richard Walsh has argued that the radical Sons of Liberty were artisans who, excluded from all governing institutions, were upset at the privations they were suffering as a result of the elite's eager consumption of British imports at the expense of their own manufactures.[32]

Yet a more thorough investigation of urban growth in the shaping of colonial South Carolinian society must cast some doubt on this reading of the roots of "popular" activism. As we have seen, while some plain folk were suffering economic hardship, many middling townspeople had done very well as a result of Charleston's explosive expansion. Quite separate from the poorest urbanites, this group had, by the late 1760s, used economic, cultural, and political channels to forge a distinct identity through the promotion of an agenda of hard work and good morals. And, although this sector of the population contained many artisans, mechanics did not have a middling monopoly. Indeed, even in artisan households, skilled labor formed only one element in the wide-ranging interests of a people who experienced few disadvantages in the face of the import trade—a trade which did not replace the need for their services and which itself offered them business opportunities. Rather than being a disgruntled lower sort, excluded from politics at all levels, this middling sort was in the process of finding its own voice within urban government, broadcasting its civic agenda through such institutions as the grand jury.

The situation of these middling men is important as we turn our attention to the dynamics of South Carolina's imperial crisis because it was precisely the same people, prominent in civic affairs and charitable fraternal organizations, who became the leading protagonists in the Sons of Liberty—Charleston's "radical" wing of revolution. Far from being dispossessed members of the lower sort, the tradesmen and service workers who formed this group had achieved economic success in the city, and often had long records of service within institutions of civic influence. Among the founders of the Sons of Liberty were such characteristic figures as Nathaniel Lebby, a shipwright, and George Flagg, an urban land speculator. When Lebby died at the turn of the eighteenth century, he left a $7,000 estate that included eighteen slaves; Flagg, also a slave-owner, had bought and sold more than ten city lots in the course of compiling his extensive property portfolio. Almost half of the Sons of Liberty were paid-up members of the Fellowship Society, and thus comfortable enough to be able to give alms to the town's less fortunate residents, and at least a fifth of them had been selected for service as town commissioners. This core group of successful tradesmen also staffed South Carolina's main Revolutionary organizations, making up 50 percent of the "mechanic" section of the 1769 non-importation committee, where they were joined by like-minded merchants with a comparable history of civic service and charitable diligence. As a result, in Charleston's case, we cannot say that economic and political marginalization was the driving force for radical Revolutionary protest.[33]

Why, then, was the radical stance so appealing to the town's Sons of Liberty? Protest against the British was, I would argue, attractive to this group on two levels. First, the conflict represented an opportunity for an emerging middling social group to build on sites of influence that they had already started to construct within the domestic political context. Thus, actions against the British government represented a new platform—beyond the one provided by the grand jury—for Charleston's middling faction to advertise their particular values to elite South Carolinians. Availed of these new channels of action, the civic lobby gradually achieved more confidence in itself as a separate class who might break free from any still-existing patronage connections to the elite.

Early on in the conflict with the British authorities, the Stamp Act crisis provided an opportunity for the middling Sons of Liberty to air their civic agenda to the urban public. Throughout their actions, the radicals sought to ensure that their deportment would be a model of the order and sobriety that they were striving to achieve as commissioners and charity-givers. Thus, Timothy's *Gazette* recounted how "Our Liberty Boys being content to keep out the Stamps, do not injure, but protect the Town."[34] Indeed, right from the formation of a John Wilkes Club, in response to the imposition of the Stamp Act, the middling "Liberty Boys" endeavored to remain shining beacons of civic responsibility. The club drank "loyal and patriotic toasts" to the "celebrated Patriot[s] of Britain or America" and "marched in a regular procession to town," being careful all the time to "preserve the same good order and regularity as had been observed throughout the day." Overall, it was impossible to drive a wedge between the principles and the personnel of this Stamp Act protest, and the motivations of those who were, simultaneously, active in urban government. Their demonstrations were, in equal measure, an expression of good order and upstanding conduct in Charleston's public spaces and a protest against the encroachments of British tyranny.[35]

At the same time, such demonstrations also provided the means by which the middling civic lobby could nurture a separate political identity, more independent from the elites whom they had hitherto relied on to represent them in the colonial government. When the Wilkes Club nominated representatives to the Commons House in 1765, they still selected like-minded social superiors, such as the dissenter and commissioner Hopkin Price, stalwart commissioner Thomas Smith of Broad Street, and, of course, Christopher Gadsden. Indeed, it would not be until after the Revolution that the middling faction completely severed their ties with elites. Yet it is clear that the additional opportunities for group action furnished by the Stamp Act crisis crystallized their awareness of themselves as a separate entity, even from those social superiors with whom they shared a political outlook. Organizational meetings of the Sons of Liberty both fostered the group's coherence and provided the opportunity for them to carry leaders from their own midst to the fore. In particular, accounts of the Sons' activities suggest that radical printer Peter Timothy was beginning to assume a leadership role almost equal to that of Christopher Gadsden. Suspected by Henry Laurens to be the driving force behind the mob that visited his house in 1765, searching for stamps, Timothy was characterized by the planter-merchant as that "malicious Villain acting behind the Curtain who could be reached only by suspicion," and, along with Gadsden, as one of the two most "industrious antiparliamentarians" in Charleston. Regularly publishing the remonstrance of the town's middling grand jury, and taking such a radical Whig stance that William Bull labeled it "the conduit Pipe of Political matters on one side," Timothy's *South Carolina Gazette* bolstered his position as a leader of the middling Patriot cause in the wake of the Stamp Act. The printer's status was then further underpinned by his election to both provincial congresses and to the First General Assembly, all as a representative for Charleston's urban parishes.[36]

However, this happy union of civic and radical interests equally stemmed from a growing tendency among the middling faction to link bad government by the elite in the domestic arena to their faulty decision-making on the imperial stage. In this respect, Charleston's urban middling sorts had a lot in common with their radical contemporaries in Britain, who frequently argued that "the sources of the war and loss of the colonies lay in the same over mighty concentrations of power in the state and locality which allowed government to pursue measures that were contrary to the sense of the people."[37]

This situation was clearly evident by 1769, when the Charleston radicals clashed with William Henry Drayton over the signing of South Carolina's non-importation agreements. Objecting to the public pressure put on non-signers of the agreement, Drayton and his supporters launched an attack on the radicals, who were fully behind the boycott. However, the invective of both sides soon "left the Subjects upon which they began to contend" and moved onto "harrowing each others private character."[38] Rather than maintaining a clear view on the merits of non-importation, radicals and elites quickly shifted the terms of the debate to the question of whether their opponents' character deemed them unfit for political service to the colony. While Drayton and his allies mocked the lack of classical education and the trading backgrounds of their opponents, the radicals hit back with criticisms that focused on Drayton's deficiencies as a leisured, elite gentleman who was little more than a sponge and a drain on society. In a letter to the *South Carolina Gazette*, the "Mechanics" mocked the "polite and courtly manner" of their foe, accusing him of not appearing "in the least to have regarded the peace and good order of that community of which he is a member." Furthermore, the authors were careful to point out that mechanics were "the most useful people in a community," able to support their families through hard work. Meanwhile, Drayton's leisured background and his probable inability to earn a living were singled out as major character flaws. Overall, the radicals took the opportunity to stress their middling values of hard work, public service, and frugality, over Drayton's faults of selfishness, laziness and luxury—all of the qualities that the civic faction had so despised in South Carolina's leaders when it came to the government of Charleston. This time, however, Drayton's flaws were further linked to the judgments he made about larger issues—his lack of regard for the health of the civic community now affecting his ability to act properly in response to imperial crisis.[39]

Continued sparring between mostly middling Patriots and elite rulers characterized the entire early 1770s, but with the Declaration of Independence in 1776 came the need for South Carolina to form its own state government. With new and pressing decisions to be made about who should govern and how they should rule, the dispute between Charleston radicals and its moderate elites over the other's deficiencies in the arena of colonial leadership reached its zenith. As a result, the lengthy conflict over the drawing up of the 1776 state constitution can be characterized as a battle between popularist, dissenting, middling men who stressed honesty and service, and a corrupt aristocracy who believed it had the right to expect their inferiors to acquiesce to their betters. Again, it was not only Revolutionary principles and Independence that were at stake, but the question of who had the right qualities for domestic governance. Arguing that the constitution handed power to Tories like John Rutledge, and sustained the sway of the chief buttress of this power— the Anglican Church—the radicals won the right to set up a committee led by Christopher Gadsden to rewrite the document. Rutledge vetoed the constitution that came out of this committee, arguing that it was too democratic and would thus prevent men of "integrity, learning and ability" from winning office.[40]

With the constitutional conflict principally being between urban radicals and ruling elites, the instruments of town government were requisitioned for continuation of the dispute. Thus, at the height of the controversy in April 1776, when Charleston's grand jurors sat down to the customary duty of writing out their grievances, the process became more about how the new state should be ruled than how the town should be ordered. Realizing that the grand jury had become the preserve of the radical civic faction, their opponents, the colonial elite, requisitioned the body as part of their campaign to pass the new constitution into law. As a result, those magistrates who signed their names after the April grievances were not the regular, conscientious, townsmen who had made the grand jury a tool of their civic agenda, but instead were the moderates drawn from the elite who had rarely shown their faces at the body's meetings since its formation some six years previously. And, rather than lecturing South Carolina's rulers about the deplorable state of the town these elites sought to instruct the civic faction in its duties and its proper relationship to its governing superiors. The pseudo-magistrates were "convinced that to live in a society without laws or a proper execution of them to restrain the licentious nature of Mankind is the greatest misery that can befal a people and must render any body of men in such a situation, but little superior to a Herd of Brutes." They further warned

that through the evil effects of anarchy and confusion, the people might become an easy prey to the several designs of their invidious Enemies. . . . We think every opposition to [the government's] operations or disregard to its authority, the worst criminality a mortal can be guilty of, highly offensive in the eyes of God, and of all just men and deserving the most exemplary punishment. And cannot but deplore the unhappy situation of any few amongst the people of this Colony who, through an ignorance of their true interests and just rights, and from a want of proper information of the real truth, may be misled by the artifice and cunning of their false and designing enemies, from a real sense of those benefits which our present Constitution has so amply provided for: Benefits, which are not confined or limited to any Ranks or degrees of men in particular but generally, equally, and indiscriminately extending to all, from the richest to the poorest, and which time and a little patient experience must soon evince.[41]

Uncouth urban radicals were thus told to stay in their place, as "every good Citizen must be happy in the Consideration of the Choice of those Officers, appointed in the Administration of our present Government." Fed up with being lectured to about their inattention to the order of their town, and now also challenged about their leadership of South Carolina in international affairs, elites had struck back at the impertinence of their "disobedient" middling inferiors using the very mouthpiece of their adversaries.[42]

The differing principles of middling urbanites and governing elites that had taken shape during the late 1750s and 1760s repeatedly played a key role in the conflicts between radicals and assemblymen after 1765. The middling faction that emerged from urban government was practically inseparable from those who were the cornerstones of the Sons of Liberty, and as such their agendas in the civic and the patriotic arenas were hard to prise apart. Anger at poor economic opportunity, or a disgruntlement born of their exclusion from the political arena, seem to have played little role in the protests of a group of radicals who were neither poor nor totally marginalized from the administration of the colony. Instead, middling townsmen rapidly came to believe that the deficiencies of the majority of their leaders in the civic arena were part and parcel of their leaders' failure to act appropriately when it came to the Revolutionary conflict.

At the heart of the emerging split between South Carolina's elites and the state's middling sorts, therefore, lay the imperatives of urban government and the ideologies of a group that had very different ideas from those held by their superiors about responsible rule and the order of society. While elites thought it enough that they should preserve their source of wealth through keeping the slave population in its place, middling sorts sought white hegemony and improvement of the morals and behaviors of blacks and poor whites. These ideas—concerned as much with the disobedience of plain folk as with slaves—did not prompt "popular collective action," but instead sparked a tussle between two relatively privileged groups of society about what principles should prevail in the keeping of order in the town and now, by extension, the colony.[43] The nature of this clash also cast Charleston's imperial crisis within a very British Atlantic mold—one in which those groups who challenged elites were very quick to link the decisions of their superiors on the international stage with their perceived deficiencies as rulers in the local, civic arena.

Unlike the rural landscape, the urban streetscape incorporates a host of shared public spaces used by the many and varied inhabitants of a town. In Charleston, as in other British Atlantic towns of the era, these spaces were full of possibility for each group of society who occupied them. For South Carolina's gentry, "improvement" represented the opportunity to construct impressive buildings that would both create a "culture of power" for the benefit of their black and white inferiors, and further bolster their status as a sophisticated provincial elite in the eyes of colonial and metropolitan visitors. Yet the physical betterment of Charleston held a parallel set of meanings among the middling whites who were partners in the project. For those artisans who participated in the many construction projects undertaken between the 1730s and the Revolution, involvement in public works brought with it considerable financial rewards and an opportunity to shape the environment in which they lived. These middling tradespeople, however, engaged in the improvement and regulation of their town in order to uphold their cultural and moral principles, as well as to make a profit, and their involvement reflected a commitment to their particular values of industry and order already forged within their household economies and their cultural lives.

Inherent in the middling sort's bid to shape their urban environment according to their particular principles as independent traders was disagreement with their gentry betters, who were engaged in the project of town improvement for quite different reasons. By the 1760s, these differing goals for Charleston lay at the heart of the civic faction's challenge to the governing elites for control of the townscape. In the colony's newspapers, on Charleston's commissions, and on its Grand Jury, middling sorts cast aside the mantra of deference to one's betters, criticizing their superiors as a self-interested and corrupt elite with little interest in the public good. As well as facing the beginnings of disorder in the backcountry, South Carolina's rice aristocracy now also confronted dissension at the very heart of its power base.

The strength of this challenge was further augmented by the ease with which the middling civic faction metamorphosed into a radical revolutionary party. In the same fashion as their counterparts in other British Atlantic towns, Charleston's urban opposition were only too keen to connect the deficiencies of their leaders in the civic arena with their perceived failures on the international stage. As a party consisting of successful tradesmen rather than poverty-stricken artisans, the Sons of Liberty found less to complain about when it came to their economic situation, but plenty that was dissatisfactory about the leaders who held sway in their home town of Charleston.

# Conclusion

WHEN the amateur poet Captain Martin wrote about the Charleston that he had encountered during his visit to South Carolina, he seemed to capture perfectly the position that the town had carved out for itself between 1740 and the Revolution. Martin saw "Black and white all mix'd together" and "Houses built on barren land." He had also encountered "Pleasant walks . . . scandalous tongues, if any mind 'em," and "Many a beau not worth a shilling / Many a bargain, if you strike it," concluding that "This is Charles-Town, how do you like it." The Low Country metropolis was a place that befuddled Martin with its various South Carolinian oddities and yet, at the same time, sections of his verse could have been describing many an eighteenth-century English-speaking town. Indeed, some forty-five years earlier, Daniel Defoe had noted analogous features of society in the provincial spa and leisure town of Tunbridge Wells, characterizing it as a place of "tattle and slander" and "walks covered with ladies completely gay and dress'd to profusion."[1] Martin had experienced, at the southern margins of the colonies, a town that was legitimately comparable to a British provincial town. Such similarities were a consequence of the pursuits of Charleston's inhabitants, who had, between 1730 and 1775, created a place that was fully integrated into an urban British Atlantic world.

As Captain Martin wrote his ditty in 1769, however, non-importation boycotts and anti-British sentiment had already gripped Charleston, beginning a conflict that would pull that British Atlantic world apart. Full-scale revolution quickly intervened to demolish the established order in town and in colony. For elites facing uprisings by white and black South Carolinians, battles with invading forces in the backcountry, and the invasion and occupation of Charleston by the British, the order of peacetime became a distant memory. In response to these challenges, South Carolina's rulers devoted themselves to the maintenance of their authority and to the ejection of the British government from their territory. Delegations sent out from the Low Country to the backcountry sought to keep Regulator settlers, who had already developed a hearty dislike for the Charleston-based authorities, in the Patriot fold. Such expeditions met with mixed success, and Loyalists proved to be a force to be reckoned with in South Carolina's more remote parts throughout the Revolutionary era. Most worrying for white South Carolinian slaveholders, however, was the determination of their slaves to take advantage of the disorder to evade the control of their masters. The colony's black majority ran away from their plantations, fled to the invading armies, headed for Charleston during the British occupation, or simply disappeared to another state. Thus was South Carolina's Revolution as much a civil war among ruling planters, slaves, and backcountry settlers as it was a conflict between American Patriots and the British government. Perhaps more than Americans' commitment to Revolutionary principles, battles between rich and poor, and black and white, guided the course of the struggle.[2]

But what of Charleston's influence over the colony in the turbulent years between 1775 and 1783? And what of its middling sorts in this era and the immediate post-Revolutionary period? This final section of our story of the rise of the town and its people traces their fortunes across these difficult years, as well as offering some suggestions as to why the nineteenth century witnessed the eclipse, and then the demise, of Charleston as a major American city.[3]

## A City Under Siege

Until its occupation by the British in 1780, a strong economy, and preparation of the city for war, ensured that Charleston's tradesmen actually continued to enjoy the prosperity to which they had become accustomed. Looking back on the conflict, the contractor Thomas Doughty claimed that "there was a good deal of business done till 1779 . . . mechanicks stood it the besst." Doughty's assessment was probably based in his recollection of the increasing number of lucrative public contracts handed out so that Charleston might better defend itself from a British attack. Men who won such work profited handsomely, and the carpenter Daniel Cannon received a SC£100,000 contract to build forts on Sullivan's Island and Haddrell's Point during the years leading up to the Revolution. At the same time, with the northern colonies embroiled in rebellion, South Carolinian traders could take advantage of still open channels of commerce in their town to monopolize the trade in European goods. For builders especially, the devastating fire of 1778 also created opportunities, as residents of the more than 250 destroyed properties looked to rebuild homes and business premises. Growing increasingly wealthy from these new prospects, townspeople traded in real estate at a rapid rate, and the price of urban lots rose faster than ever. All of the possibilities that had previously favored the urban entrepreneur seemed heightened by the North's troubles, the threat of war, and the possibility of another urban conflagration.[4]

While their businesses remained on course, the town's middling radical Patriots were (as we have seen) still locking horns with governing elites over the nature of the independent state's first constitution. But, already in 1775, other events were underway that would emphasize the similarities, rather than the differences, between Charleston's middling sorts and their elite bedfellows. Chief among these uniting forces was slavery. All in equal danger of losing livelihoods and lives in the face of a slave uprising, South Carolina's middling and elite whites came together on the question of how they should react to a slave population alert to rumors of revolution and freedom. More sensitive to the humanity of their slaves, the attitude of urban middling sorts toward the Africans in their homes and workplaces was, until the 1770s, often distinguishable from the majority opinion of planters toward the faceless laborers who toiled on distant lands. As grand jurors, town tradesmen had shown a particular concern for the morals of Charleston's slaves, a concern probably often stemming from their commitment to a dissenting Christianity willing to embrace blacks in its fold. At the same time, tradespeople's last testaments persistently recognized slaves as individuals when they gave Africans their freedom, with a number of artisan slaveholders writing a will that freed a slave: the decision of Joseph Roper, a Congregationalist turner, to free his slave Rose, along with her children David and Sarah, was not uncommon.[5]

However, as they watched an increasing stream of their slaves attempt escape to the British ships moored off Charleston, and living at the hub of a black information network that rapidly spread gossip about new chances for freedom, some city dwellers proved only too keen to shift their priorities firmly over to their own safety, and so began fully cooperating with elites in the suppression of black aspirations. Town militiamen conscientiously took on extra duties, "principally to guard against any hostile attempts that might be made by our domesticks."[6] Even those black townsmen who had subscribed to the model of the hardworking, godly, and responsible citizen propagated by Charleston's ruling middling men fell afoul of their newly suspicious white compatriots: the free black Thomas Jeremiah, a long-serving harbor pilot, fisherman, and Christian, could not be saved by the governor from hanging and burning after his groundless conviction for fomenting an uprising in the town.[7] At the same time, white tradesmen who revealed too plainly their recognition of Africans as anything more than soulless pieces of property rapidly attracted the censure of both elites and middling sorts. When the shoemaker Patrick Hinds permitted Lady Huntingdon's Methodist envoy David to preach to a black crowd in his yard, the Charleston grand jurors fully endorsed the protests that followed, citing Hinds "for entertaining & admitting negroe Preachers in his House & on his Grounds, where they deliver Doctrines to large numbers of Negroes dangerous to & subversive of the Peace Safety & Tranquility of this Province."[8]

As the expectation of war pushed rural and urban slaveholders together in defense of their security, townspeople confronted the second challenge to their community—the British occupation of the city, from June 1780 to December 1782. The issue now foremost in Charlestonians' minds was the large number of enemy troops in their midst. Cut off from the remainder of South Carolina, and indeed from the entire Lower South, Charleston could no longer stand at the center of the region's political systems. And, although the town still continued as a social and economic hub, its role in this respect was much reduced. Instead, the main action took place in the backcountry, where Patriots, slaves, and British troops wrestled for control over the future of mainland colonial America's richest landscape.

Charleston's occupation splintered the urban community. Townspeople who came out strongly for the Patriots were forced to abandon all property and business in town, either fleeing the province or joining up in defense of the new nation. Those who chose to stay on and conceal their Patriot tendencies were, within the year, deported to St. Augustine by the British, who were quick to recognize the possibility that they might incite a rebellion in the town. Reflecting further on the wartime situation, the contractor Doughty recalled that such "people here were so much taken up in military duties that they could not well attend to anything else."[9] On returning to their hometown, once-successful tradespeople quickly discovered that their estates had been dismantled, the war bonds they had bought were unprofitable, and the value of their rental properties had plummeted as their tenants fled. Writing his will, the wealthy town jeweler John Paul Grimke lamented that it had been his "full intention to have bequeathed a considerable legacy to my nieces . . . and I should have certainly fulfiled my intention if calamities attending the late war had not reduced my estate to much less than one third its former value." Grimke was also left hoping in vain for legislation to recover depreciated paper money, and was prevented from giving his son SC£2,000 upon his marriage because the cash was tied up in treasury indents whose value had crashed.[10]

As well as being separated by distance when they departed their home town, Patriot Charlestonians also became ideologically divided from those fellow townspeople who chose to remain neutral, or to actively support the British forces. With occupation, political allegiances were sure to be thrown into stark relief. When faced with choosing sides, some townspeople made a decision based on their economic interests, believing that compliance was the best route to preserving their livelihoods. Thomas Elfe Jr. signed the Address of Charleston welcoming the British to the town after he had been told, "in a violent and threatening manner," that he would be "removed from his Family, business, and Friends" if he refused to put his name to the document.[11] By appealing to the very heart of Elfe's interests as an urban trader, the British persuaded him to accept their presence in the town. Following his endorsement, Elfe appears to have kept a relatively low profile. By staying on in the city, tradespeople like this cabinetmaker succeeded in scraping a living from the custom of the British forces and the needs of the elite white men, women, and children who sought refuge in Charleston from the ravages of war.[12]

Elfe's response, however, did not just separate him from the committed Patriot townspeople; it also set him apart from Charleston's ardent Loyalists. A significant group, these tradespeople seem to have kept their opinions on the American rebellion to themselves until the arrival of the British, when events were to place them in the limelight and widen the gap between them and their fellow Patriots. The Loyalists first found prominence with the decision of the British to establish a Board of Police, a body designed to keep order in the town by perpetuating the existing instruments of urban government. Loyalist middling sorts were only too keen to demonstrate their still strong commitment to civic regulation by volunteering for the onerous task of policing a city that was now a major gathering place for escaping slaves. Operating according to their long-held principles, middling commissioners embarked on a mission to regulate Charleston's markets, to keep the streets clean and clear of debris, to put any masterless slaves to work on the town's fortifications, to feed and clothe the poor, and to ensure that bakers met with a good supply of flour and did not cheat customers by demanding high prices for underweight loaves. Even though Charleston's middling community had been rent asunder by Revolution, its values were thus perpetuated through the years of greatest turmoil by those who chose to stay and serve their British masters.[13]

For these conscientious townsmen, however, prominence quickly turned to notoriety. With their willingness to work under the Crown's administration, Loyalists had clearly identified themselves to their rebellious contemporaries, and they were placed in an impossible position at the withdrawal of British troops in 1782. When Patriot townspeople arrived back to assess the damage to their property, Loyalists had no choice but to run for their lives. Chartering boats out of Charleston bound for London or the Caribbean, these families were forced to leave behind urban estates built up over decades of hard work; rental properties, warehouses, timber yards, suburban plantations, shipyards, and workshops stood empty, account books listed pages of debts never to be claimed, and skilled blacks were abandoned to their struggle to avoid re-enslavement by a new owner. A significant proportion of these men and their families would never see Charleston again, their property auctioned off to those townspeople who returned after the British had left in 1782.[14]

## Regrouping after the Troubles

In 1784, the wife of Loyalist house carpenter James Cook was forced to make a public appeal in the Charleston newspapers to end the "compleat misery of my innocent family. . . . My health is going fast, by constantly fretting; the frights and insults are not to be described which I receive in my family, by mobs and parties with swords and clubs, who have surrounded my house, to add to the distress of myself and my poor child." The contractor John Wyatt's ambivalence to the Patriot cause made for equally difficult times for him in the wake of the conflict, and he sought refuge in St. Augustine until late 1784. Those Charleston Loyalists who, following American victory in 1783, risked their lives to reclaim their livelihoods, quickly discovered that schisms in the urban community wrought by war were not easily mended. Indeed, it took intervention by the mayor of a newly incorporated Charleston to preserve the safety of citizens who had cooperated with the British.[15]

Conflicts that divided the urban community in war spilled over into peace-time disagreements, and the agenda of a revivified party of middling activists centered on their post-conflict economic grievances. Battles about the rights of British merchants to trade in the city, the restoration of estates to former Loyalists, the refusal of elites to pay high prices of goods and services, and the cancellation of wartime debts, provided new rallying points for a civic faction still determined to bring elites to account. Now with the full confidence to eject pre-Revolutionary leader Christopher Gadsden altogether from their party, the most vocal middling Patriots sought a radical champion from their own midst.[16] Thus, it was under the tutelage of Alexander Gillon—Charleston merchant, member of the Fellowship Society, and former Charleston grand juror—that the party honed its agenda. Gillon soon gathered additional adherents to his cause. Anne, the wife of the deceased pre-Revolutionary radical printer Peter Timothy, provided the voice for the faction in her newspaper. Support to the radical cause also came from the Palmetto Society, formed in 1777, and the Carpenters' Society, established in 1783. Once again, therefore, the faction was characterized by its public-minded, middling membership. Such was the force and coherence of the faction's protests in this fraught, post-occupation, environment that the middling merchant Arthur Bryan reflected that "a violent opposition almost totally ruined the Aristocracy, for if they now carry anything in the assembly it is by deception."[17]

As Bryan's observation suggests, the invective of Gillon and his fellow travelers moved quickly to conflate the stance of elites on economic issues with their self-interested approach during the Revolution. Arguing that "enormous wealth is seldom the associate of pure and disinterested virtue," the civic faction labeled themselves in the turbulent 1784 corporation election as a party of "Democracy and the Revolution" that sought victory over "Tories and Aristocrats." In *Timothy's Gazette*, "Old Homespun" railed against the "gentlemen of property," and "Amicus" was disquieted by the "aristocratic influence (both IN and OUT of legislature)." The 1785 and 1786 corporation elections were characterized by an equal dose of polemic.[18] Becoming ever bolder, the middling faction also challenged the authority of their superiors face-to-face, the most direct confrontation between the two sides occurring in March 1784. When the tavern keeper Captain William Thompson failed to pass on a message from John Rutledge, conveying that he would be unable to dine with the Sons of Saint Patrick, Rutledge demanded to know why Thompson had not at least "suffer[ed] his servant to deliver his Message." Taking offence, Thompson angrily confronted Rutledge and demanded an apology for Rutledge's (this "haughty Lordling") treatment of him as a "wretched vassal." The Marine Anti-Britannic Society formally thanked Thompson for his refusal to bow to a corrupt aristocracy who supposed it was their natural right to govern, and moved to publish thanks for his "manly and patriotic" conduct in the matter.[19]

By 1785, however, the radical movement had petered out. At first it had gained a valuable foothold on the newly incorporated city's government, with the unwillingness of some radical wardens to put a stop to anti-Loyalist protests sponsoring the ongoing unrest in the city. Yet, when Alexander Gillon put himself up for the post of city intendant in 1785, he won only a third of the votes against the incumbent, Richard Hutson. With all eligible voters (including Tories) allowed to participate in the election, the radicals had discovered that their campaign was too violent to be attractive to a majority of Charleston's middling voters, who for so long had campaigned for city government so that good order—not chaos—might reign in their home town.[20] And with the encouragement of a peaceful political scene and returning economic prosperity, Charleston's middling sorts quickly reestablished the parameters of their pre-war community.

Already in 1790 John Wyatt's Charleston friends and business associates were willing to recall him in the character of an honest and hard-working tradesman, his years in hiding in St. Augustine seemingly brushed aside as a moment of madness by an otherwise upstanding member of the community. At the same time, the Patriot leanings of Wyatt's business partners, Thomas and Barnard Richardson, counted for little when it came to a dispute over who should inherit the lion's share of the company's considerable assets. Since witnesses remembered the Richardsons (who were only journeymen when they joined the firm) as a pair of lazy sponges who drank away the firm's profits and passed most of their time carousing at the Wyatts' beach house, they were unwilling to see surviving relatives inherit the fruits of their friend's labor.[21] As Wyatt's circle had done, other middling social networks established before

1776 also regrouped following the conflict. Charleston shipwright George Buckle took Miss Betsy Wood, the daughter of a local bookbinder, as his wife before Independence, and then, at his death in 1800, had arranged for a venduemaster, a shipwright, and a carpenter to be his assessors, and for his cousin, the blockmaker Thomas Baas (and his wife) to be executors, calling upon a shipwright and two merchants as witnesses.[22]

The ease with which Wyatt and other middling tradesmen resolved their differences was indicative of the speedy reemergence of the broader, pre-Revolutionary dynamic that had existed between Charleston, the state of South Carolina, and the English-speaking Atlantic. First, economic trends characteristic of earlier decades were reestablished as the town continued to grow into its role as the region's service center: businesses became ever more complex, expanding their workforces and developing a more industrialized character than in the years before 1776. At the center of such change was John Wyatt's carpentry enterprise. Records show that between 1784 and 1797 the concern was made up of no less than three master artisan partners, eleven slaves owned by Wyatt and often put to work in his business, and about seventeen carpenters and a clerk of accounts—a capacity probably not previously achieved by any skilled business, but increasingly common during the last decades of the eighteenth century, when almost half of Charleston's artisans were part of workshops with ten or more free and unfree employees.[23]

Wyatt organized his considerable labor resources along ever more capitalist lines, and the company's journeymen carpenters filled out timecards and were paid a weekly wage for their work. What is more, Wyatt, Richardson & Richardson seemed aware that by pooling their assets and increasing the scope and scale of their operations, they might be able to win out over their local competitors. To this end, John Wyatt planned to set up a sawmill to allow his concern to "get what lumber we wish and . . . have the advantage of others."[24] Following the successful establishment of this mill in suburban Charleston, the partners purchased additional lands at one of the city's wharves, where they enlarged their premises with a counting house, stores, a depot for their carting business, a brewery, and new workshops. To a greater extent than Thomas Elfe some thirty years before, Wyatt and Richardson had created a complex, vertically integrated, enterprise that demonstrated how industrial change elsewhere in the British Atlantic world had continued to impact the structure of Charleston's economy even after political independence.

As businesses expanded and evolved, they also continued to pursue avenues that had brought profits and wealth in the previous decades. In particular, Charleston's builders displayed an ongoing penchant for the kind
of speculative house construction that had brought them success from the
1740s onward. Building leases persisted as a popular method of sponsoring
such work, and some town speculators took on larger projects than they had
attempted in the pre-Revolutionary era. Returning from service in the Continental Army, the carpenter Daniel Cannon abandoned the small-scale town-
center land deals that he had favored earlier in the eighteenth century, instead
devoting himself to the development of his suburban Cannonborough tract.
Most likely surveyed in 1794, Cannonburgh's first lands were sold in 1795, and
at the time of his death, Cannon had managed to sell about half of the seventy
lots that he had planned.[25]

Not wishing to confine themselves to their main trades, but still preferring to reside in Charleston, urban traders also continued to channel their
entrepreneurial talents toward the opportunities on offer in the Low Country's domestic markets, much as they had done since the town economy had
first emerged as a profitable proposition in the decades after 1740. Taking the
domestic provisioning trade to a new level of integration was the grocer John
Addoms, who actively coordinated his rural and urban businesses. Addoms
"opened a grocery and commission store—on Jervey and Walter's wharf—
[with] articles in the grocery line for sale wholesale, retail, for cash or produce," and was seeking "a careful and very industrious man to go on shares
in raising stock, cutting lumber firewood etc at a plantation in St Thomas
Parish—situated on a bold landing." In all likelihood, it was this enterprise
that furnished some of the "excellent hams and butter" that were for sale at
Addoms's town grocery store.[26] Setting their sights beyond the limits of the
South Carolina, Charlestonians also continued to look for business possibilities further afield, augmenting the town's position as the hub of multiple trading systems. Thomas Bennett advertised that with only eight weeks notice his
Charleston mills could supply "particular lumber for the West-India use, such
as windmill arms, points, beams, house frames &c. of the best pine."[27]

As a consequence of this ongoing entrepreneurial activity among the
town's independent traders, Charleston's role as a provincial service and leisure
center became ever more evident in its overall economic profile. Such developments were first of all visible in the physical landscape. By 1790, Charles-

ton's commercial downtown streets had become clearly demarcated according to the services offered by its tradesmen. Home to 583 different businesses, Charleston's nine main downtown thoroughfares were lined with the premises of merchants, shopkeepers, and artisans. However, the city's traders were distributed across these streets according to an identifiable pattern. For example, Broad Street was devoted to merchants and artisans in the luxury and clothing trades while King Street, with its many artisans and shopkeepers, had clearly become the main location of general retail. Lined with the evidence of its principal role as a provincial service center, Charleston's streets marked out distinct zones in which South Carolinians could engage with a local economy.[28]

What is more, Charleston's character as a provincial service town now also had a discernible impact on its merchant community. Merchants, of course, came in many different guises, from the wealthiest slave traders down to the most marginal petty dealers. By the late eighteenth century, this community had come to be classified using a standardized nomenclature common to most city directories published across the English-speaking urban Atlantic. These directories reveal that the precise composition of a merchant community depended on the nature of the town in which they operated. As major port cities, both the Philadelphia and Liverpool trading communities of the late eighteenth century were comprised of relatively large numbers of merchants—resident men with substantial capital and the capacity to coordinate the import and export of goods on an international scale. Especially in Liverpool, those hucksters, shopkeepers, and auctioneers, who were further down the distributive chain, formed a minority of the trading community.[29]

Overall, a similar proportion of Philadelphia, Liverpool, and Charleston business owners were merchants. However, the members of this trading community who were actually transatlantic merchants were far fewer in the Low Country town than in either the American or British port cities of the era. Rather than having the typical trading community associated with a port town, Charleston had developed as a place that acted as a regional distribution center for goods and a location in which factors might commission on behalf of merchants.[30] The larger quantity of shopkeepers and auctioneers show that the city was an important nodal point for distribution of goods to customers. Perhaps to an even larger degree than in the colonial era, Charleston's economic character was determined by its domestic marketing functions, as opposed to its international connections.[31]

As such a town, Charleston found it hard not to continue in its role as a provincial cultural center in a British Atlantic urban system, despite the fact that this entity had, politically, been broken apart. Many Charlestonians still worked in reference to the metropole, exposing their ongoing respect for it to the scrutiny of an American audience. Under the title "Modern Anecdotes," one author related the gaiety and brilliance of London society to Low Country newspaper readers with an enthusiasm that befitted a British subject rather than an American citizen. At the same time, cabinetmaker Thomas Wallace boasted of his London training, and Charles Stewart could not resist mentioning that he had "met with encouragement from people of property in Britain." Musical instrument maker and sheet music retailer John Speisseger had little hesitation in revealing his English roots, with an explanation that he was "late with Messrs. Longman and Broderip in London." Even while their presence caused political upset, an influx of new British factors into the city in the years after the Revolution only reiterated the town's commercial ties to the metropole. All, of course, were able to take advantage of the revivified social season that once again flourished in the months leading up to Easter; races at the Newmarket course attracted their biggest crowds yet, and the Charleston dancing assembly entered a new era as it appointed its own master of ceremonies.[32]

While elites once more enjoyed glittering social lives, middling sorts continued to distinguish themselves from their betters using the cultural modes they had favored before war had temporarily divided their community. White male Charlestonians pressed forward with the charitable associations that they had committed themselves to earlier in the century with the incorporation of the South Carolina and Fellowship Societies. In 1792, the construction of the new Orphan House signaled the development of poor assistance, from a relatively informal system of handouts and subsidized housing to a coordinated effort to feed, accommodate, and provide needy white children with a trade. Of those taking the initiative in this new project, the vast majority had shown a strong pre-Revolutionary commitment to the charitable cause, and the city corporation appointed two long-standing building partnerships, Cannon & Doughty, and Crosby & Toomer, to draw up plans and supervise construction of the Orphan House. On this occasion, some of Charleston's most civic-minded sub-contractors even worked for free, in lieu of paying a subscription toward the new orphanage.[33]

Daniel Cannon had no doubt won yet another lucrative contract in part because he had managed to seal his prominence in urban circles with his election to the city corporation. Cannon's ascent to the very top of Charleston's government was representative of how the civic faction had at last won control of their environment. Cannon's rise was also indicative of the city's ability to nurture a middle class that had reached maturity in an environment that continued to favor their efforts as independent traders. However, the contractor's prominence was facilitated by the fact that the state's governing elites now no longer viewed Charleston as their main seat of political power: in 1786, they had introduced a bill to relocate the state's capital to Columbia. With the westward shift of state government, emblematic of a larger shift in South Carolina's epicenter, Charleston and its middle class would continue to exist for a while yet, but they would ultimately cease to matter.

## Declining Influence

In 1790 the first United States Census revealed that Charlestonians were now a much smaller percentage of the South Carolina population than they had been during the colonial era. By 1800, Charleston had fallen to fifth in the population rankings of America's cities, a downward trajectory that would never be reversed.[34] Furthermore, these hard demographic facts were preceded, from the late 1760s onward, by a new and conspicuous challenge, originating in the state's backcountry, to Charleston's importance. The rapidly growing population of the backcountry region had begun to make a very substantial contribution to the economy of South Carolina, and, with their embrace of slavery, to the creation of a much more extensive plantation society. As the effect of these westward shifts begun to make themselves felt in Low Country society after 1775, Charleston lost its privileged position as the epicenter of South Carolinian affairs. While American independence removed the city from a British world, rural growth worked also to separate it from an urban Atlantic.

With so many settlers arriving in South Carolina to grow profitable staple crops for export, it quickly became evident that the new state's destiny would be as an overwhelmingly agricultural society. In the decade after 1770, the population of South Carolina's backcountry regions quadrupled. These thousands of new settlers were drawn to this distant land both by a market in

need of crops for domestic consumption and export, and by the recent success of white authorities in displacing the Southeast's Indians even further to
the west. Bringing knowledge with them from the colonies to the north, from
whence a large proportion had come, South Carolina's newest residents first
made their living by growing tobacco and wheat, the majority of which was
then exported through the Charleston market. The new crops would enhance
Charleston's existing role as a service center; however, they would do nothing
to encourage any further industrial development, as the only processing they
required took place at rural inspection stations and mills established across
the state.[35]

By the 1790s, with markets for both wheat and tobacco in decline, planters
switched to cotton. With the invention of the cotton gin and other new farming techniques, the change to cotton further assured that innovation in the
new state would now take place in a rural setting. In upcountry workshops
situated either in villages or out on the land, the workhorse of South Carolina's
new "white gold" was built and maintained. Even though his social and cultural life centered on the Charleston community, for example, the free black
cotton-gin maker William Ellison now lived and worked among the wealthy
white planters of Sumter District, close to his customers and the dynamism
of the emerging cotton economy. On South Carolina's new plantations themselves, economic innovation also drifted farther west, when recent upcountry settlers began to deploy the farming methods brought with them from the
Chesapeake in aid of cotton production. Replacing the hoe with the plow permitted larger crops to be cultivated by fewer slaves, who now worked under
the heavily regulated gang-system. Hemmed in by patrols and overseers who
ensured that they remained on the plantation, there were fewer opportunities
for these new enslaved South Carolinians to engage with urban markets and
to escape the restrictions of the rural economy. As well as keeping slaves from
Charleston, the new Cotton South began to draw some white city dwellers
away from their home town. When he died in 1809, city blockmaker Thomas
Baas maintained his town business, but he was also growing cotton on his
Dorchester plantation.[36]

Accompanying this period of economic transition away from the coastal
Low Country was a growing backcountry population who took up an ever
larger share of influence over the political and cultural direction of South

Carolina. This westward shift is particularly evident in the development of the South Carolina Baptist movement during this era. In 1775, the Baptist's main organization, the Charleston Association, had twelve member churches, of which four were in the backcountry. In 1789, the association had expanded to twenty-two members, of which eleven were in the backcountry. The evangelical church was becoming more of a statewide, as opposed to an urban, phenomenon, melding into a Second Great Awakening that began in the rural South in the last fifteen years of the eighteenth century. More and more, it was difficult to equate religious dissenters in the Low Country with the urban British Atlantic middling sort who had provided the bulk of the evangelical's membership before 1780, and easier to view evangelicalism as a rural movement embracing yeoman and poor planters in a typically southern manner.[37]

However, this transition to a more rural, yeoman, membership was not an easy one for the Charleston Association to make, and the difficulties that the group encountered as a result of the shifting terrain of dissent highlighted the way in which backcountry expansion was transforming cultural conflict in South Carolina. The building of bridges between Charleston's dissenters and its elites had begun during the Revolution, as urban religious leaders realized that they needed to appeal to a growing number of rural dissenters if the Patriot cause they supported was to triumph in South Carolina. The roots of this unification lay in the Reverend Oliver Hart's 1775 mission to the backcountry Loyalists, a tour made in the company of William Henry Drayton and the Reverend William Tennant. Even though three years later Hart would publish his sermon condemning elite overindulgences as disastrous for South Carolina's war effort, the expediencies of managing a new backcountry population in a Revolutionary situation had forced Hart to temporarily overcome his dislike of the colony's rulers.

After the Revolution, the growing success of the evangelical movement continued to force a rapprochement between middling dissenters and elites. Importantly, Charleston's less radical, middling Regular Baptists confronted, in the backcountry, a more radical New Light sect. As a result, elite–middling conflict was put to one side as Regular Baptists encountered a socially inferior, and potentially disruptive, new wing of the faith, one that had the ability to challenge their values from below through its adherence to uneducated, upstart ministers, and their worrying embrace of female elders. As historian

Rachel Klein has explained, the Charleston Association was thus forced into redirecting its attentions away from condemnations of a profligate and corrupt elite, and made to refocus on keeping the New Lights in their place at the bottom of the social ladder.[38] As part of the disputes over the vesting of state authority in the Anglican Church during the drawing up of South Carolina's 1776 Constitution, dissenters had sought the downfall of the Low Country's overly powerful elites. By the later 1780s, however, such battles were put to one side as middling Baptists switched their efforts toward the bringing of Separates into the fold, recognizing that this new, backcountry, group now represented the greatest challenge to both of their situations.

The shifting terrain of religious dissent was accompanied by the appearance area of political conflict to the west. In 1775, Charleston had been the absolute epicenter of South Carolina politics. Practically every assemblyman came from the Charleston district, and until the establishment of the circuit courts in 1772, there were no institutions of secular government in the backcountry at all. As the apportionment of representatives in some of South Carolina's various governing bodies shows, however, Charleston's supremacy collapsed over the course of the Revolutionary era. In the Provincial Congress that was called in November 1774, the backcountry received a third of the 184 seats on offer. The end of a long period of turmoil was marked, in 1790, by the election of the first and second state congresses under the new South Carolina constitution. In the first congress, Charleston's two parishes of St Philip's and St Michael's held 16 percent of representatives; by the second congress of the same year, that figure had tumbled to 10 percent.[39]

As the level of Charleston's representation gradually began to fall into line with its actual share of the white population, there was an almost inevitable westward shift of the main political action. Until at least 1775, it is legitimate to argue that the conflict between Charleston's civic faction and the colonial elite was of greatest importance because the town was the center of politics. Entering stage left, however, were the backcountry planters and their representatives. At various moments, Charleston radicals and certain among the newer backcountry faction found common ground and, for a while, they joined together to mount protests against the power of the elites. Rulers' unwillingness to enact legislation to cancel war debts and relieve those laboring under their heavy weight, for example, brought urban tradesmen and poorer backcountry planters together during the 1780s. In the early 1790s, support for the

French Revolutionary cause again united planters in the newer rural areas with their fellow South Carolinians in Charleston, as they used international events to highlight the continued corruption and self-interested actions of the state's own "aristocracy." Even in 1800, sectional tensions over the presidential elections created a statewide Republican Party that toasted "the yeomanry, mechanics, and manufactures of the United States, whose intelligence and patriotism support our Constitution, as their labors do our lives," against the Federalists, who unashamedly offered up elite candidates for election.[40]

But, although the protests of Republicans deployed a rhetoric that had long characterized the conflict between middling townspeople and elites, the disagreements between free white South Carolinians now had nothing to do with the issues and communities nurtured by the urban environment. Wealthy planters of the early nineteenth century shared much more with their opponents than they ever had done before, when urban interests conflicted with rural factions, middling dissenters ran up against Anglican elites, and civic politicians harried those who cared more about order in their own households than within the town. Now, planters were pitched against farmers, staple-producers against staple-producers, and evangelical Christians against fellow Baptists.

Then, as the nineteenth century progressed, economic stagnation worked just as hard as had earlier success to undermine Charleston and its middling sorts. In the antebellum decades, the fate of the city and its full-time residents was sealed. The War of 1812 caused the first of a long line of depressions that seriously affected South Carolina's trade, dented planter profits, and brought the previously expanding demand for luxury goods and services in the Low Country to a grinding halt. Whereas eighteenth-century Charleston had experienced constant growth in response to the ever increasing clamor for the accoutrements of gentility, the nineteenth century brought no such opportunity. With this familiar avenue of expansion closed off, Charleston's provincial service economy found it almost impossible to change direction in favor of the industrial future that might have brought opportunity to those independent trading households who had done so well until 1800. Used to servicing ships, not building them, and to making up suits from British fabric, not weaving the material themselves, city traders could not grasp the opportunity to establish shipyards or cotton mills. Perhaps in light of the series of economic depressions and the continuing attractions of planting, these were opportunities that looked too risky even for the most daring and experienced urban entrepreneur. With circumstances colluding to prevent the town and its population from responding to a changing world, Charleston remained an eighteenth-century city in a nineteenth-century world—an anachronism forever living in the shadow of its glorious past. Now, South Carolina really had become a place whose whole character was determined by its staple crops.[41]

# Tabular Appendix

Table A.1. Population growth in selected British and British American towns

| Town | Population ca. 1700 | Population ca. 1800 |
|------|--------------------|--------------------|
| Boston | 7,500 | 24,937 |
| Bristol | 13,482 | 61,153 |
| Charleston | 1,500 | 18,824 |
| Colchester | 6,647 | 11,520 |
| Glasgow | 18,000 | 77,058 |
| New York | 4,500 | 60,489 |
| Newcastle | 11,617 | 33,048 |
| Philadelphia | 2,450 | 51,938 |
| Shrewsbury | 6,867 | 14,739 |

*Sources:* Nash, *Urban Crucible,* appendix (table 13); Clowse, *Measuring Charleston's Overseas Commerce,* table A-11; Nash, "The Social Evolution of Preindustrial American Cities," table 1; Langton, "Urban Growth," 473–74 (table 14.4).

**Table A.2. Origins and political roles of members of 1769 "Committee of Thirty-Six," in response to the Massachusetts Circular Letter**

| Origin | Name | Affiliations |
|--------|------|--------------|
| Planters | Thomas Lynch | — |
| | Wm. Williamson | — |
| | Thomas Ferguson | — |
| | Benjamin Elliot | — |
| | John McKenzie | — |
| | Peter Porcher | Fellowship Society |
| | Barnard Elliot | — |
| | Benjamin Huger | — |
| | Wm. Moultrie | — |
| | John Parker | — |
| | Charles Elliot | — |
| | Daniel Legare | Magistrate |
| | Isaac Lesesne | — |
| Merchants | John Neufville | Committees; Magistrate |
| | John Edwards | Committees; Magistrate |
| | John Laurens | Committees |
| | Daniel D'Oyley | Committees |
| | Thomas Shirley | — |
| | Peter Bacot | Committees; Magistrate; Fellowship Society |
| | John Ward | Committees; Magistrate |
| | John Abbot Hall | Magistrate |
| | John Coram | Fellowship Society |
| | Aaron Loocock | Committees |
| | Andrew Lord | Magistrate |
| | Roger Smith | Magistrate |
| | Wm. Price | Magistrate |
| Mechanics | Daniel Cannon | Committees; Magistrate; Fellowship Society |
| | John Price | — |
| | Cato Ash | Committees; Magistrate |
| | John Fullerton | Magistrate; Fellowship Society |
| | Joseph Verree | Committees; Magistrate |
| | Simon Berwick | Fellowship Society |
| | John Matthews | Committees; Magistrate |
| | Theodore Tresevant | Committees; Magistrate; South Carolina Society |
| | Thomas Young | — |
| | Tunis Thebout | — |
| | Wm. Trusler | — |

*Sources:* McCrady, *History of South Carolina under the Royal Government,* 651; Records of the Fellowship Society, South Caroliniana Library; St. Philip's Vestry Minutes, 1742–83, South Caroliniana Library. My thanks to Rebecca Starr for providing the McCrady reference.

Table A.3. Charleston households by occupation or status of household head, 1790

| Occupation/Status | Number of households | Whites in household | Slaves | Free blacks | Total number in household | % of total Charleston population |
|---|---|---|---|---|---|---|
| Tradespeople[a] | 491 | 2,313 | 1,642 | 32 | 3,987 | 25.4 |
| Merchants[b] | 394 | 1,591 | 1,399 | 31 | 3,021 | 19.3 |
| Service providers and government employees[c] | 255 | 1,361 | 1,310 | 30 | 2,701 | 17.2 |
| Widows or spinsters[d] | 212 | 810 | 1,059 | 18 | 1,887 | 12.0 |
| Planters | 112 | 613 | 1,134 | 5 | 1,752 | 11.1 |
| Free blacks | 106 | 3 | 77 | 414 | 494 | 3.1 |
| Unknown[e] | 229 | 1,076 | 750 | 37 | 1,863 | 11.9 |
| Total | 1,799 | 7,767 | 7,341 | 567 | 15,705 | 100.0 |

*Sources:* Charleston County, Parishes of St. Michael and St. Philip, in U.S. Bureau of the Census, *Heads of Families at the First Census of the United States, Taken in the Year 1790. South Carolina; Charleston City Directory, 1790,* Charleston County Public Library.

[a] Tradespeople include men and women working in the following trades: apothecary, artist, baker, bandbox maker, blacksmith, blockmaker, bookbinder, brass founder, brewer, bricklayer, butcher, buttonmaker, bottlemaker, cabinetmaker, carpenter, carter, carver, chairmaker, chocolatier, cigarmaker, clocksmith, confectioner, cooper, currier, distiller, drayman, engraver, fisherman, fruitier, gardener, grocer, gunsmith, harnessmaker, hatter, liveryman, mantuamaker, milliner, musical instrument maker, painter, perfumier, perukemaker, printer, ropemaker, saddler, sailmaker, sawyer, scrivener, seamstress, ship chandler, shipwright, shoemaker, silversmith, staymaker, stonemason, sugar baker, tailor, tallow chandler, tanner, tinsmith, tobaconnist, turner, umbrellamaker, upholsterer, vintner, waggoner, and wheelwright.

[b] Includes merchants, shopkeepers, or factors.

[c] Includes the following categories: teacher, schoolmaster, boardinghouse owner, innkeeper, dancing master, music teacher, attorney-at-law, doctor or physician, members of the clergy (and their assistants), and any town dweller identified as holding a city, state, or federal government post.

[d] Includes households where a woman is named as the head of household and is not assigned any other trade or profession.

[e] Includes male heads of household and their dependents who are listed in the census but who are either listed in the city directory without a trade or profession or are not listed at all.

Table A.4. Size of artisan workshops in Charleston, 1790

| Number of employees[a] | Number of households | Number of potential employees | % of total employees |
|---|---|---|---|
| 1 | 99 | 99 | 3.8 |
| 2–4 | 207 | 566 | 21.7 |
| 5–9 | 111 | 738 | 28.3 |
| 10+ | 74 | 1,207 | 46.2 |

*Sources:* U.S. Bureau of the Census, *Heads of Families at the First Census of the United States, Taken in the Year 1790. South Carolina; Charleston City Directory,* 1790, Charleston County Public Library.

Note: This table has been compiled by cross-referencing the 1790 City Directory with the Federal Census of the same year, allowing identification of the complete composition of artisan households. Using the household arrangement of John Wyatt as a precedent (journeymen, apprentices, and slaves sharing the master's house), the number of adult white males has been added to the number of slaves to calculate the size of the workforce available to the master. Although this may count female and child slaves who were not used as workshop labor, it omits potential apprentice boys below age sixteen. Such boys were numerous in the trading household, but it is not possible to distinguish them from the master's own children. Thus, it must be hoped that the overcounting of slaves is cancelled out by the undercounting of apprentices.

[a] Includes adult white males plus slaves (see note above)

Table A.5. Distribution of commercial premises in Charleston's major thoroughfares, 1790

| Commercial premises | East Bay | Broad Street | Church Street | Elliott Street | King Street | Meeting Street | Queen Street |
|---|---|---|---|---|---|---|---|
| Merchants | 33 | 30 | 12 | 12 | 8 | 10 | 5 |
| Shopkeepers | 22 | 3 | 12 | 3 | 72 | 11 | 18 |
| Artisans: | | | | | | | |
| Luxury/Clothing | 7 | 16 | 20 | 10 | 23 | 20 | 14 |
| Food/Service | 8 | 5 | 2 | 7 | 23 | 16 | 3 |
| Construction | 15 | 4 | 6 | 1 | 30 | 20 | 16 |
| Total | 85 | 58 | 52 | 33 | 156 | 67 | 56 |

*Sources: Charleston City Directory,* 1790, Charleston County Public Library; U.S. Bureau of the Census, *Heads of Families at the First Census of the United States, Taken in the Year 1790. South Carolina.*

Table A.6. Internal composition of the trading communities of three Atlantic Seaboard cities, 1790–1796

| | Percentage of traders in: | | |
| --- | --- | --- | --- |
| Type of trader | Charleston 1790 (N = 392) | Philadelphia 1791 (N = 928) | Liverpool 1796 (N = 1,253) |
| Auctioneer | 3 | 1 | 0.5 |
| Broker | 1 | 2 | 7.0 |
| Factor | 11 | 1 | 0.5 |
| Grocer | 4 | 18 | 9.0 |
| Merchant | 30 | 39 | 53.0 |
| Shopkeeper | 45 | 39 | 22.0 |
| Storekeeper | 6 | 0 | 8.0 |

Source: Charleston City Directory, 1790, Charleston County Public Library; Haggerty, "Trade and Trading Communities in the Eighteenth-Century Atlantic."

# Notes

### Abbreviations

CC     Special Collections, College of Charleston, Robert Scott Small Library, Charleston, SC

CCPL     Charleston County Public Library, Charleston, SC

CLS     Charleston Library Society, Charleston, SC

LCP     Library Company of Philadelphia, Philadelphia, PA

LOC     Library of Congress, Washington, DC

LRP     *The Letterbook of Robert Pringle*, ed. Walter B. Edgar, Columbia, SC, 1972

MESDA     Museum of Early Southern Decorative Arts, Winston-Salem, NC

NAS     National Archives of Scotland, Edinburgh

NHS     Newport Historical Society, Newport, RI

NYPL     New York Public Library, New York City, NY

*PHL*     *The Papers of Henry Laurens*, ed. Philip M. Hamer et al., 16 vols., Columbia, SC, 1968–2002

*SCDA*     *South Carolina Deed Abstracts*, ed. Clara A. Langley, 4 vols., Easley, SC, 1983

SCDAH     South Carolina Department of Archives and History, Columbia, SC

SCHS     South Carolina Historical Society, Charleston, SC

SCL     South Caroliniana Library, University of South Carolina, Columbia, SC

SHC     Southern Historical Collection, University of North Carolina, Chapel Hill, NC

### Introduction

1. Braudel, *Structures of Everyday Life*, 479.

2. The most comprehensive comparisons of colonial urban population appear in Nash, "Social Evolution of Preindustrial American Cities," 115–45, and Price, "Economic Functions and the Growth of American Port Towns," 175 (appendix A).

3. For a chronology of Charleston's development and a detailed exploration of its physical expansion, see Poston, *Buildings of Charleston.* Other histories of Charleston include Sellers, *Charleston Business on the Eve of the Revolution;* and Rogers, *Charleston in the Age of the Pinckneys.* For details of urban speculative development, see *PHL,* vol. 5, 589–95.

4. On towns and urban settlement in South Carolina, see Piker, *Okfuskee;* Ernst and Merrens, "Camden's Turrets Pierce the Skies!"; and Migliazzo, "A Tarnished Legacy Revisited." On the dominance of Charleston within South Carolina, see Rogers, *Charleston in the Age of the Pinckneys,* 11–13.

5. See the tabular appendix in this volume for a comparison of urban populations across

the eighteenth-century Atlantic World. See also Nash, *Urban Crucible*, appendix (table 13); Price, "Economic Functions and the Growth of American Port Towns," 175; U.S. Bureau of the Census, *Heads of Families at the First Census of the United States, Taken in the Year 1790, South Carolina*, 38–44; Langton, "Urban Growth and Economic Change," map 14.1.

6. Edelson, *Plantation Enterprise*, 4.

7. On Charleston's function as a socioeconomic hub, see Pearson, "Planters Full of Money," 299–321; DalLago, "City as Social Display"; Earle and Hoffman, "Urban Development"; Coclanis, *Shadow of a Dream*; Coclanis, "The Sociology of Architecture"; and Nash, "South Carolina and the Atlantic Economy." On Charleston's role as a center of government, see Greene, *Quest For Power*; Sirmans, *South Carolina Politics*; and Olwell, *Masters, Slaves, and Subjects*, 57–101.

8. The principal scholars who have written on Low Country slave society in the colonial period include Morgan, *Slave Counterpoint*; Olwell, *Masters, Slaves, and Subjects*; Wood, *Black Majority*; Morgan, "Black Life in Eighteenth-Century Charleston"; and Herman, *Town House*, 119–54. The term "slave society" is applied to the Low Country in Berlin, *Many Thousands Gone*, 142–76.

9. On the link between staple agriculture and settlement patterns elsewhere in the colonial American South, see Earle, *Evolution of a Tidewater Settlement System*; Ernst and Merrens, "Camden's Turrets Pierce the Skies!"; and Farmer, "Persistence of Country Trade."

10. Price argues that because Charleston's "autochthonous business community" was smaller than that of northern cities, the town was "reduce[d] to the level of a mere 'shipping point' rather than a real 'commercial center' or 'general entrepôt.'" See Price, "Economic Function," 162–63; see also Nash, *Urban Crucible*, ix. Even a recent and exciting addition to the scholarship on the colonial city—Benjamin Carp's study of cities and revolution—makes Charleston's part-time residents, the elites, the major focus (though the lower ranks of urban society receive attention in Philadelphia, Boston, Newport, and New York). See Carp, *Rebels Rising*. Some scholars have focused their attention on the non-staple sector of the Charleston community; notable among these are Walsh, *Charleston's Sons of Liberty*; Sellers, *Charleston Business on the Eve of the Revolution*; and Martin, *Divided Mastery*, 20–25. However, these snapshots of various sectors of the urban community do not add up to a thorough assessment of Charleston's influence over South Carolina during the colonial period.

11. For example, Welch, *Slave Society in the City*, and Burnard, "The Grand Mart of the Island."

12. The staple narrative of colonial economic development is exemplified by McCusker and Menard, *Economy of British America*. Peter Coclanis also favors the staples theory insofar as it has focused attention on the export sector and its role in wealth-creation and growth. But, he argues, it is going too far to "suggest that either the production function for that staple or the social concomitants arising therefrom is somehow fixed" (Coclanis, *Shadow of a Dream*, 92). R. C. Nash has further argued, "It was the cost efficiencies derived from focusing the rice trade on a single colonial market that led to Charleston's rapid development" (Nash, "Urbanization in the Colonial South," 10).

13. Bridenbaugh, *Cities in Revolt*, 420; Nash, *Urban Crucible*; Carp, *Rebels Rising*; Doerflinger, *Vigorous Spirit of Enterprise*; Salinger, *To Serve Well and Faithfully*; and Smith, *The Lower Sort*. One recent work that escapes this chronological framework is Middleton, *From*

*Privileges to Rights.* In this study of New York artisans through the years of Dutch and English colonial rule, Middleton demonstrates how changes in the working lives and political outlook of tradespeople were interwoven with a transformation in the urban political economy long before 1776. This shift had more to do with the cultural inheritance of the city's rulers, as well as with the long-term vicissitudes of the local economy, than with a common experience of immiseration at the hands of an advancing capitalist economy.

14. Peter Clark has argued that "the British town emerged as the chief laboratory of a modernizing world," as these towns "forged new patterns of leisure, time, taste and sensibility, and created new perceptions of modernity through a stress on public and private improvement, and through refashioned notions of the built environment." See Clark, introduction to *The Cambridge Urban History of Britain,* 2–3. Other major works on the topic include Borsay, *English Urban Renaissance;* Hunt, *Middling Sort;* Wilson, *Sense of the People;* Earle, *Making of the English Middle Class;* Langford, *A Polite and Commercial People;* Sweet, *English Town;* Barry and Brooks, *The Middling Sort of People;* and Clark, *British Clubs and Societies.*

15. This is a framework that David Armitage has suggested may be especially suitable for urban history, as "the history of a particular place . . . in relation to the wider Atlantic world" may be able to overcome the artificial divisions created by regional studies between places and societies. See Armitage, "Three Concepts of Atlantic History," 21–23. Other recent works that have usefully deployed such a framework include Hatfield, *Atlantic Virginia;* Coclanis, *The Atlantic Economy;* Hancock, *Citizens of the World;* and Haggerty, *British Atlantic Trading Community.*

16. In 1748 Bridgetown's population was 23 percent free white, 35 percent free black, and 42 percent slave. By 1773, less than 20 percent of inhabitants were free whites and almost 40 percent were free black. Welch, *Slave Society in the City,* 95.

17. Here, and in all following sections, I will use the term tradesman, tradeswoman, tradesperson, tradespeople, or tradesfolk to describe those who made a living by manufacturing and/or trading goods and services. Most Early American historians have divided commercial people into subgroups by labeling them artisans, craftsmen (or craftspersons), mechanics, and merchants/shopkeepers. However, as Elizabeth McKellar has argued for the case of early modern London, contemporaries did not deploy such terminology. Indeed, both "mechanick" and "craftsman" carried negative connotations throughout the eighteenth century. In his *Dictionary,* Samuel Johnson defined *mechanick* as "bred to manual labour," or "mean, servile; of mean occupation," and a *mechanick* as "a manufacturer; a low workman." Meanwhile, Johnson defined craft in a problematic way too, explaining that it not only meant manual art or trade but also suggested fraud, cunning, or artifice. The term *craftsman* was thus not widely used by contemporaries. At the same time, *trade* was said to be "occupation; particular employment, whether manual or mercantile, distinguished from the liberal arts or learned professions," while *tradesfolk* were "people employed in trades." Further, in this book I argue that Charleston's middling sorts made their way through a mix of trade and manufacturing; thus, to distinguish them as mechanics, craftsmen, or merchants does not accurately represent their economic identity. See McKellar, *Birth of Modern London,* 96–97; Johnson, *Dictionary of the English Language.*

18. The schisms that emerged in white Revolutionary society in Virginia are the main subject of two recent books: Holton, *Forced Founders;* McDonnell, *Politics of War.*

19. Hemphill, "Manners and Class in the Revolutionary Era," 349. Stuart Blumin has, for example, argued that "the contradictions and ambiguities of middling status were . . . irreducible" in colonial America. See Blumin, *Emergence of the Middle Class,* 30–38. For early America as a middle-class society, see Hartz, *Liberal Tradition,* and Brown, *Middle Class Democracy.* Studies that have based their discussions around the binary perception of colonial society include Rock and Gilje, *American Artisans;* Nash, "Artisans and Politics"; Nash, *Urban Crucible;* and Isaac, *Transformation of Virginia.* Another body of scholarship argues that we must wait until the Revolution for the transformation of America's social structure into a more complex entity. See, for example, Wood, *Radicalism of the American Revolution,* and Appleby, "Social Consequence of American Revolutionary Ideals."

20. Thompson, *Making of the English Working Class.* The difference between older and more recent definitions of class has been very ably summed up in a recent forum on the issue in the *William and Mary Quarterly.* Writing an introduction to the articles therein, Simon Middleton and Billy G. Smith outlined that a newer definition of class would be "manifest as much in the needs and loyalties it nurtures as in the aspirations and behavior it condemns and prohibits. As such, social power is best conceived not as a linear imposition by which one group drives another toward an objective but as a field of relationships and interactions that pulls as much as pushes men and women into social and cultural arrangements with particular economic outcomes while remaining constantly in flux: contested, negotiated, and rarely, if ever, static. Adopting a class perspective on the past, then, requires the investigation of the innumerable ways in which the peoples of early North America and the Atlantic world considered, discussed, and acted within and against the unequal societies to which they belonged." Middleton and Smith, "Class in Early America." Such definitions of class are further developed in McDonnell, *Politics of War,* and Hemphill, *Bowing to Necessities.*

21. For the debate about social and economic development in Jacksonian America, see Sellers, *Market Revolution in Colonial America;* "Symposium on Charles Sellers' 'The Market Revolution'"; Stockes and Conway, *Market Revolution in America;* Ryan, *Cradle of the Middle Class;* and Blumin, *Emergence of the Middle Class.*

22. As stated by Ned Landsman, who has argued that "over the course of the eighteenth century, [American colonists] would identify themselves increasingly as provincial Britons, citizens of the British provinces, with a particularly provincial point of view." Landsman, *From Colonials to Provincials,* 3. There are many competing models in existence seeking to explain the nature of the relationship between colonial British America and Britain itself. Jon Butler, who supports the idea that early America was exceptional and unique, has argued that "a vigorous secular life emulated European models yet moved to New World rhythms and concerns" and that transformations before 1776 "made the direction of American history unmistakable, even if they did not make it inevitable." Butler, *Becoming America,* 3–4. Jack P. Greene has similarly argued that, between 1720 and 1780, "out of . . . [a] steady process of convergence emerged the beginnings of an American cultural order that was waiting to be defined during and immediately after the era of the American Revolution." Greene, *Pursuits of Happiness,* 171. Other scholars have eschewed the idea of American cultural exceptionalism, in favor of a model that stresses colonial emulation of the metropole. This idea is outlined in a South Carolinian context by Waterhouse, *New World Elite.* Focusing on colonial American's consumption of British manufactures, while overlooking the role of

local manufacturers and service providers, T. H. Breen has also implicitly emphasized the emulative aspect of colonial material culture before 1765. Breen, *Marketplace of the Revolution.* My study, however, seeks to elaborate on Ned Landsman's argument, hitherto rooted only in the sphere of intellectual and religious culture, that provinciality provides the best framework for understanding the cultural relationship between British subjects in the New World and those in the Old World.

23. Peter Coclanis has argued that "the evolution of Charleston, the center of low-country civilization, reflected . . . the growing wealth of the area," a wealth founded on "rice and blue dye produced by black slaves." Coclanis, *Shadow of a Dream,* 7. Jacob Price has described Charleston as a "shipping point" for the staple economy and classifies all other mainland colonial towns as ports. Price, "Economic Function," 175. Carl Bridenbaugh stressed that colonial mainland America's "five seaports were above all else commercial centers. Overseas, coastal, or internal trade determined the economic well-being of the inhabitants." Bridenbaugh, *Cities in Revolt,* 419. S. Max Edelson has highlighted Charleston as a "marketplace of identity" dominated by planters, who, through their transatlantic commercial activities in the town, fought for "cultural legitimacy on Britain's colonial periphery." Edelson, *Plantation Enterprise,* 168.

24. Peter Clark has explained how "the older tripartite hierarchy of London, 'great and good towns' (the regional and county centres) and small market towns was replaced by an increasingly diffuse and polycentric system." Clark, Introduction to *The Cambridge Urban History of Britain,* 9–10.

25. The literature addressing early America's transition to capitalism is voluminous but is most ably summarized in Matson, "A House of Many Mansions"; Merrill, "Putting 'Capitalism' in its Place"; and Appleby, "The Vexed Story of Capitalism." As these review essays point out, disagreements about what constitutes *capitalism* have mostly served to confuse the debate: hence my decision to omit this loaded term and to concentrate instead on the nuts and bolts of economic change.

26. Historians of early America have yet to decide how the opportunities of an advancing consumer culture influenced the colonial and early republican economy. I would argue that consumption did, as Cathy Matson has suggested, "provide a creative impetus toward trade and craft production," especially among the middling townspeople who most commonly serviced the emerging consumer economy. However, such opportunities did not prompt all middling sorts to emulate the elite. Although some middling traders did embrace the lifestyle that they were selling, many others kept a "professional distance" from this new consumer culture, shunning the more extravagant facets of fashion in favor of more frugal values. On the potential for consumption to shed new light on old debates about early American economic development, see Matson, "House of Many Mansions," 39, and Appleby, "Vexed Story of Capitalism," 10–13. My argument here also draws on a recent resurgence in the popularity of Max Weber's theories concerning work and Protestantism. Weber's revival is discussed in Appleby, "Vexed Story of Capitalism," 9, and Hancock, "Rethinking the Economy of British America," 101. Weber's ideas have been applied in a New England context by Vickers, "Competency and Competition"; Newell, *From Dependency to Independence;* and Stephen Innes, *Creating the Commonwealth.*

27. Richard L. Bushman addresses the emergence of polite urban cultural amenities in his study of American refinement, noting that models for the polite city had their roots

in Renaissance planning and that many developments had parallels in London. However, Bushman does not inquire into the precise relation of colonial American urban politeness to its British counterpart. Bushman, *Refinement of America*, 139–80.

28. Borsay, *English Urban Renaissance*; Sweet, *Urban Histories*; and Berry, "Promoting Taste in the Provincial Press."

29. Barry, "Bourgeois Collectivism?"; Rogers, "The Middling Sort in Eighteenth-Century Politics"; and Sweet, *English Town*, 75–140. Kathleen Wilson has also argued for a strong link between these provincial contests for power and the shape of national disputes, explaining that "in the public culture of the period, political articulacy lay in the eye of the beholder, and political consciousness was a many-splendored thing, forged as strikingly through the involvement of individuals in localized contests for power as through participation in national movements that aimed at ousting a minister or reforming the state." Wilson, *Sense of the People*, 15.

30. Weir, "The Harmony We Were Famous For"; Starr, *School for Politicks*; Greene, *Quest for Power*; and Olwell, *Masters, Slaves, and Subjects*.

## 1. "To plant in towns"

1. The fullest recent account of Carolina's proprietary period is Roper, *Conceiving Carolina*, 4–5. See also Weir, "Shaftesbury's Darling," and Clowse, *Economic Beginnings*.

2. On the French Huguenot experience, see Hirsch, *Huguenots of Colonial South Carolina*, and McClain and Ellefson, "A Letter from Carolina, 1688."

3. On the Barbados connection, see Greene, "Colonial South Carolina and the Caribbean Connection"; Coclanis, *Shadow of a Dream*, 21–23; Sirmans, *Colonial South Carolina*, 19–128; and Roper, *Conceiving Carolina*, 51–67.

4. On the importance of Africans to early economic activity in South Carolina, see Wood, *Black Majority*, 96–130; Littlefield, *Rice and Slaves*; Carney, *Black Rice*; and Edelson, *Plantation Enterprise*, 53–91.

5. On the experiences of Native Americans and Africans in the early years of South Carolina, see Merrell, *The Indians' New World*, 1–91; Wood, *Black Majority*, 271–330; and Littlefield, *Rice and Slaves*, 74–114.

6. On early settlement in Virginia, see Kupperman, *The Jamestown Project*, 210–328. For details of Pennsylvania's early decades, see Nash, *Quakers and Politics*. On Carolina's first years, see Roper, *Conceiving Carolina*, 16–49.

7. The spelling of Charleston underwent a number of changes before 1790. It was first named Charles' Towne but, as the eighteenth century progressed, the "e" was dropped and the apostrophe disappeared, leaving it as Charles Town, and sometimes CharlesTown. After the Revolution, the name was formerly changed to Charleston. For the purposes of clarity, this book will use Charles Towne to discuss the town's early years in this first chapter, and then will switch to Charleston.

8. On the Fundamental Constitutions, see Roper, *Conceiving Carolina*, 29–50. For discussion of James Harrington and his seventeenth-century followers, see Pocock, *Machiavellian Moment*, 361–422. In Maryland and New York, the manorial system was deployed as a unit of settlement. For a history of manorial settlement, see Kim, *Landlord and Tenant*. New England towns were mentioned in charters but not legislated into existence. See, for example, Connecticut's "Fundamental Orders of 1639."

9. As quoted in Haley, *First Earl of Shaftesbury*, 249. For a contemporary discussion of the benefits of the classical urban plan, see Wren, *Parentalia*, 267.

10. "The Fundamental Constitutions of Carolina: March 1, 1669," Article 44.

11. As quoted by Roper, *Conceiving Carolina*, 48.

12. Haley, *First Earl of Shaftesbury*, 186. The most comprehensive contemporary accounts of the fire's impact on London's elite and upper-middling sorts are available in Latham and Matthews, *Diary of Samuel Pepys*, 7, and in *Diary of John Evelyn*, 3.

13. Great Britain and Pickering, *Statutes at Large*, vol. 8, Article 7 and Article 5, 235.

14. McKellar, *Birth of Modern London*, 31. McKellar's discussion of London's rebuilding is the most recent, and definitive, treatment of the process and its impact. For the continuing repercussions of new urban construction in the eighteenth century, see Corfield, *Impact of English Towns*, and Chalklin, *Provincial Towns of Georgian England*. The rebuilding also had an impact on the New World, as in part it was responsible for the diminished supply of white indentured labor to the Chesapeake. See Menard, "From Servants to Slaves."

15. "Merchandise and trade unto the said Province, or out of the same shall depart, shall be laden or unladen onely at such Ports as shall be erected and constituted by the said William Penn, his heires and assignee, any use, custome, or other thing to the contrary notwithstanding" ("Charter for the Province of Pennsylvania—1681"). For discussion of William Penn's urban plans, see Nash, *Quakers and Politics*, 38−39, as well as Nash, "Framing of Government in Pennsylvania," 187−88.

16. Clowse, *Economic Beginnings*, 96.

17. Welch, *Slave Society in the City*, 53 (table 3.1); Clowse, *Economic Beginnings*, 165−66; and Hirsch, *Huguenots of Colonial South Carolina*, 47. Bertrand van Ruymbeke has estimated that 54 percent of Huguenot settlers were either artisans or merchants, while only 14 percent were yeomen. Further, he shows that most tradespeople chose to establish themselves in an urban setting. Ruymbeke, "Huguenots of Proprietary South Carolina," 32−39.

18. Account book of Nicholas de Longuemare, 1703−1708, Charleston Museum. List of initial buyers of Charleston Grand Modell lots, misc. ms., SCHS.

19. Morris, *Illustrated Journeys of Celia Fiennes*, 114, 176, 86−87. For the spread of urban development to the English provinces, see Borsay, *English Urban Renaissance*. For contemporary illustrations of Philadelphia, see Nash, *First City*, fig. 17, 46.

20. Welch, *Slave Society in the City*, 60−68; Greene, "Changing Identity in the British West Indies," 29−30; Nash, *Urban Crucible*, table 13, 407, 54−75; and Sweet, *English Town*, 10−14. On the connections between trade, wealth, and urban growth in London, see Earle, *Making of the English Middle Class*. For Bristol, see Morgan, *Bristol and the Atlantic Trade*

21. Cooper, *Statutes at Large*, 2:283.

22. For details of Wren's post-fire achievements and the church rebuilding project, see Downes, *Christopher Wren*; Port, *Commissions for Building Fifty New Churches*.

23. Clowse, *Economic Beginnings*, 195−200; Sirmans, *Colonial South Carolina*, 143.

24. Merrens and Terry, "Dying in Paradise," 542−46. For in-depth discussion of the Yamassee War and its ramifications, see Haan, "The Trade do's not Flourish as Formerly"; Ramsey, "Something Cloudy in their looks." On the importance of Charleston's early fortifications, see Saunders, "As regular and fformidable."

25. Clowse, *Economic Beginnings*, 82−87; Wood, *Black Majority*, 30−32.

26. Elizabeth Sindrey, account book, 34/355, SCHS.

27. In his will of 1698, Pawley described himself as a "carpenter of Charles Towne," but he had become a "planter of Berkeley County" by 1714. S.v. "Pawley, Percival," Index of Artisans, MESDA. This index contains primary references to over 76,000 artisans working in the South in 126 different trades. On file cards are full-text quotations and facts extracted from pre-1821 newspapers, city directories, court records, estate and private papers, and other primary sources, all organized by artisan name. Names of the 2,074 artisans active in Charleston during the eighteenth century were obtained from this index using MESDA's Craftsman Database, and all available information on these tradespersons was then extracted. See also Daniel Defoe as quoted in Earle, *Making of the English Middle Class*, 3. For a discussion of the relationship between trade and urban growth in the very early years of settlement, see Stumpf, "A Case of Arrested Development." For early economic opportunity in the northern colonial town, see Nash, *Urban Crucible*, 33–64, and Hunter, *Purchasing Identity*, 14–70.

28. Clowse, *Economic Beginnings*, 95–108, 130; Clowse, *Measuring Charleston's Overseas Commerce*, table B-21, 57; and Coclanis, *Shadow of a Dream*, tables 3, 14, 83.

29. Clowse, *Measuring Charleston's Overseas Commerce*, tables B-51, B-52, B-53, B-61, and A-21.

30. Carolina's 1701 slave code made it abundantly clear that Charles Towne had already developed into a principal gathering place for the colony's African Americans, noting that "a great number of slaves which do not dwell in Charlestown do on Sundays resort tither" and bestowing extra powers on the town's constables to attempt to put an end to this activity. See "An Act for the better ordering of Slaves," reproduced in Roper, "The 1701 Act for the better ordering of Slaves." On African American's early favoring of Charleston, see also Wood, *Black Majority*, 195–217.

31. Robert Pringle to Andrew Pringle, Charleston 29 December 1740, *LRP*, vol. 1. Evidence of destruction and rebuilding in the wake of the fire can be found in contemporary land conveyances. See, for example, executors of Moses Wilson to Daniel Bourget, Book 5, 293, 8 and 9 April 1741, Lease and Release, "houses lately standing thereon having been destroyed by the dreadful fire"; Thomas Dixon to John Meek, Book W, 34, 15 September 1741, agreement, "Meek agrees to build on the lot, at his own cost, within 4 months, a 3 storey brick house"; Thomas Cooper to Isaac Holmes, Book B-B, 29, 5 and 6 June 1745, Lease and Release, land including "the tenement lately destroyed by the great fire in Charleston," *SCDA*, vol. 2.

32. Proceedings for 25 January 1744 in *Journal of the Commons House of Assembly*, 4:547. Slave-ownership data among inventoried artisans residing in Charleston is extracted from the Index of Artisans, MESDA. Historians have argued that slaves stymied the emergence of a skilled economy in Charleston, but this study disputes that contention. For details of this argument, see Morgan, "Black Life in Eighteenth-Century Charleston"; Edelson, "Affiliation without Affinity." For further discussion of the ways in which slavery encouraged the growth of skilled enterprises in Charleston, see chapters 3 and 4. Shipbuilding in the colony was not a major industry, but as the volume of shipping increased, so did the demand for shipwrights to repair and restock boats that had been built elsewhere. See Clowse, *Economic Beginnings*, 224–26, on the state of shipbuilding in this period.

33. Robert Pringle to John Erving, Charleston, 16 April 1739, *LRP*, vol. 1.

34. Colonial Records, CUST 1, Exports to Carolina from London and Outports, 1735, National Archives. For statistics on artisan arrivals in Charleston, see table 1.

35. Robert Pringle to Andrew Pringle, 5 February 1743, *LRP*, vol. 2.

36. *South Carolina Gazette*, 26 April 1739; *South Carolina Gazette*, 19 May 1739.

37. Robert Pringle to John Smith, Charleston, 23 March 1741, *LRP*, vol. 1.

38. Edelson, *Plantation Enterprise*, 126–65.

39. Menard, "Economic and Social Development of the South," 275–81; Edelson, *Plantation Enterprise*, 111–12.

## 2. "A floating market"

1. For a summary of the relationship between the governor and the Commons House of Assembly, see Greene, *Quest for Power*, 31–39. The idea of salutary neglect was introduced by Henretta in *Salutary Neglect*. The concept has been given a more recent treatment in Steele, "The British Parliament and the Atlantic Colonies."

2. For statistics underlining Charleston's trading supremacy, see Clowse, *Measuring Charleston's Overseas Commerce*, and McCusker and Menard, *Economy of British America*, 169–88.

3. On the role of merchants in the Charleston economy, see Nash, "Urbanization in the Colonial South." On the shaping of a South Carolinian commercial culture based around rice, see Edelson, *Plantation Enterprise*, 166–99. On the influence of staples on patterns of trade in the colonial South, see Price, "Economic Function," 162–63. On the influence of staples over the economy of the Upper South, see Price, "Last Phase of the Virginia-London Consignment Trade," and Price, "Buchanan & Simson, 1759–1763."

4. James Glen, "Governor James Glen's Valuation, 1751," in Merrens, *Colonial South Carolina Scene*, 184.

5. Isaac Hayne Ledger, 1765–1781, 34/561, SCHS.

6. For a consideration of American consumer markets that places British imports at the very center of analysis, see Breen, "Baubles of Britain," and Breen, *Marketplace of Revolution*. Although I share Breen's opinion that colonial self-sufficiency is a best forgotten myth (Breen, *Marketplace of Revolution*, 17–18), I believe that the nature of the "empire of goods" that incorporated Britain and America cannot be understood only by examining colonial consumption of British manufactures. Instead, a British Atlantic World of goods was created when Britons and Americans grew, manufactured, processed, or recycled material possessions that were ultimately the product of colony *and* metropole. Acknowledging the richness of America's domestic consumer market actually furthers Breen's thesis by underlining the degree to which consumer boycotts were political statement rather than real sacrifice for the majority of colonists. Indeed, it was the high level of colonial market development beyond the importation trade that permitted these boycotts to be effective at all. Low Country residents certainly did not fear shortages when the boycotts were announced, and when Charleston merchant Josiah Smith worried about the privations that might come as a result of the 1775 boycott, he only discussed possible shortages of slave clothing, which, he surmised, might be prevented by the industry of the Low Country's own weavers. See Smith to George Appleby, Bristol, 14 March 1775, Letterbook of Josiah Smith Jr., ms. no. 3018, SHC.

7. On the evolution of the merchant community, see Nash, "Urbanization in the Colonial South"; Rogers, *Charleston in the Age of the Pinckneys*, 3–25; and Greene, *Pursuits of Happiness*, 146. On the slave trade into Charleston, see Morgan, "Slave Sales in Colonial Charleston"; Littlefield, "The Slave Trade to Colonial South Carolina"; and Richardson, "The British Slave Trade to Colonial South Carolina."

8. Throughout the colonial era, South Carolina currency, here distinguished as SC£, had an exchange rate of SC£7 to £1 sterling. I have not converted sums quoted in contemporary sources in SC£ into pounds sterling, but have left them in the original currency.

9. Daybook of Alexander Nisbet and John Blackwood, 1727, GD237/1/151, NAS; Inventory of Thomas Corker, February 1771, vol. 94A, 231, CCPL.

10. James Poyas Daybook, 1764–1766, 34/0325, SCHS; accounts of the Estate of James Hartley, misc. records, CCPL; and Baker-Grimke receipts, 11/538/1, SCHS.

11. As stated by in Nash, "Urbanization in the Colonial South," 11. An often needed luxury item that was impossible to acquire from Britain was mourning jewelry and clothing. Such items were personalized and required at short notice, making importation from the metropole totally impractical. For the purchase of mourning goods, see William Ancrum's 1779 letter mentioning the "rings for the ladies" that he was having made in Charleston. Sets of such items were usually for either mourning or commemoration. William Ancrum to Parker Quince, 16 August 1779, William Ancrum account book and Letterbook, Ms. P, SCL. Stressing the need for the services of white tradespersons (and their slaves) provides a counterweight to the more commonly held view that South Carolina's plantation owners managed to avoid reliance on urban artisans by training up their own skilled slaves. For discussions of this point of view, see Morgan, "Black Society in the Low Country," 97, 102–3, and Edelson, "Affiliation without Affinity," 229–31.

12. Data extracted from the Index of Artisans, MESDA. Since this database records all mentions of artisans in Charleston in newspapers, court records, church records, private papers and wills, and inventories, tradespeople who did not usually advertise (the poor or those in the building trades, for example) are counted. Relying only on newspaper advertisements, a number of scholars have underestimated the size of the town's manufacturing sector. R. C. Nash has argued, on the basis of newspaper advertisements alone, that "Charleston's manufacturing was retarded in comparison with the northern cities." Nash, "Urbanization in the Colonial South," 10. Carl Bridenbaugh also believes the town's artisan contingent comparatively small, stating that "this city of twelve thousand did not nourish an outstanding craft or produce a single eminent workman before the Revolution." Bridenbaugh, *Colonial Craftsman*, 122.

13. Account book of Henry Laurens, entries for April 1769 and January 1771, ms. 17, CC. Although the timing of Laurens's switch to Hinds (September 1768) suggests that the non-importation movement may well have been involved, Laurens's correspondence shows that he was a long-time supporter of Hinds's efforts to establish himself in business. Therefore, it may be misguided to attribute the decision solely to the boycott. For the merchant's earlier dealings with Hinds, see Henry Laurens to Robert and John Thompson, 20 April 1757, *PHL*, vol. 2.

14. Miller and Cannon vs. John Harvey, 1756, vol. 42A, no. 102A; William Harvey vs. Jacob Axson, 1769, vol. 81B, no. 7A, Judgment Rolls, SCDAH. And see Baker-Grimke receipts, 11/538/1, SCHS.

15. Benjamin Hawes vs. Nathaniel Bulline, 1767, vol. 69A, no. 69A; Weyman and Carne vs. Joseph Feltham, 1768, vol. 77A, no. 157A; Jonathan Sarrazin vs. Thomas Harvey, 1769, vol. 83A, no. 148A; Hawes and Flagg vs. James Duthie, vol. 83A, no. 110A; John Paul Grimke vs. Micajah Smith, vol. 41A, no. 169A, Judgment Rolls, SCDAH. See also Baker-Grimke receipts, 11/538/1 SCHS.

16. On the importance of clothing to identity in colonial America, see Waldstreicher, "Reading the Runaways"; Baumgarten, *What Clothes Reveal*; inventory and book debts of Alexander Smith, n.d., vol. 74, CCPL; bill of Alexander Smith, s.v. "Sarrazin, Moreau," Index of Artisans, MESDA; and inventory of Alexander McCormack, 4 November 1773, vol. 94, Book B, CCPL. Of the patrons of Charleston tradesmen included in table 2.1, fifty-five hailed from Charleston, fourteen from the parishes directly surrounding Charleston, and seventeen from secondary and backcountry areas. For a breakdown of the various zones of settlement in colonial South Carolina, see Edelson, *Plantation Enterprise*, Table 4: Geography of South Carolina Settlement Zones.

17. Mancall et al., "Indians and the Economy of Eighteenth-Century Carolina"; "Indian Expenses: 1764, John Dodd for gunsmiths work, 18.17.6. Thomas Tew for Taylors work, 5.10.0," in Journal of the Public Accounts, Records of the Public Treasurers of South Carolina, Ledger A, 1759–1768, SCDAH. Here and elsewhere, such figures as 18.17.6 or 5.10.0 refer, in order, to SC£ (pounds), shillings, and pence.

18. Inventory of George Ross, Inventories Vol. B, 8 October 1790, CCPL. Inventories of the possessions of Ross's metalworking contemporaries regularly listed the specialist tools for casting silver, punching out tin buttons, and drawing silver and gold wire. See, for example, inventory of Frances Gottier, Inventories Vol. A, 23 October 1784, CCPL; inventory of John Miot, Inventories Vol. B, 16 February 1792, CCPL; and Governor Glen's Report on South Carolina, 1751, "An Account of Houses and Lotts Fronting the river on the Bay in Charlestown in South Carolina Together with the Trades and professions of the occupiers thereof and the rents paid annually for the same," in Merrens, *South Carolina Scene*, 185. For a description of the more typical color of a colonial port city's seafront, see Gilje, *Liberty on the Waterfront*, 3–32.

19. Discussions of secondhand and repair markets in the British Atlantic world are few and far between. The best examples include Baumgarten, *What Clothes Reveal*, 139; O'Connor, "The Measure of the Market," 227–82; and Lemire, *Fashion's Favorite*. For a twenty-seven-year period from 1756 to 1783, seventy-six receipts have survived for services provided to Richard Baker by local artisans. See Baker-Grimke Papers, 11/538/1, SCHS, and Richard Hart vs. Benjamin Perry, 1770, vol. 87A, no. 108A, Judgment Rolls, SCDAH.

20. McInnes, "Emergence of a Leisure Town: Shrewsbury, 1660–1760," table 1, 56; Stobart, "An Eighteenth-Century Revolution?"; and Stobart, "Leisure and Shopping."

21. This relationship between domestic economy and the import sector was common in other parts of colonial British America. For a discussion of such a relationship between the production of homespun fabric and the quantity of certain types of cloth imported into the colonies, see Smith, "The Market for Manufactures in the Thirteen Colonies, 1698–1776," and Hood, *Weaver's Craft*, 112–39.

22. Price, "Economic Function," 163; Edelson, *Plantation Enterprise*, 403. The best brief summary of South Carolina's transatlantic trade remains McCusker and Menard, *Economy of British America*, 169–88. One study that does much to stress the depth and complexity of

urban markets (among other things) is Cathy Matson's study of lesser New York City merchants during the colonial period. See Matson, *Merchants and Empire*, 215–64.

23. The major exception here was of course the market for African slaves. Although slaves could be purchased at auction and on Charleston's wharves, slave sales tended not to be conducted in marketplaces commonly used for the trading of consumer durables and foodstuffs.

24. For a fulsome account of Kershaw's activities and the evolution of Camden, see Ernst and Merrens, "Camden's Turrets Pierce the Skies!"

25. *Georgia Gazette,* 15 August 1765, advertisement by Hugh Sym, saddler relocated from Charleston; *Georgia Gazette,* 8 April 1767, advertisement of Thomas Coleman, upholsterer previously working at Charleston; *Georgia Gazette,* 3 September 1766, "to be sold by publick outcry at the vendue house in Charlestown—Georgia lands in Christ Church Parish"; and *Georgia Gazette,* 12 April 1769, "plantation for sale—enquire of John Gordon esq merchant at Charleston."

26. *Georgia Gazette,* 25 October 1764.

27. Captain Hinrichs, a Hessian soldier, explained in 1780 that "trade with the backcountry people who have settled near and beyond the Appalachian Mountains is carried on from the middle of September to the first of January, during which time these People come to Charleston in throngs with loaded wagons carrying the surplus of their products, which they exchange for imported wares." Diary of Captain Hinrichs, in Uhlendorf, *Siege of Charleston,* 337. See also Thorp, "Doing Business in the Backcountry." By the end of the colonial era, Wilmington, North Carolina, had grown large enough to become another node in Charleston's urban network. See Wood, *This Remote Part of the World,* 227–29. On rural marketing systems elsewhere in colonial America, see Shammas, *Pre-Industrial Consumer,* 197–266. Efforts by Jonathan Bryan in the 1740s to raise the profile of Port Royal and reduce Charleston's monopoly on trade failed, revealing how Charleston's dominance was clearly appreciated by contemporaries, some of whom felt it problematic. For details, see Gallay, "Jonathan Bryan's Plantation Empire," 256.

28. Clowse, *Measuring Charleston's Overseas Commerce,* table C-41, 121–23. For a discussion of involvement in this domestic trade, see Stumpf, "Trends in Charleston's Interregional Import Trade," and Stumpf, "South Carolina Importers of General Merchandise." For an analysis of the rum trade, see McCusker, *Rum and the American Revolution.* It should also be noted that Charleston was the hub of a considerable trade in smuggled goods. Details of this trade are, inevitably, sketchy, but Hessian officer Captain Hinrich claimed that South Carolina's "principal commerce, which consists largely of smuggling, is carried on between Charleston and St. Eustatius, where in defiance of English laws the merchants of Charleston trade their products to the Dutch in exchange for wares which should be imported only from England. These in turn, by surreptitious trade, they sell at a profit in the Carolinas, boosting their prices by as much as the merchants in England would have to add to theirs on account of internal duties and excises if they should export these commodities . . . No other province besides South Carolina makes such excessive profits by contraband trade." Diary of Captain Hinrichs, in Uhlendorf, *Siege of Charleston,* 321.

29. Clowse, *Measuring Charleston's Overseas Commerce,* table C-41.

30. Entries for September 1771 and April 1774, Daybook of Thomas Elfe, CLS; listing for Legare and Greenwood as merchants, in the first *Charleston City Directory* (1782), CCPL;

advertisement of Bolsover and Sherman, *South Carolina Gazette and Country Journal,* 16 November 1773; and receipt book of Isaac Motte and Co., 34/358, SCHS, entry for January 1769. Henry Laurens also shipped house frames from his Mepkin plantation to Grenada via Charleston; see Edelson, *Plantation Enterprise,* 355. See also Steen, "Pottery, Intercolonial Trade, and Revolution," 62–72.

31. Robert Pringle to John Erving, 9 September 1740; Robert Pringle to Michael Lovell, 24 April 1740; Robert Pringle to Isaac Norris, 27 December 1740, in *LRP,* vol. 1; Moses Lopez to Aaron Lopez, Charleston, 3 May 1764, in which Moses sells a boat and buys pitch and rice, Aaron Lopez Papers, folder 622, NHS. For a similar business empire built on re-exportation, see Smith, "Gedney Clarke of Salem and Barbados."

32. William Wilson Letterbook, undated letters 1757 and 1758, and New York, 14 December 1758, ms., NYPL.

33. Robert Pringle to Thomas Morison, Charleston, 28 December 1738, *LRP,* vol. 1

34. Inventory of Thomas Gates, shopkeeper, 29 September 1741, vol. 71, Book K-K, and inventory of John Patient, shopkeeper, undated 1761, vol. 87, Book B, Charleston County Inventories, CCPL.

35. T. H. Breen has been one of the few scholars to discuss vendue sales and their role in the distribution of goods. However, Breen has only addressed the importance of these sales as a conduit for newly imported British goods, and has argued that only unbroken parcels of such manufactures were sold at them; however, in Charleston the reality was much more complex. See Breen, *Marketplace of the Revolution,* 140–43. See also Doerflinger, *Vigorous Spirit of Enterprise,* 171, for a brief mention of vendue sales of discounted British goods. For the variety of goods on offer in Philadelphia's vendues, see advertisements in the *Pennsylvania Gazette,* 1730–80, of which over five thousand were for vendue sales of secondhand wares, items from the Indian trade, land, real property, horses, and slaves and servants.

36. *LRP,* 2:480, 530, 592, 629, 645, 658, 669, 676, 685, 721, 780, 804, 841. Estate sales were advertised in the *South Carolina Gazette* on an almost weekly basis. Records of which goods were sold to whom in an estate sale sometimes followed an inventory, and this provides the only glimpse into what is otherwise an invisible secondhand market. See Inventory of Elizabeth McKenzie, 5 December 1748, Inventories vol. 77, Book A; Inventory of Benjamin Heap (where widow Heap purchased back some goods), Inventories vol. 77, Book A; "Account of the Sales of the goods and effects of David Villaret sold at public vendue," Inventories vol. 71, K-K; "Sale of Sarah Saxby's effects," Inventories vol. 74; "Account of sales of the estate of Ichabod Winborn," Inventories vol. 74, CCPL.

37. *South Carolina Gazette,* 26 July 1774. See letter from Egerton Leigh to Henry Laurens, London, 6 February 1765, *PHL,* vol. 7. This letter reads, in part, "Please to purchase at Mr. Graeme's Sale the following Furniture on my account, which he will give me Credit for till I once more settle among you. 1. The Windsor Chairs in the Hall 2. Some or all of the Dining-Room Glasses, as you think proper 3. A handsome Marble slab and Stand 4. Twelve good Parlour Chairs 5. Kitchen-Furniture generally, if good of the Kind 6. A mahogany desk 7. Ditto Bedstead 8. Good feather-bed 9. Such Ornaments &c. as suiting the House you may think worth retaining." Leigh was to rent this Charleston house for three years on his return to Charleston.

38. For a detailed discussion of the activities of female consumers in late colonial and early national Charleston, see O'Connor, "Measure of the Market," 227–82. For a discussion

of the period before 1750, during which the terms of slaves' market activities were set, see Wood, *Black Majority*, 195–217.

39. For an extensive treatment of slave-marketing activities in Charleston between 1740 and 1775, see Olwell, *Masters, Slaves, and Subjects*, 141–80. For black economic activity in other Atlantic towns, see Dantas, "Black Townsmen"; Wood, "White Society and the Informal Slave Economies." Blacks were also a vital force in the urban market of Kingston, Jamaica. For a discussion of their activities, see Simmonds, "The Afro-Jamaican and the Internal Marketing System." On informal marketplaces in other British and American towns, see Haggerty, *British Atlantic Trading Community*, and Lemire, "The Theft of Clothes."

40. Edelson, *Plantation Enterprise*, 166–99.

41. Defoe, *Complete English Tradesman*, chapter 15: "Of Tradesmen ruining one another by rumour and clamour, by scandal and reproach."

42. Ibid., chapter 24: "Of credit in trade, and how a tradesman ought to value and improve it: how easily lost, and how hard it is to be recovered." The loss of reputation came through the inability to treat customers properly, slander, or recklessness (lack of financial credit), a term also blurred with *character*.

43. Breen, *Tobacco Culture*, 84–124. Breen fully acknowledges that the "commercial friendships" forged by Virginia planters conflicted with the versions adhered to by the British merchants they dealt with. The most famous colonial fraudster was Tom Bell; for a discussion of his career, see Bullock, "A Mumper among the Gentle." The universal breakdown of guild regulation in the British Atlantic town placed further emphasis on the importance of the commercial friendship. On the decreasing influence of guilds and livery companies over city traders in an English context, see Earle, *Making of the English Middle Class*, 250–60.

44. Advertisement of John Cleator, *South Carolina Advertiser and General Gazette*, 27 April 1770; advertisement of Edward Tash, *City Gazette and Daily Advertiser*, 8 January 1798.

45. Advertisement of Richard Clark, *South Carolina Gazette*, 2 June 1767; advertisement of Richard Singleton, *City Gazette and Daily Advertiser*, 13 March 1789.

46. Advertisement of Thomas Legare, *South Carolina Gazette*, 27 November 1740; advertisement of John Ward, *South Carolina Gazette*, 26 November 1767; and advertisement of John Mason, *South Carolina Gazette*, 2 February 1765. Over half of all artisan advertisers in the South Carolina newspapers between 1732 and 1800 made a claim about price or quality (statistic culled from the Index of Southern Artists and Artisans, MESDA).

47. Excerpts from *Caledonian Mercury*, 13 January 1741, and from *Edinburgh Advertiser*, 4 July 1783. Other quotes extracted from the Index of Artisans, MESDA.

48. Advertisement of John Parkinson, *South Carolina Weekly Gazette*, 22 March 1783. Local planters did patronize Parkinson, or at least it is known that William Moultrie ordered picture frames from him. See Henry Ravanel Ledger, 34/0322, SCHS. Blacksmith Seth Gilbert, for example, wrote that he would be able to do work "cheap as any where in Charles-Town" in his advertisement in the *South Carolina Gazette and Country Journal*, 19 August 1766.

49. Henry Laurens to Francis Bremar, London, 27 March 1748/9, *PHL*, vol. 1. Laurens included three merchant houses in this list, but artisans were in the majority.

50. Henry Laurens to John Lewis Gervais, Westminster, 7 December 1773, *PHL*, vol. 9. Laurens knew the Henries through a "very worthy gentlemen" with whom he had become friendly in London. Henry Laurens to James Laurens, Bath, 3 January 1774, *PHL*, vol. 9. See also account book of Henry Laurens, CC.

51. Henry Laurens to William Cowles, Charleston, 4 June 1771, *PHL*, vol. 7. As the editors of Laurens's papers explain, the "broad ax" was a tool used by naval and mercantile shipwrights in the Royal Yards at Greenwich and is used here by Laurens to tell his correspondent that Rose had a background as a King's shipbuilder. Henry Laurens to John Coming Ball, 7 January 1763, *PHL*, vol. 3.

52. William Ancrum to John Chesnutt, 29 August 1777, and other entries, William Ancrum Letterbook, mss P, SCL.

53. Wells, *Journal of a Voyage*. Wells told this story, she said, to highlight how Charlestonians were in "want of British Manufactures." Clearly, this did not mean they were in want of everything.

### 3. "Stupendous works"

1. Article in the *South Carolina Gazette*, 16 June 1766.

2. Elizabeth McKellar explicitly addresses this issue, arguing that urban development "was a new area of business which attracted new men." See McKellar, *Birth of Modern London*, 38–53.

3. Menard, "Financing the Low Country Export Boom."

4. For a summary of these changes, see McKellar, *Birth of Modern London*, 71–113.

5. This building industry might be termed "modern," not in the sense of reflecting our present-day equivalent, but in the sense that Charleston's builders were au fait with the latest in eighteenth-century practice, as opposed to working in modes that had guided English-speaking builders for a century or more.

6. Salmon, "Women and Property in South Carolina"; Olwell, *Masters, Slaves, and Subjects*, 57–102; Morris, *Southern Slavery*, 37–60.

7. See Hunter, *Purchasing Identity*, 130–31, for a discussion of the Boston fire and its ramifications for the urban landscape. For a discussion of the impact of Charleston's fire and a reckoning of its financial costs, see Mulcahy, "The Great Fire of 1740," and Scott, "Sufferers in the Charleston Fire."

8. For discussion of these fires and the subsequent rebuilding, see Borsay, *English Urban Renaissance*, 80–114.

9. The text of the fire act was published in the *South Carolina Gazette*, 18 December 1740. Issues of the *South Carolina Gazette* for 15 April 1745 and 16 December 1745 show that the Charleston authors of this act were serious in their implementation of it, as they issued ongoing warnings to residents that, if they continued to erect wooden houses, they would have such houses pulled down.

10. Great Britain and Pickering, *Statutes at Large*, 8:235.

11. The best discussions of the varying types of urban property titles can be found in Chalklin, *Provincial Towns of Georgian England*, 135–39 and 142–45, and McKellar, *Birth of Modern London*, 93–113.

12. Shortly after the devastating fire of 1740, merchant Robert Pringle wrote to Andrew Pringle, his brother, "I am again to desire you'll endeavour to procure me a carpenter ser-

vant, & instead of two as mention'd in my last, to procure me a bricklayer in the room of one of them. They may depend on good encouragement." Robert Pringle to Andrew Pringle, Charleston, 29 December 1740, *LRP*, vol. 1.

13. Land conveyance between Francois Guichard, pastor of the French Church, and John Vaun; advertisement of John Vaun, *South Carolina Gazette,* 5 March 1743/4, s.v. "Vaun, John," Index of Artisans, MESDA. The term "tenement" usually referred to a property erected for rental. The tenement would usually be smaller than the average house, and would probably be attached to its neighbors.

14. Lease between Richard Beresford and Frederick Kaufman, Book F-3, 100, 20 April 1762, *SCDA*, vol. 3.

15. Advertisement of Christopher Gadsden, *South Carolina Gazette,* 6 July 1769.

16. Sugarman and Warrington, "Land Law, citizenship, and the invention of 'Englishness.'"

17. Sale of lot 3 on the East Bay by Nathaniel Fuller to Edward Fenwicke, esq., Book G3, 456, 25 May 1765, *SCDA*, vol. 3. This document explained that the lot was being sold as a mortgage was due to a Charleston doctor on the property, but as Fuller was a minor, he was to be "foreclosed of [his] equity of redemption in sd property." See also Release of Reversion and Equity of Redemption by David Christina to Gabriel Guignard on a lot on the Broad Path leading to Charleston, Book HH, 129, 28 September 1750, *SCDA*, vol. 2.

18. S.v. "Lingard, James" and "Theus, Jeremiah," Index of Artisans, MESDA.

19. McKellar, *Birth of Modern London,* 86–87.

20. Figure derived from the Index of Artisans, MESDA.

21. Memorandum and sketches dated 19 February 1750, Papers of Charles Pinckney, mss. 1127, 2104, and 3900, SCL.

22. Peter Manigault to Daniel Blake, Charleston, 6 March 1770; Peter Manigault to Ralph Izard, esq., not dated but estimated by Crowse as September 1765; and Peter Manigault to Ralph Izard, esq., Charleston, 9 October 1765, Peter Manigault Letterbook, transcribed by Maurice A. Crowse, MESDA. At about this time, many of these builders bolstered their stature within the Charleston economy by also taking on the management of large-scale public projects, such as the raising of St. Michael's Church and of the Exchange. For further details of these works, see chapter 6.

23. For a discussion of these terms and their usage, see McKellar, *Birth of Modern London,* 81–89.

24. Jacob Axson Jr. vs. William Clay Snipes, 1771, vol. 99A, no. 255A, Judgment Rolls, SCDAH; Thomas Robinson vs. Luke Stoutenburgh, esq., 1768, vol. 88A, no. 173A, Judgment Rolls, SCDAH; expense of Building Mrs. Ann Middleton's House and kitchen 1799–1800, 43/118, SCHS.

25. Because accounts have not survived, we do not know the precise course of development, but as Carolina Wyche Dixon has argued, Waite is linked to the house through an intersection between patterns of wood carving in the books listed in his inventory and the surviving interior of the house. See Dixon, "The Miles Brewton House."

26. Advertisement of Ezra Waite, *South Carolina and American General Gazette,* 18 August 1769.

27. Dixon, "The Miles Brewton House." Discussion of these connections can be found in Simons and Simons, "The William Burrows House of Charleston."

28. In December 1758, five bricklayers were used for a day by Thomas Gordon at a cost of £4.2.6., total £71.17.6., 1767, information summarized from vol. 68B, no. 10A, Judgment Rolls, SCDAH; James Cook, vol. 87(1), reel no. 86, mfm., LOC; Thomas Harrison vs. Jervey and Walter, 1785, vol. 119A, no. 318A, Judgment Rolls, SCDAH.

29. For the most complete assessment of relations between black and white artisans in colonial Charleston, see Morgan, "Black Life in Eighteenth-Century Charleston."

30. Act for Rebuilding Charleston, published in the *South Carolina Gazette*, 18 December 1740.

31. "Memoirs of Boston King," 4 June 1796, accessed at http://collections.ic.gc.ca/black loyalists/documents/diaries/king-memoirs.htm.

32. Number derived from all types of records that name a slave skilled in these trades owned by an artisan from Charleston. I have included slaves named in inventories or wills up to the year 1800, on the assumption that they would have been working in the city during the lifetime of their owner. Records from Index of Artisans, MESDA.

33. Company accounts of Wyatt, Richardson, and Richardson, included as evidence in the case of Wyatt vs. Richardson, Chancery Court Records, bundle 10, Box 1, 1797, SCDAH.

34. See McKellar, *Birth of Modern London*, 155–87, for a discussion of London house plans, and Herman, "Slave and Servant Housing in Charleston," for a discussion of Charleston house plans. Many historians have pointed to the Charleston "single house" as evidence of the emergence of a unique architectural form suited to the requirements of a hot climate. These historians have argued that this was evidence of an adaptation of English building customs to the Low Country. Two matters eliminate the relevance of the single house to discussions here. First, the single house did not become widespread until the third quarter of the eighteenth century; before then, housing stock was much more in line with that in other English-speaking towns. Indeed, in Charleston the single house did not reach maturity as a form until the beginning of the nineteenth century. For a full discussion of these issues, see Herman, "The Charleston Single House."

35. Across all studies of wealth-creation in colonial America, urban land has tended to be passed over. The rents yielded by urban land, and the nonownership of urban property, have been considered a method of measuring poverty by Salinger and Weatherell, "Wealth and Renting in Pre-Revolutionary Philadelphia." However, historians have stuck to rural land, trade, and, rarely, manufacturing, when looking for ways that early white Americans generated wealth. This is commensurate with the favoring of the staples-led thesis of growth as stated by McCusker and Menard in *Economy of British America*, though these two authors nevertheless call for more work on the colonial construction industry (*Economy of British America*, 316). For the impact of rural land speculation on colonial wealth and society, see John Frederick Martin, *Profits in the Wilderness*. On the shortage of land in New England, see Lockridge, "Land, Population, and the Evolution of New England Society." Historians of the antebellum period have been more adventurous in looking at the urban landscape as a source of innovation and wealth; for the best example, see Rilling, *Making Houses, Crafting Capitalism*.

36. Chalklin, *Provincial Towns of Britain*, 229. Statistic derived from Index of Artisans, MESDA, showing that 50 percent of Charleston carpenters appeared in the land records.

37. For documentation of Verree's ownership, see Poston, *Buildings of Charleston*,

67–68, s.v. "Chalmers, Gilbert," Index of Artisans, MESDA. Chalmers advertised the real estate in the *Charleston Gazette and Daily Advertiser,* 10 November 1796, as "a lot of land . . . at the corner of Boundary and King with all the buildings."

38. S.v. "Deans, Robert," Index of Artisans, MESDA.

39. Will of Anthony Toomer, vol. 27, Book C, 507, CCPL.

40. Plat number 182, Plan of the Lands of Anthony Toomer, McCrady Plat Collection, SCDAH.

41. S.v. "Thebout, Tunis," Index of Artisans, MESDA.

42. S.v. "Grimke, John Paul," Index of Artisans, MESDA.

43. All figures derived from Daybook of Thomas Elfe, CLS.

44. For an assessment of renting and rental prices in British towns, see Clark, "Shelter from the Storm"; Urdank, "Consumption of Rental Property." While assessing the economic situation in Charleston shortly before the British occupation, Josiah Smith Jr. spoke of those "who live comfortably by house rents" but were suddenly "obliged to break into their principle sums." Such a statement clearly underlines the existence of a widespread custom among wealthier townspeople of accumulating rental properties with the goal of achieving a regular income. Josiah Smith Jr. to unknown correspondent, 29 January 1779, Letterbook, SHC.

45. Governor Glen's report on South Carolina, 1751–1753, "An Account of Houses and Lotts Fronting the river on the Bay in Charlestown in South Carolina Together with the Trades and professions of the occupiers thereof and the rents paid annually for the same," in Merrens, *South Carolina Scene,* 257.

46. James Murray to his mother, 1 August 1754, Murray of Murraythwaite Muniments, NAS.

47. Entries for April and September 1758, William Ancrum account book and Letterbook, mss. P, SCL; advertisement for Jonathan Sarrazin's property, *South Carolina and American General Gazette,* 18 September 1777; advertisement of Anthony Toomer, *South Carolina Gazette and Country Journal,* 26 January 1773.

48. Advertisement of Barnard Elliott, *South Carolina Gazette and Country Journal,* 24 May 1774; memorial of John Rose, vol. 132(2), reel 134, Loyalist Claims, LOC.

49. On the difficulties of estimating urban land values and yields, see Menard and Ryden, "South Carolina's Rural Land Market." I should like to thank David Ryden for supplying me with a copy of this article in advance of its publication. Dabook of Thomas Elfe, CLS.

50. Glen, "An Account of Houses and Lotts," Merrens, *Colonial South Carolina Scene,* 257. The varying estimates of returns on the cultivation of rural land are discussed in Menard, "Financing the Low Country Export Boom," 663–65.

51. "A 1768 Tax Account," in Merrens, *Colonial South Carolina Scene,* 248–52. The prices of all Charleston land sold between 1767 and 1773, as listed in Langley, *South Carolina Deed Abstracts,* were compared against table 8.2, "Average Annual Value and Destinations of Commodity Exports from the Lower South, 1768–1772," in McCusker and Menard, *Economy of British America,* 174.

52. For details of Barbon's career, see McKellar, *Birth of Modern London,* 42–46. On John Wood's activities, see Mowl and Earnshaw, *John Wood.*

53. Sarah Meek widow and her son Thomas Brickles to Mathew Webb, a free negro,

butcher, Book C3, 770, 24 August 1764, *SCDA*, vol. 3; Feoffment in Trust of Judith West to John Mitchell, Book RR, 137, 30 August 1756, *SCDA*, vol. 2. See U.S. Bureau of the Census, *Heads of Families at the First Census of the United States, Taken in the Year 1790, South Carolina*, 38–44. For a discussion of the living conditions and arrangements of Charleston's black residents in the early national period, see Hermann, *Town House*, 119–54.

54. Advertisement of Claudius Guillaud, *South Carolina Gazette*, 5 July 1773.

55. Inventory of William Carruthers, 20 June 1775, vol. 94, Book A; inventory of William Randall, 22 October 1755, vol. 82, Book B, Charleston County Wills, CCPL.

56. After the death of merchant Thomas Corker, Josiah Smith Jr. described Corker's Charleston real estate to his brother in England, outlining how there were "two wooden tenements" that were "ancient and of so bad a construction that they will never admit tenants of much note. Consequently the rent will not be so large and perhaps often short paid." Smith added that the tenants currently in one tenement were "a family in low circumstances." Josiah Smith Jr. to Mr. John Corker at Uttoxeter, Staffs., Charleston, 10 October, 1771, Letterbook, SHC.

57. All land deed records are from Langley, *South Carolina Deed Abstracts*, vols. 1–4.

58. Among the merchants who most often bought and sold urban land were Josiah Smith Jr., Thomas Corker, William Ellis, William Banbury, and Francis Bremar.

59. See Berg, "Small Producer Capitalism," tables 5 and 6, 31–32. See also wills of Charleston artisans before 1800 as gathered in the Index of Artisans, MESDA.

60. Altogether, 279 transactions out of a total of 438 listed for Charleston in Langley, *South Carolina Deed Abstracts* between 1756 and 1773 provide locations that can be pinpointed to a precise place in the town.

### 4. Urban Households, Economic Opportunity, and Social Structure

1. Company accounts of Wyatt, Richardson, and Richardson, and testimony of Violetta Wyatt, included as evidence in the case of Wyatt vs. Richardson, Chancery Court Records, bundle 10, Box 1, 1797, SCDAH.

2. "Journal of Josiah Quincy, Jr.," 439.

3. For wealth-distribution figures, see Waterhouse, "Economic Growth," and Jones, *Wealth of a Nation to Be*, table 7.1, 220. As Jones's statistics show, there were regional variations, with New England's wealth distribution more even than that of the Middle Colonies or the South. Both of these works use inventories to gauge the wealth of South Carolinians in, respectively, the wider Charleston County and the colony as a whole. These figures, for a historian of Charleston, are frustratingly vague. However, the dearth of sources means that I have been unable to produce any more meaningful statistics concerning wealth distribution within the limits of Charleston. No census data survives before 1790 and surviving tax records for Charleston from the 1760s provide a guide to the overall property and wealth of the town in comparison to South Carolina's rural parishes, but do not include any individual tax returns. What is more, it is often difficult to guess whether an inventory belongs to a person who actually lived in Charleston, or in the surrounding county, as the documents frequently fail to make a distinction.

4. Nash, *Urban Crucible*, 250–335. Works that divide urban society according to occupation include Nash, "Artisans and Politics in Eighteenth-Century Philadelphia"; Rock and Gilje, *American Artisans;* Doerflinger, *Vigorous Spirit of Enterprise;* Wright and Viens, *Boston*

*Business Community;* and Hunter, *Purchasing Identity.* Stuart Blumin has explicitly argued that "the contradictions and ambiguities of middling status were . . . irreducible in the eighteenth-century American city." See Blumin, *Emergence of the Middle Class,* 30 and 31–38. On class versus racial divisions in Charleston and colonial South Carolina, see Philip D. Morgan, *Slave Counterpoint,* 257–317. While fully acknowledging that class was a source of conflict between "patriarchs and plain folk," Morgan uses a model of "paired polarities" (ibid., 316) to explore this relationship, also placing white-black relations at the center of his story. For other treatments of southern society that rely on binary models of interaction, see Edmund Morgan, *American Slavery, American Freedom;* Isaac, *Transformation of Virginia,* 161–77.

    5. Earle, *Making of the English Middle Class,* 335; D'Cruze, "Middling Sorts in Eighteenth Century Colchester," 184 and 188–89; Hunt, *Middling Sort,* 139; and Berg, "Small Producer Capitalism."

    6. Scholars who have contributed to this picture of the early American household and its economic activities include Ulrich, *Good Wives,* 13–50; Lockridge, *A New England Town;* Shammas, "Anglo-American Household Governance"; Shammas, *History of Household Government,* 1–108; Hood, *Weaver's Craft,* 30–111; Henretta, "Families and Farms"; McCusker and Menard, *Economy of British America,* 329; Stephen Innes, *Work and Labor in Early America,* 31–41; and Vickers, "Competency and Competition." On the structure of the southern household, see McCurry, *Masters of Small Worlds,* and Genovese, *Within the Plantation Household.* The British eighteenth-century household was similar in composition; see Tadmor, "Concept of the Household-Family."

    7. Earle, *Making of the English Middle Class;* de Vries, "The Industrial Revolution and the Industrious Revolution." Edward J. Perkins has also emphasized the importance of entrepreneurship to the early American household; see Perkins, "Entrepreneurial Spirit in Colonial America." On the importance of women to the household economy, see O'Connor, "Measure of the Market"; Wulf, *Not All Wives,* 119–53; and Hunt, *Middling Sort,* 22–46. Although some historians of colonial America have focused on a "narrowing down" of opportunity for women as colonial society matured, this study seeks to place women's work in a family framework and so does not attempt to measure the levels of freedom afforded to women by their situation. Those who have focused on women's opportunities include Norton, "Evolution of White Women's Experience," and Carr and Walsh, "The Planter's Wife."

    8. MESDA has traced 297 artisans active in Charleston in 1770. In 1790, according to the first federal census, there were on average seven dependents for every artisan head of household, and so I have used this figure to estimate a household total of eight individuals in 1770. See "Governor William Bull's Representation of the Colony" in Merrens, *Colonial South Carolina Scene,* 262.

    9. Studies that stress these developments in the context of the early stages of the British industrial revolution include McKendrick, "Josiah Wedgwood"; Hudson, *Genesis of Industrial Capital;* Berg, "Women's Work, Mechanization and the Early Phases of the Industrialization in England"; Berg, "Small Producer Capitalism"; and O'Brien and Quinault, *Industrial Revolution.*

    10. The question of competition from the labor of skilled slaves is one that has received some attention from historians, who have usually concluded that the existence of such slaves reduced opportunities for free white artisans and prompted an antagonistic relationship

between the two parties. For details of these arguments, see Bridenbaugh, *Colonial Crafts-man*, 120, and Morgan, "Black Life in Eighteenth-Century Charleston," 205. Likewise, Rich-ard Walsh has argued that artisans "resorted to slave labor" and constantly regretted their decision when they realized that they had created stiff competition for work. See Walsh, *Charleston's Sons of Liberty*, 23. This study emphasizes that slavery was extremely useful to Charleston's artisans, having positive benefits for white employers even when it brought little for its black victims. See "Governor William Bull's Representation of the Colony," in Merrens, *Colonial South Carolina Scene*, 262.

11. See table 4.1, this volume. Philip Morgan's figures on overall slaveholding in Charles-ton inventories between 1730 and 1800 reveal some noteworthy contrasts between the slaveholding of artisans and that of the overall population. Artisans were more likely to own between one and nine slaves, and between 1750 and 1769, 78 percent of artisans held this many slaves, whereas only 45 percent of the overall population fell into this bracket. How-ever, where roughly 50 percent of the population held between ten and nineteen slaves, only 24 percent of artisans had this many. See Morgan, "Black Life in Eighteenth-Century Charleston," table 2, 190. Advertisement of Thomas Bennett, *South Carolina and American General Gazette*, Charleston, 4 June 1778. Artisans seem to have largely ignored a regulation that there must be one white apprentice or journeyman for every two slaves in their enter-prise. For a complete discussion of the legal restrictions on skilled black labor, see Morris, *Government and Labor*, 184–85.

12. For biographical details of Elfe's career, see Burton, *Charleston Furniture*, and Hum-phrey, *Thomas Elfe, Cabinetmaker*.

13. The structure of Elfe's enterprise was deduced from entries in his daybook (Day-book, CLS). For some specific examples of this structure in operation in the English cabi-netmaking trade circa 1755, see Kirkham, "Samuel Norman." For the ubiquity of these struc-tures in other urban trades, see Berg, "Small Producer Capitalism." Berg uses a study of the metalworking trades of Sheffield and Birmingham during the eighteenth century to argue for the "very important place of a dynamic core of small- and medium-scale producers." She further makes a plea for the explosion of the "attendant historical myths of artisan and fac-tory production" that place the two work environments at opposite ends of the scale.

14. Berg, "Small Producer Capitalism," 30.

15. Advertisement of John Boomer, *South Carolina Gazette*, 18 August 1758; advertise-ment of Logan and Williams, *South Carolina Gazette*, 17 May 1760.

16. Inventory of Alexander McCormack, 4 November 1773, vol. 94, Book B, CCPL.

17. See table 4.1, this volume. See chapter 3 for a discussion of Pinckney's house-building activities.

18. John Ruger vs. Benjamin Hawes and Uz Rogers, 1768, vol. 81A, no. 492A; John Mar-ley vs. Thomas Ralph, 1760, vol. 51A, no. 192A; James Kirkwood vs. Robert Cochran, 1757, vol. 30A, no. 62A, all in Judgment Rolls, SCDAH.

19. Daybook of Alexander Crawford, 1785–1795, 34–347, SCHS.

20. Memorial of Robert Beard, vol. 25(2), bundle 125, Loyalist Claims, LOC; *Royal Gazette*, 13 July 1782; *Royal Gazette*, 1 August 1781. See also William Ancrum to Thomas Cracker, esq., 15 May 1778 and 13 October 1778, William Ancrum account book and Letter-book, mss. P, SCL.

21. In the British case, Shani D'Cruze has noted how "correlations between occupa-

tional criteria and social status are fraught with difficulty" in eighteenth-century towns where economic diversification obfuscated the link between a person's trade and his or her identity. See D'Cruze, "Middling Sort," 184. Gary Nash has recognized the difficulties inherent in classifying early American urban-dwellers by occupation. See Nash, "Artisans and Politics in Eighteenth-Century Philadelphia," 243–68.

22. Advertisements of Charleston artisans, as extracted from Charleston newspapers in the Index of Artisans, MESDA. The reasons for diversification can be seen in two opposing ways. In some cases, rural or small-town traders diversified because there was not enough business for their main trade in a stagnating market; for examples with a southern American context, see Russo, *Free Workers in a Plantation Economy,* and Daniels, "Wanted: A Blacksmith who Understands Plantation Work." However, other cases—such as the situation of Charleston tradespeople, who were working in a growing *urban* economy—cannot be viewed in the same light; diversification as part of such a rapidly expanding and lively economy, I would argue, should instead be viewed as a consequence of the array of possibilities on offer, the willingness of entrepreneurial people to take advantage of them, and the lack of government regulation that might prevent this.

23. Advertisement of Joshua Lockwood, *South Carolina Gazette,* 29 October 1772. See also advertisement of Lockwood, *South Carolina Gazette,* 20 December 1773, where he explains that he had "a jeweller and silversmith in constant employ, [and] should be obliged to such of [his] friends as to have anything to do in that way." Advertisements of William Rigby Naylor, *South Carolina Gazette,* 13 June 1771; *South Carolina and American General Gazette,* 10 August 1772.

24. See *South Carolina Weekly Gazette,* 23 August 1783. According to his wife and acquaintances, John Wyatt had also exported mahogany from the Caribbean to England via Charleston. See testimony of Violetta Wyatt and of Thomas Doughty, company accounts of Wyatt, Richardson, and Richardson, included as evidence in the case of Wyatt vs. Richardson, Chancery Court Records, bundle 10, Box 1, 1797, SCDAH.

25. Elfe usually kept approximately SC£1,000 worth of these goods in stock at any one time. See Daybook of Thomas Elfe, CLS. For further jobs undertaken by tradespersons, see advertisement of Michael Muckinfuss, *South Carolina Gazette,* 9 May 1768; Muckinfuss was a blacksmith who opened an inn. See also the case of artist Jeremiah Theus, who was paid for making German translations of documents for the colonial government, in Journal of the Public Accounts, Ledger A, 1759–1768, SCDAH.

26. Hunt, *Middling Sort,* 58–62. On growing numeracy among American tradespeople, see Patricia Cline Cohen, "Reckoning with Commerce," 324.

27. Advertisement of John Blott, *South Carolina Gazette and Country Journal,* 29 January 1768; William Whiting vs. Laughton and Bookless, 1769, vol. 84A, no. 190A, 1769, Judgment Rolls, SCDAH; testimony of Violetta Wyatt in the case of Richardson vs. Wyatt, South Carolina Chancery Court Records, bundle 10, no. 1, 1797, SCDAH; memorial of Daniel Manson, vol. 131(2), Reel 133, Loyalist Claims, LOC.

28. For the most fully worked out discussion of separate spheres in the middle-class context, see Davidoff and Hall, *Family Fortunes,* 272–315. Only eighteen wives of Charleston's artisans were mentioned as practicing the same trade as their husbands, or as continuing the trade after the husband's death. Of these women, six appear not to have worked at the trade themselves, but to have used their skilled slaves to carry on the workshop. An equal number followed a different from their husband's. Information extracted from Index

of Artisans, MESDA. Women did also perform so-called incidental work, such as look-ing after boarders who had been taken into the household for extra income. For examples, see testimony of Violetta Wyatt in the case of Richardson vs. Wyatt, South Carolina Chan-cery Court Records, bundle 10, no. 1, 1797, SCDAH, and advertisement of John Blott, *South Carolina Gazette and Country Journal*, 29 January 1768. Thomas Elfe's account book also indicates that he let out single rooms to boarders in his house, and it is unlikely that he undertook the extra household duties incurred by their presence. Daybook of Thomas Elfe, CLS.

29. John Stevens to William Mann, Jamaica, 20 October 1768; John Stevens to John Ste-vens Jr., Jamaica, 20 October 1768; John Stevens to William Burrows, Charleston, 11 April 1769; John Stevens to Paul Whitehead, Twickenham, near London, 6 December, 1770, all in John Stevens Letterbook, 1768–1770, mss, LCP. My thanks to Mr. Phil Lapsansky for bring-ing this manuscript to my attention. For a similar career path of another middling service provider, see Cobau, "The Precarious Life of Thomas Pike."

30. Advertisements of Agnes Lind, *South Carolina Gazette*, 29 May 1762 and 1 June 1 1766; inventory of Elizabeth McKenzie, 5 December 1748, vol. 77, Book A, Charleston Inventories, CCPL; advertisements of Francis Ramadge, *South Carolina Gazette*, 21 Sep-tember, 1765; *South Carolina Gazette and Country Journal*, 15 December, 1767; *South Caro-lina Gazette and General Advertiser*, 2 May 1783; *The City Gazette, or the Daily Adver-tiser*, 11 February 1791; and *City Gazette*, 20 November 1804. For an account of Ramadge's career, see Kierner, *Beyond the Household*, 24–25. For details of the life of Ann Cross, see O'Connor, "The Measure of the Market," 79–84.

31. Lists of liquor licenses granted, in *South Carolina Gazette*, 24 April 1762, 11 May 1767, 3 May 1773, and 27 May 1783.

32. *South Carolina Gazette*, 6 February 1762. When the tavern had been under the care of "Mr. Cannon," it had also been run by his wife Mary, as noted in Estes, "Daniel Can-non," 22.

33. Remonstrance of John Daniel, John Yerworth, George Heskett, John Scott, and David Brown, 25 January 1744 in *Journal of Commons House of Assembly*, 4:547. This remon-strance was a response to a petition by non–slave-owners to the South Carolina govern-ment, complaining that "by reason of . . . slaves they could meet with no work or encourage-ment." However, five other shipwrights, led by John Daniel (who had a workforce of fifteen slave carpenters), dismissed these protests on the grounds that it was not competition from enslaved workers that had resulted in the lack of work, but the laziness of the complainants and a tendency to take advantage of the free market by demanding "extravagant wages" for the work they did.

34. Daybook of Thomas Elfe, CLS.

35. Testimony of Violetta Wyatt, included as evidence in the case of Wyatt vs. Richard-son, Chancery Court Records, bundle 10, Box 1, 1797, SCDAH.

36. Memorial of James Cook, vol. 87(1), reel no. 86, Loyalist Claims, LOC; inventory of Francis Gottier, 23 October 1784, vol. A, 1783–87, 254, SCDAH; inventory of Esaie Brunet, 22 November 1757, vol. 84, Charleston County Wills, CCPL; inventory of Alexander Petrie, 16 March 1768, 10:365, SCDAH.

37. Testimony of George Flagg included as evidence in the case of Wyatt vs. Richard-son, Chancery Court Records, bundle 10, Box 1, 1797, SCDAH.

38. Testimony of Violetta Wyatt included as evidence in the case of Wyatt vs. Richard-

son, Chancery Court Records, bundle 10, Box 1, 1797, SCDAH; s.v. "Blott, John," Index of Artisans, MESDA. See also Sarah Perkins vs. Benjamin Hawes, 1766, vol. 66A, no. 135A, Judgment Rolls, SCDAH, which details a dispute over payment for a slave painter hired for a year by Hawes and not paid for. See also Daybook of Thomas Elfe, CLS, where Elfe agreed to a yearly payment to a widow in Charleston for the labor of her slave on his suburban plantation at Daniel's Island.

39. Wade, *Slavery in the Cities,* 243–83.

40. Edelson, *Plantation Enterprise,* 200–54; McCusker and Menard have argued that "economically rational residents of the Lower South who had a choice raised rice," since "plantation agriculture, not trade or manufacturing, afforded the best chances for success." See McCusker and Menard, *Economy of British America,* 188.

41. Advertisement of Stephen Cater, *South Carolina Gazette,* 12 February 1753. Abraham Roulain had begun his career in the Low Country as a Charleston cabinetmaker but had moved on to become a planter after a number of years at his trade. Roulain's appraisers were Joseph Fogartie, Vincent Guerin, and Oswell Eve, all of whom were planters. S.v. "Roulain, Abraham," Index of Artisans, MESDA; inventory of Abraham Roulain, 3 July 1788, vol. A, 1783–87, SCDAH; memorial of John Rose, vol. 132(2), reel 134, Loyalist Claims, LOC; Letterbook of John Stevens, mss., LCP.

42. Margaret Hunt has highlighted the ambivalent attitude of English middling sorts toward the rural life. See Hunt, *Middling Sort,* 1–2. The relationship between land, wealth, status, and economic dynamism is assumed in Morgan, *Slave Counterpoint,* and in McCusker and Menard, *Economy of British America,* 169–88. On the changing nature of the Low Country plantation enterprise, see Edelson, *Plantation Enterprise,* 92–125.

43. William Murray to his mother, 6 March 1757, Murray of Murraythwaite muniments, NAS.

44. William Murray to John Murray, 27 March 1755; John Murray to his mother, 31 March 1763; Cousin Murray to William Murray, 21 August 1762, all in Murray of Murraythwaite muniments, NAS.

45. Advertisement of Gilbert Chalmers, *Charleston Gazette and Daily Advertiser,* 24 January 1798; s.v. "Horlbeck, Peter," Index of Artisans, MESDA; s.v. "Crosby, Timothy," Index of Artisans, MESDA; advertisement of Stephen Shrewsbury, *South Carolina and American General Gazette,* 28 April 1775.

46. See table 4.2, this volume. For a discussion of the development of a provisioning market in the Chesapeake, see Walsh, "Provisioning Tidewater Towns."

47. Advertisement of Eleazer Phillips, *South Carolina Gazette and Timothy's and Mason's Daily Advertiser,* 5 November 1795. See table 4.5, "Charges on Expenses credited to plantations . . . Henry Laurens' Plantation Enterprise," in Edelson, "Planting the Low Country," 345, where the cash sums obtained for wood sales are directly comparable to the records for Milner's sales spanning 1772 and 1773, while Laurens's account book runs from 1766 to 1773. For Milner's sales, see John Milner vs. John Imrie, 1775, vol. 103A, no. 79A, Judgment Rolls, SCDAH. For other examples of Charleston residents exploiting timber reserves, see advertisement of John Cart, *South Carolina Gazette,* 23 June 1749, and s.v. "Carwithin, William," Index of Artisans, MESDA.

48. Advertisement of John Rose, *South Carolina Gazette,* 2 October 1766.

49. Advertisement of Timothy Crosby, *South Carolina Gazette,* 24 February 1759;

advertisement of Edward Hanahan, *South Carolina Gazette*, 4 February 1759; *South Carolina Gazette*, 7 August 1762; *South Carolina Gazette*, 31 December 1763; *Charleston Daily Advertiser*, 26 April 1783.

50. Advertisement of George Milner, *City Gazette or the Daily Advertiser*, 1 November 1791; advertisement of Daniel Cannon, *South Carolina Gazette and Country Journal*, 22 November 1768.

51. Daybook of Thomas Elfe, sundry entries, 1768–75, CLS. Although I would have liked to have delved more deeply into the role of women in the running of these suburban farms, it has not proved possible, as I was unable to find any evidence highlighting the relationship between urban women and such enterprises.

52. Inventory of Cato Ash, n.d., vol. 100, 1776–84, Charleston County Wills, CCPL.

53. On the economic roles of poorer women in Charleston, see O'Connor, "The Measure of the Market," 66–128. On the contrasting roles of elite planter women in a domestic setting, see Anzilotti, "Autonomy and the Female Planter," and Kierner, "Hospitality, Sociability, and Gender."

54. Philip Morgan has argued that, "where a large group of plain folk existed, as preeminently in Virginia, but to a lesser degree also in South Carolina, masters courted their support and generally received their recognition." Morgan, *Slave Counterpoint*, 316.

55. Smith, "Inequality in Late Colonial Philadelphia," 643; Bielinski, "A Middling Sort"; Pencak, "Social Structure in Revolutionary Boston," 267–78; Waterhouse, "Economic Growth"; and Jones, *Wealth of a Nation To Be*, table 7.1, 220.

56. Inventory of Anthony Toomer, 15 October 1799, vol. C, 1793–1800, SCDAH; inventory of Francis Morand, 7 October 1766, vol. 88, Book B; inventory of William Rigby Nailor, 26 October 1773, vol. 94, Book B; inventory of Robert Fairweather, 2 July 1763, vol. 87, Book B; inventory of William Williams, 12 July 1770, vol. 94, Book A, Charleston County Inventories, CCPL. Of 100 artisan inventories from the period 1730–80, 15 listed personal property in excess of £640 sterling, the urban average for southern artisans, and 52 listed wealth higher than the £137.8 sterling average for artisans. For average wealth, see Alice Hanson Jones, *Wealth of a Nation To Be*, table 7.5, 224.

57. Will of Anthony Toomer, 10 September 1800, vol. 30, Book C, Charleston County Wills, CCPL; inventory of Jeremiah Theus, s.v. "Theus, Jeremiah," Index of Artisans, MESDA; will of Thomas Weaver, s.v. "Weaver, Thomas," Index of Artisans, MESDA; inventory of Martin Pfenninger, s.v. "Pfenninger, Martin," Index of Artisans, MESDA.

58. Inventory of Samuel Lacey, 12 April 1749, vol. 77, Book A, and inventory of Robert Landall, 15 June 1773, vol. 94, Book B, Charleston County Wills, CCPL. On the material culture of the poorer Virginia yeomen, see Isaac, *Transformation of Virginia*, 45–46.

59. During the occupation of Charleston, vestrymen complained that they had been overwhelmed by demands for poor relief, and they estimated that they would have to give food, shelter, and clothing to about seventy men, women, and children—but this was a mere one percent of the town's white population. Without doubt, there were those who struggled; there were a few whites who died with very little, or with nothing at all, after debts on their estates had been paid. However, this level of poverty was low compared to that experienced in contemporary Boston, where the city's overseers were spending an ever-increasing proportion of the budget on relief, so that by 1775, 15 percent of monies were disbursed in this manner. For sums spent from Charleston's poor-relief funds, see St. Philip's Vestry Minutes,

SCL, and minutes of the Charleston Board of Police, CO/15, National Archives, London. For sums spent on poor relief in Boston, see Nash, *Urban Crucible,* table 10, "Poor Relief in Boston, New York, and Philadelphia, 1700–1775," 402–4.

60. Daybook of Thomas Elfe, entry for November 1772, CLS; inventory of John Paul Grimke, 15 March 1791, vol. B, page 391, SCDAH; and inventory of Anthony Toomer, 15 October 1799, vol. C, 1793–1800, SCDAH. A more comprehensive survey of credit and debt networks among Charleston's tradespeople would be desirable, but the sources are somewhat sparse. Most pertinently, Thomas Elfe's daybook is the only surviving set of accounts from this sector of the urban community, making it impossible to trace in any great detail the networks of financial obligation among trading people. The only other window on financial networks (other than the mortgages discussed below) are the lists of debtors or creditors sometimes appended to inventories. However, the inclusion of such material is infrequent and far from comprehensive.

61. Daybook of Thomas Elfe, "Bonds and Notes, 1768," CLS; South Carolina mortgages, 1730–83, as transcribed into the Index of Artisans, MESDA. In total, 229 mortgages had a town trader as one party. The property mortgaged usually comprised slaves, but sometimes included real estate, household furnishings, or stock in trade.

62. A total of 379 marriages of known Charleston residents were traced, using Salley, *Marriage Notices in the South Carolina Gazette and Its Successors,* and the Index of Artisans at MESDA, where the marriages of all Charleston artisans were listed. The professions of the bride's family, for these unions, was traceable in 209 cases. Inventory of Charles Desel, s.v. "Desel, Charles," Index of Artisans, MESDA.

63. Altogether, twenty-two townsmen took planters' daughters or widows as their spouses between 1732 and 1777. Other examples include Peter Manigault to Elizabeth Wragg in 1755, William Doughty to Rachel Porcher in 1770, Richard Peronneau to Anne Ball in 1767, and William Glen Jr. to Martha Miller in 1770. All from Salley, *Marriage Notices.*

64. Will of Thomas Nightingale, s.v. "Nightingale, Thomas," Index of Artisans, MESDA; will and inventory of John Watson, s.v. "Watson, John," Index of Artisans, MESDA; Charleston County Inventories drawn up in 1783, SCDAH. The exceptions in the 1783 sample were the wealthiest planter-merchants, whose estates spanned country and city.

65. Henry Laurens to Robert and John Thompson and Co., Charleston, 20 April 1757, *PHL,* vol. 2, where Laurens took up the cause of Hinds to obtain a £150 refund for him. See U.S. Bureau of the Census, *Heads of Families at the First Census of the United States, Taken in the Year 1790, South Carolina,* 38–44, entry for Patrick Hinds.

### 5. Criminal Pleasures and Charitable Deeds

1. The best account of this gentrification process is Bushman, *Refinement of America.* See also Breen, *Marketplace of Revolution;* Carson et al., *Of Consuming Interests;* and Hunter, *Purchasing Identity,* 107–46. For discussions of the primacy of a rural locus of southern gentry culture, see Isaac, *Transformation of Virginia;* Rozbicki, *Complete Colonial Gentleman;* Burnard, *Creole Gentlemen,* 205–36; and Chaplin, *An Anxious Pursuit.* Bushman also stressed the rural aspect to genteel life in eighteenth-century Delaware, in *Refinement of America,* 3–29.

2. Waterhouse, *New World Gentry,* 86.

3. Hamilton, "Itinerarium," as quoted in Bushman, *Refinement of America,* 79–81 and

181–87. The best exposition of the power of emulation in a British context is Brewer et al., *Birth of a Consumer Society.*

4. S. Max Edelson has discussed how a "marketplace of identity" gave these staple producers "the means with which to fashion a corporate identity" making "the work of planting . . . as much cultural as it was economic, social, and environmental." See Edelson, *Plantation Enterprise,* 282; also Burnard, *Creole Gentlemen,* 205–36. On the adaptive aspects of middling culture, see Hemphill, *Bowing to Necessities,* 65–86, and Hemphill, "Manners and Class."

5. On the role of provincial towns in the formation of national cultures in eighteenth-century Britain, see Borsay, *English Urban Renaissance;* Sweet, *English Town,* 219–66; Sweet, *Writing of Urban Histories,* 236–75; and Clark and Houston, "Culture and Leisure, 1700–1840," 575–614. For a discussion of the importance of the British provincial contribution to colonial American culture, see Landsman, *From Colonial to Provincials,* 31–122.

6. On the cultural relationship between the gentry and the town in Britain, see Borsay, "The Landed Elite and Provincial Towns in Britain." On elite culture and the town in a colonial American context, see Hunter, *Purchasing Identity,* 107–47.

7. Berry, "Promoting Taste in the Provincial Press"; Barry, "The Press and the Politics of Culture." On the colonial American newspaper as a forum of culture, see Shields, *Civil Tongues and Polite Letters,* 46–54 and 262–65, and Waldstreicher, "Reading the Runaways."

8. Although tradespeople produced goods in a manner demanded by their customers, by the eighteenth century they possessed a substantial body of specialist knowledge that gave them some power to dictate fashions. The *London Tradesman,* a guide to apprenticeships for parents, repeatedly stressed the importance of the craftsperson in this respect. To complete his work satisfactorily, the gatesmith who made ironwork for the country houses of the gentry needed "tolerable taste and judgment," the author noted, and described the upholsterer as a "man upon whose judgment I rely in the Choice of Goods," and who therefore needed to possess "taste in the Fashions, and skill in the workmanship." See Campbell, *London Tradesman,* 166–70. Richard Bushman has also noted the appearance of tradespeople and their shops in colonial America, but has read this as a move toward a novel, colonial material world, rather than as the bearer of any British Atlantic trends. Further, Bushman doubts that elites much visited the shops of local craftspersons—a doubt that the evidence in chapter 2 would seem to dispute. See Bushman, "Shopping and Advertising."

9. Advertisement of Rachel and William Lawrence, *South Carolina Gazette,* 9 August 1774; advertisement of Richard Bird, *South Carolina Gazette,* 18 September 1762; advertisement of Robert Frogg, *South Carolina Gazette,* 22 November 1773; advertisement of Elizabeth Hall, *South Carolina Gazette,* 20 November 1762; advertisement of Logan and Ward, *South Carolina Gazette,* 24 May 1760; advertisement of John Barnes, *South Carolina Gazette,* 6 November 1752.

10. Advertisement of Mary Baker, *South Carolina Gazette,* 6 March 1762; advertisement of Eleanor Dryden, *South Carolina Gazette,* 21 June 1760; advertisement of Mary Cranmer, *South Carolina Gazette,* 30 September 1756; advertisement of Peter Butler, *South Carolina Gazette,* 5 February 1750; advertisement of Philip Tidyman, *South Carolina Gazette,* 18 February, 1764; advertisement of Walter Mansell, *South Carolina Gazette,* 22 January 1756; and advertisements of Richard Herbert, *South Carolina Gazette,* 9 January 1742 and 10 October 1743.

11. See, for example, advertisement of John Oliver, *South Carolina Gazette*, 18 February 1764, and advertisement of John Brown, *South Carolina Gazette*, 14 July 1773.

12. Advertisements of Joshua Lockwood, *South Carolina Gazette*, 21 March 1761, 7 April 1760, 11 June 1763, and 26 February 1763.

13. Through his discussion of the role of the townscape in elite culture, Richard Waterhouse has already highlighted Charleston's importance to Low Country culture. However, Waterhouse describes an almost pathological desire among colonial elites to copy English cultural models. Here, I would like to stress how the growth of the town enabled gentry and townspeople to fashion a provincial urbane culture, of the sort also found across Britain among those who were not colonial plantation owners. See Waterhouse, "The Development of Elite Culture." Other studies have tended to focus on the plantation as the principal locus of elite culture in colonial South Carolina. See Robert Olwell's treatment of the political economy of the plantation for an excellent discussion of the role of the "country seat" and its slave society in the elite culture in the Low Country. Olwell, *Masters, Slaves, and Subjects*, 181–221.

14. Campbell, *London Tradesman*, 14. On new developments in consuming practice and etiquette, see Berry, "Polite Consumption"; Walsh, "Shops, Shopping, and the Art of Decision Making." For a discussion of the provincial shopping experience in Britain, see Stobart, "Shopping Streets as Social Space."

15. Daybook of Alexander Crawford, 1785–95, 34–347, SCHS. Crawford, a Charleston painter and glazier, repeatedly used these phrases to record the nature of the work that he undertook for his town customers. Crawford's daybook contains references to bow windows, which had become typical of shops and were used to display wares to customers. For details of such developments in the British retail landscape, see Mui and Mui, *Shops and Shopkeeping*, 221–48.

16. Baker-Grimke receipts, 11/538/1, SCHS. This collection of receipts includes preprinted examples from silversmith Philip Tidyman and merchants Mansell, Corbett, and Robinson. See advertisement of Thomas Bradford, *Charleston Courier*, 8 February 1788.

17. Diary of Eliza Wilkinson, National Library of Scotland; "Meddler's Club," as quoted by Shields in "Early Cities of America: Charleston." Wilkinson's autonomy as an elite urban consumer appears to have been representative of South Carolinian women of her status. The records kept by merchant-planter Henry Laurens, straddling the year in which his wife Eleanor died, are especially informative. While she was alive, Laurens gave his wife SC£100 (£14 sterling) per month for household purchases. What Eleanor purchased was not recorded in Henry Laurens's accounts, but after his wife's death, in July 1770, he began to take over her shopping responsibilities. Laurens's first venture into the "female" purchasing sphere was his visit to a Mrs. Breedlove in Charleston, who made mourning gowns for his two daughters. From there on, the merchant began to concern himself with the acquisition of picture frames, stays, cutlery, shoes, mantuas, tin pudding cans, and gown patterns from Charleston tradesmen and tradeswomen. From the changing consumption patterns of Henry Laurens, we can see that Eleanor Laurens had patronized tradesmen and women based in Charleston for, probably, many years. See account book of Henry Laurens, CC. The receipts of the Bakers of Archdale Hall demonstrate a similar distribution of purchasing responsibilities and a tendency among wives and daughters to embark on shopping expeditions into Charleston. See Baker-Grimke receipts, 11/538/1, SCHS. For an assessment of the

shopping practices of women in the revolutionary and early national period, see O'Connor, "Collaborative Consumption."

18. As Linda Sturtz has argued, Virginia women could be independent consumers, but the rural nature of the store system—and the crudeness of many stores—prevented these establishments from becoming sites of leisured consumption for women, as Charleston was for the Low Country's elite consumers. See Sturtz, *Within Her Power*, 111–40. See also Daniel St. Jennifer to unknown, 22 May 1764, in Galloway Papers, NYPL: "If Miss Galloway is not yet provided with a piece of white fustian please tender her my compliments and acquaint her that I have by ? a piece of 40yds and if by the next post you can send down word, which quantity will go it shall be sent up by his return."

19. As Peter Borsay shows, only the largest cities actually had purpose-built assembly rooms, with balls and assemblies in smaller provincial towns usually taking place in inns or other public buildings such as courthouses. See Borsay, *English Urban Renaissance*, appendices 1–7.

20. *Charleston Gazette and Daily Advertiser*, 4 April 1784.

21. For a discussion of the season in its provincial British context, see Clark and Houston, "Culture and Leisure." On the emergence of a season in Boston and Salem, see Hunter, *Purchasing Identity*, 107–10.

22. See, for example, *South Carolina Gazette*, 18 January 1734, for "a tragedy," and also *South Carolina Gazette*, 15 November 1750, for a ball held by Henry Holt. Advertisement of Ann Shepherd, *South Carolina Gazette*, 7 July 1748; *South Carolina Gazette and General Advertiser*, 3 February 1783.

23. *South Carolina Gazette*, 7 October 1763 and 15 April 1766. Charleston's provincial preeminence was reinforced by its ability to draw in Georgia elites, whose own social activities in Savannah never achieved the same sophistication as those of South Carolina. Indeed, social events in Charleston were often reported in the Georgia newspapers; see, for example, *Georgia Gazette*, 17 November 1763.

24. "Journal of Josiah Quincy, Jr.," 441–42.

25. Hewitt, *An Historical Account*, 312; "Journal of Thomas Griffiths," in Merrens, *Colonial South Carolina Scene*, 246.

26. "An Account of Our American Settlements," *Gentleman's Magazine*, no. 25 (January 1755): 16–17. Metropolitan commentators' opinions of Charleston's elite culture seem to have contrasted quite strongly with those of elites elsewhere in the southern colonies. For further opinions about Chesapeake elites, see Rozbicki, "The Curse of Provincialism."

27. On the material culture of town traders in Britain, see Weatherill, *Consumer Behaviour and Material Culture*, 70–90 and 166–90, and Smollett, *Expedition of Humphry Clinker*, 37.

28. For a discussion of urban merchant gentility, see Hunter, *Purchasing Identity*, 107–46; Kierner, *Traders and Gentlefolk*, 128–64; and Bushman, *Refinement of America*, 100–80.

29. John Murray to his mother, undated, probably 1750s, and John Murray to his mother, 7 January 1750, both in Murray of Murraythwaite muniments, NAS.

30. For an excellent treatment of Dale's "case history," see Shields, *Civil Tongues and Polite Letters*, 276–301.

31. Stevens's status is especially suggested by his inability to get Low Country elites

to pay bills owed to his wife, requests for money being repeatedly rejected. Following one such demand, John Brewton responded only with an "extraordinary ungenteel note." Subsequent appeals to relative Miles Brewton for the cash appear to have been equally unsuccessful. See John Stevens to Mr. John Brewton, 27 November 1770, and to Miles Brewton, esq., 3 December 1770, in Letterbook of John Stevens, 1768−70, LCP.

32. For a lengthy discussion of these issues in a British context, see Hunt, *Middling Sort*, 101−24; Clark, *British Clubs and Societies*; and Wilson, "Urban Culture and Political Activism."

33. Hunter, *Purchasing Identity*, 132, and Bridenbaugh, *Cities In Revolt*, 322.

34. Hewitt, *An Historical Account*, 299.

35. Rules and membership list of the South Carolina Society, 1748, misc. records, vol. 75, Book B, CCPL; membership rolls of the Fellowship Society, SCL. It should also be noted that, while elites joined these societies, they were rarely the most active members, membership not necessarily denoting ardent endorsement of the principles. Thus, while some members of the Fellowship Society were drawn from the elite, none of the prerevolutionary officers in this organization (presumably its most active participants) were members of the governing elite. A representative group of officers were the 1771 cohort: president was carpenter James Brown; junior warden was goldsmith Thomas Harper; treasurer was carpenter Blake Leay White; secretary was merchant Edward Legge Jr.; and senior steward was tailor John Rantowle.

36. For the hearing of sermons, see minutes of the Fellowship Society, 20 September 1769: for alcoholic overindulgence, see minutes for 13 June 1770; for sending of leftovers to the jail, see minutes for 6 December 1769. The minutes of the society for 19 April 1769 record, "received from Mr Blake Leay White a donation of £50 currency . . . the thanks be returned . . . by publishing it in the newspaper." The membership rolls of the Fellowship Society include many names against which the word "excluded" had been entered, and minutes include discussions to eject members on the grounds of drunk and disorderly behavior, suggesting the importance of upstanding behavior to these societies. Records of the Fellowship Society, SCL.

37. Will of John Prue, vol. 15, Book B, page 413, Charleston County Wills, CCPL; see also Josiah Smith Jr. to John Corker Jr., Charleston, 12 June 1771, Letterbook of Josiah Smith Jr., SHC.

38. Miscellaneous petitions to the South Carolina Legislature, SCDAH. With their charitable goals, these societies were modeled on the emerging British institution of the box, or benefit, club, which looked forward to newer associational forms rather than backward to the extinct guilds. For a discussion of benefit clubs, see Clark, *British Clubs and Societies*, 350−87.

39. In 1769 the society's chief officers and some of its members had turned out in public at the Baptist meeting to mourn the passing of Charles Motte, according to the Fellowship Society minutes, 16 June 1769. For church membership information for the Circular Congregational Church, see account ledger 1777−1806, 28/690/9, SCHS. On the dissenting church in South Carolina, see Klein, *Unification of a Slave State*, 42−45, and Little, "Adding to the Church Such as Shall be Saved." On the links between urban middling sorts and dissenting religion in Britain, see Gilbert, *Religion and Society in Industrial England*, 59−61; Gilbert explains that Wesley himself recognized most of his converts to be neither elite nor

paupers. In the second half of the eighteenth century, wealthier middling sorts also became drawn to the evangelical message; for a discussion of this attraction, see Bebbington, *Evangelicalism in Modern Britain,* 25–26.

40. Records of the Circular Congregational Church, account ledger 1777–1806, 28/690/9, SCHS.

41. Kierner, *Beyond the Household,* 32–33; minutes of the Fellowship Society, 1 April 1770, SCL; Congregational Church, Records; 1732-(1802), SCHS.

42. Mechal Sobel has argued that, "After 1750, spiritual revival was widespread in Virginia. It began in response to the needs of the lower class, to their conflicts in values and to their longings for coherence." See Sobel, *World They Made Together,* 85. Rhys Isaac has posited, "Opposites are intimately linked not only by the societal context in which they occur but also by the very antagonism that orients them to each other." See Isaac, *Transformation of Virginia,* 163. For more on these conflicts elsewhere in the early South, see Morgan, *Slave Counterpoint,* 260–300, and Burnard, *Creole Gentleman,* 205–36.

43. On the clash between older cultural practices and the imperatives of a newer urbane gentility, see Borsay, *English Urban Renaissance,* 284–308.

44. Ramsay, *History of South Carolina,* 403.

45. Account of the celebrations for the King's Birthday, *South Carolina Gazette,* 8 November 1760.

46. Thomas Pike, *South Carolina Gazette,* 18 September 1765. Entrance tickets for the event cost 30/—a day's wages for a blacksmith was £1. For wage rates, see Walsh, *Charleston's Sons of Liberty,* appendix 2, "Daily Wages, 1710–1783"; Borsay, *English Urban Renaissance,* 292.

47. Morgan, "Black Life in Eighteenth-Century Charleston."

48. Most often, objections were voiced at the quarterly meetings of the Charleston grand jury, where magistrates railed ineffectively against what they saw as the disorderly and improper behavior of the town's working people. See Presentment of the Grand Jury, as published in the *South Carolina Gazette,* 15 April 1745, for example: "officers of the watch for entertaining seaman and negroes at unseasonable hours and carrying juggs of liquor for his watchmen on duty." For accounts of African American and poor Charlestonians gathering to drink in such establishments, see the following in Complaints of the Grand Jury, SCDAH: October 1769, "many licenced dram shops and tipling houses in Charleston"; January 1770, "Daniel Caine behind beef market for keeping a disorderly tipling and gaming house where apprentices and other youth are entertained, and William Holliday on the Bay for keeping a disorderly house and suffering youth to game therein"; April 1770, "William Wayne up the path tavernkeeper for keeping a disorderly house and secreting and entertaining youth to the corruption of their morals"; January 1771, "great number of dram shops and tipling houses in Charleston such as entertain negroes and other disorderly persons and that the magistrates residing in Charleston would be more vigilant in suppressing such of them as they find contrary to good order"; April 1771, "habit of watchmen and their wives keeping dram shops." It is important to note that middling sorts and elites appear to have objected to the behavior of their black and white social inferiors for different reasons. For a discussion of these, see chapter 6, this volume. Interracial liaisons also formed an important element in this mixed, urban culture; for details, see Morgan, *Slave Counterpoint* 398–412.

49. On transatlantic luxury debates and their place in the early South, see Micklus,

"History of the Tuesday Club." On more general colonial debates on luxury, see Greene, "Search for Identity"; Breen, *Marketplace of Revolution*, 148–94. On the concept of luxury itself, see Sekora, *Luxury*.

50. Rhys Isaac has charted the growth of evangelical adherence in colonial Virginia. See Isaac, *Transformation of Virginia*, 161–77. However, because the dissenting churches' position in Virginia vis-à-vis the established Church of England was less clear than in South Carolina (where there was little dispute that dissent was legitimate), their challenge was more critical. In South Carolina, dissenting sects did not prima facie represent an outright challenge to authority, but, rather, an alternative way of life—much as it did in the metropole.

51. For details of the Bryans and their evangelical commitments, see Gallay, *Formation of a Planter Elite*, and Gallay, "Origins of Slaveholders Paternalism."

52. Entries for Saturday 15 March, Sunday 16 March, and Monday 17 March, 1740, *George Whitfield's Journals*. Whitefield's initial description of the dissenting congregation that he met with suggests a middling congregation, composed of successful tradespeople, rather than one of lower sorts; he describes the people as "very polite" and comments on their "gaiety of dress" (see entry for 6 January 1739, *George Whitfield's Journals*, 401–2, 384).

53. Garden's anti-Whitefield and anti-Methodist message was put forward in a number of pamphlets and sermons, including Garden, *Six letters*; Garden, *Regeneration and the testimony of the spirit*; and Garden, *A brief account of the deluded Dutartres*.

54. Smith, *The Burning of Sodom*.

55. Hart, *Dancing Exploded*.

56. Josiah Smith Jr. to James Poyas, Charleston, 25 January 1774, Letterbook, SHC. Writing to Poyas, who was in England after his spell as merchant in Charleston, Smith was sure that "times differ'd with them since you left Charles Town." Looking back on the era, Alexander Hewitt also observed that "even the spirit of luxury and extravagance, too common in England, was beginning to creep into Carolina." See Hewitt, *Historical Account*, 294, and will of Frederick Struebell, vol. 10, Book B, 1760–67, 473, Charleston County Wills, CCPL.

57. *South Carolina Gazette*, 1 March 1773.

### 6. "A Very Essential Service to this Community"

1. Peter Timothy to Benjamin Franklin, Charleston, 3 September 1768, in Hennig Cohen, "Four letters from Peter Timothy."

2. Beeman, "Deference, Republicanism, and the Emergence of Popular Politics," 422. The paradigm of deference that is used in discussions of colonial life, and especially of colonial politics, has remained a perennial framework, especially within the South. For a comprehensive discussion, see "Deference or Defiance in Eighteenth-Century America?"

3. The emphasis on domestic harmony and deference is reinforced by a tendency to discuss South Carolina's colonial and revolutionary politics only on the level of elite-metropolitan interaction. See Weir, "The Harmony We Were Famous For"; Menard, "Slavery, Economic Growth, and Revolutionary Ideology"; Greene, *Quest for Power*; Klein, *Unification of a Slave State*; Nadelhaft, *Disorders of War*; Starr, *A School for Politicks*; and Mercantini, *Who Shall Rule at Home?*

4. Nash, *Urban Crucible*, 184. Thanks to a succession of excellent studies of revolutionary Virginia, its colonial elite have now emerged as an anxious bunch, often under

siege from both within and outside their colony. See Isaac, *Transformation of Virginia*, 243–95; Holton, *Forced Founders*, 131–63; McDonnell, *Politics of War*. On the politics of Charleston's artisans, see Walsh, *Charleston's Sons of Liberty*. In South Carolina, it is generally agreed, the slightly later Regulator movement represented the greatest threat to elite power between 1780 and 1860. This conflict between backcountry settlers and coastal elites, although beginning in the 1760s, matured during the Revolution and came to fruition in the Early Republic and antebellum period. See Klein, *Unification of a Slave State*, 47–108; Brown, *South Carolina Regulators*.

5. Henry Laurens to James Grant, Charleston, 23 March 1767, *PHL*, vol. 5.

6. On the improvement movement and its intersections with urban politics, see Jones and Falkus, "Urban Improvement and the English Economy"; Barry, "Bourgeois Collectivism"; Rogers, "Middling Sort in Eighteenth Century Politics"; Sweet, *English Town*, 75–140; Innes and Rogers, "Politics and Government, 1700–1840."

7. *Gentleman's Magazine*, June 1753, and Lounsbury, *From Statehouse to Courthouse*.

8. John Murray to his mother (undated, probably, 1750s), Murray of Murraythwaite Muniments, NAS; "Charleston in 1774" in Merrens, *Colonial South Carolina Scene*, 281–82; "Short Description of South Carolina," George Milligan Johnson, 1765, add.29973, Manuscript Room, British Library. Celia Fiennes described the Kent town of Sandwich as a "sad old town"; see Morris, *Journeys of Celia Fiennes*. In his *Tour Thro' the Whole Island of Great Britain*, Daniel Defoe praised Ipswich as an "airy, clean, and well govern'd town," with modern amenities such as walks and parks, whereas Norwich had "antient and decayed" public edifices.

9. Public Accounts, Records of the Public Treasurers of South Carolina, Ledger A, 1759–1768, SCDAH. Work on Charleston's fortifications proved another area of influence for some of the town's largest building contractors. The bricklaying and carpentry firms of Deans and Baker and Richard Moncrieff managed to make themselves indispensable to the construction of Charleston's defenses from 1755 onward, with the town's fortification committee accounts showing that, although there must have been many artisans capable of fulfilling contracts (and indeed many who applied to do so), the same two partnerships repeatedly garnered work. Both firms received over SC£8,000 for work done constructing the Charleston barracks, a 30 percent share of the SC£53,000 paid out to town tradesmen in the building of defenses between 1755 and 1763. See Journal of the Commissioner of Fortifications, 1755–1764, SCDAH.

10. Figures calculated from the records of the Public Treasurers of South Carolina, 1725–1730 and 1759–1768, SCDAH; petition of Samuel Axson, 25 January 1757, *Journal of the Commons House of Assembly*, 10:305–6; and petitions for position of house messenger, 4 July 1769, *Journal of the Commons House of Assembly*, vol. 38, SCDAH.

11. Ramsay, *History of South Carolina*, 73; *South Carolina Gazette*, 6 July 1769; advertisement of John Clements, *South Carolina State Gazette*, 22 February 1793; petition from the residents of Comings Point, Journal of the Commons House of Assembly, mfm Reel 19, A1b, 1769–75, LOC (a week later, a similar request from the residents of Ansonborough was granted). See also the advertisement of Thomas Cole, *City Gazette and Daily Advertiser*, 17 May 1788, in which Cole made efforts to establish a new marketplace in Charleston's suburbs.

12. Journal of the Commons House of Assembly, 5 June 1766, Milton S. Eisenhower Library, The Johns Hopkins University.

13. Campbell, *London Tradesman*, 153.

14. Batty Langley's *Builder's Jewel* could be bought at George Wood's bookstore in Charleston; inventory of George Wood, 2 June 1777, vol. 99, Book B, Charleston County Inventories, CCPL.

15. Bills of the Commissioners for St. Michael's Church, 50–257B, SCHS.

16. Vestry Minutes of St. Michael's Parish, 50–257B, entries for 27 January 27 1766 and 7 May 1766, SCHS.

17. Journal of the Commons House of Assembly, 26 February 1767, Milton S. Eisenhower Library, The Johns Hopkins University.

18. Henry Laurens to William Cowles and Co., Charleston, 9 May 1768, *PHL*, vol. 5; Henry Laurens to William Cowles and Co., Charleston, 4 April 1769, *PHL*, vol. 6. In the busy years of Charleston's expansion, the practices established with the building of St. Michael's Church and the Exchange spread to include most major public works, with collaboration, cooperation, and negotiation between skilled middling townsman and gentleman planter becoming the customary method of construction. At the time that the Exchange was going up, William Rigby Naylor and carpenter James Brown had been contracted to supervise the construction of a new watch house, master builder Daniel Cannon was laying plans, for a poorhouse and hospital, before the assembly, and bricklayers Crosby and Toomer had a contract to build a stone bridge across one of the many canals that flowed into Charleston. For details of these projects, see *South Carolina Gazette*, 5 October 1767.

19. Glen explained how it was "customary in Great Britain in Acts of this Nature when Commissioners have been appointed for the purposes in the said Acts that the Nomination of such Commissioners has been left to the Crown and a time has been limited for their Continuance," as quoted in Greene, *Quest For Power*, 254. The clash over the power of the commissions was part of a larger tussle between the Royal Council and the Assembly over the issue of money and disbursement of public funds. Previous historians have summarily dismissed the importance of Charleston's commissions, and Rebecca Starr has argued that "what local authority existed" in South Carolina "was the creation and creature of the legislature"; see Starr, *School for Politicks*, 140. In his discussion of public works in Charleston, Carl Bridenbaugh also emphasized elite authority over the cityscape, and explained that "the fundamental misfortune of Charleston's condition" was "the absence of any properly constituted local authority." Refusal of the Commons House of Assembly to provide a prison was also, according to Bridenbaugh "a civil disgrace." Bridenbaugh, *Cities in Revolt*, 372 and 385.

20. "Bull's Representation of the Colony, 1770," Merrens, *Colonial South Carolina Scene*, 269.

21. Rogers, "Middling Sort in Eighteenth-Century Politics," 149, 160.

22. Edgar and Bailey, *Biographical Dictionary*, was used to determine who served in the colonial government.

23. S.v. "Cannon, Daniel," Index of Artisans, MESDA; membership rolls of the Fellowship Society, SCL; St. Philip's Vestry minutes, 1732–1783, SCL. Cannon also laid out a suburb of Charleston, called Cannonborough, during the 1790s. Other examples of so-called civic-minded practitioners of public works included blockmaker Barnard Beekman, and carpenters Joseph Verree and Richard Moncrieff, who were all appointed firemasters in the fire commission of 1756; by the next decade all three had made their services to the public

indispensable. Beekman, the biggest earner, derived SC£1,630 between 1760 and 1768 for work primarily related to the upkeep of Charleston's fire engines, but also included contracts concerning the town's pumps and public wells. Moncrieff and Verree made slightly less money during the same period, with the former receiving SC£583, the latter, SC£176. See Journal of the Public Treasurer, account ledger, 1759–1768, SCDAH.

24. Simpson, *Practical Justice.*

25. Ibid.

26. *South Carolina Gazette,* 31 October 1774.

27. Letter from "A Tradesman," *South Carolina Gazette,* 26 January 1765. See also John Carpenter, *South Carolina Gazette,* 26 February 1763.

28. See entries for Peter Timothy, Daniel Crawford, Samuel Brailsford, George Austin, Benjamin Dart, John Edwards Sr., Benjamin Guerard, Hopkin Price, Thomas Savage, Benjamin Smith, Charles Pinckney, Christopher Gadsden, and Henry Laurens in Edgar and Bailey, *Biographical Dictionary.*

29. Complaints about Charleston had been part of the agenda before this period, but had not dominated as they did following the creation of the town's own jury. Further, presentments only began to appear in the *South Carolina Gazette* on a regular basis after 1772.

30. Presentments of the Charleston County Grand Jury, 1770–1776, SCDAH.

31. Presentments of the Charleston County Grand Jury, 16 May 1775, 15 February 1774, 16 February 1773, in SCDAH.

32. Richard Walsh asserted that "mercantilism, with its anti-colonial manufacturing and tight money policy, put [the artisan] at a distinct disadvantage and placed him ordinarily on the side of the revolutionaries." Walsh, *Charleston's Sons of Liberty,* 25. Although historians have highlighted the connection between civic protest and radical revolutionary protest, they have tended to assume that the protestors were not middling but "popular," in the sense of being drawn from lower ranks of urban society. See Waldstreicher, *In the Midst of Perpetual Fetes,* 24–25; Carp, "Fire of Liberty"; and Nash, *Urban Crucible,* 339–84. Pauline Maier has pointed out that the Sons of Liberty "seemed to grow out of a series of earlier groups" with charitable, civic, and evangelical goals, but she too views them as a popular, rather than as a middling, force. See Maier, *From Resistance to Revolution,* 85–87.

33. Inventory of Nathaniel Lebby, 1800, s.v. "Lebby, Nathaniel," Index of Artisans, MESDA; land transactions of George Flagg, s.v. "Flagg, George," Index of Artisans, MESDA. Richard Walsh has noted that some town artisans suffered financial difficulties between 1766 and 1770 (Walsh, *Charleston's Sons of Liberty,* 35), but it is clear that such difficulties rarely led to a loss of middling social status. Walsh demonstrates that Nathaniel Lebby certainly suffered during this period but, as Lebby's inventory shows, he had resources ultimately sufficient to withstand the lean times. See tabular appendix for breakdown of nonimportation committee members and their professions and interests. Rebecca Starr has argued that this committee was very important, insofar as it influenced the configuration of South Carolina politics; see Starr, *School for Politicks,* 88–90. Henry Laurens also observed that "the mob" who invaded his house looking for stamped paper consisted of some "hearted Jacks" but also many "towns men" who tried to disguise their more respectable social status with "soot, Sailors habits, slouch hats &c." See Laurens to James Grant, Charleston, 1 November 1765 and Laurens to Joseph Brown, Charleston, 28 October 1765, both in *PHL,* vol. 5.

34. As quoted in Maier, "Charleston Mob," 176. Maier also notes the ongoing quest for law and order among the Revolution's popular supporters. However, she does not see this wish for order as stemming from the protestors' domestic concerns but, rather, from inherited English ideas about political behavior and popular protest.

35. As quoted in Walsh, *Charleston's Sons of Liberty*, 32.

36. Henry Laurens to Joseph Brown, Charleston, 28 October 1765, and Henry Laurens to John Lewis Gervais, Charleston, 29 January 1766, both in *PHL*, vol. 5; entry for Peter Timothy in Edgar and Bailey, *Biographical Dictionary.*

37. Wilson, *Sense of the People*, 236. The parallels between the political experiences of urban middling sorts in provincial Britain and in Charleston are striking. In her study, Wilson explains how, in Newcastle, a group of middling, dissenting tradesmen—forced to the margins of civic power by an entrenched, Anglican, elite—identified civic corruption with the actions of George III and his ministers. Beginning with the 1760s, this faction mixed a radical Wilkite agenda, and patriotic support for Americans (whom they perceived as the victims of corrupt government), with their own quest for supremacy in Newcastle's civic affairs. This blatantly political challenge to the city's ruling elites had gradually evolved from the 1750s onward. First, with the advent of improvement bodies and voluntary hospital associations, a separate civic political culture was forged. Then the Wilkite agenda, Wilson argues, provided the groups, starting in the 1760s, with a "language of rights and liberties and a model of political activism—that of resistance." Finally, the War of Independence swelled the fray, as national issues and local conflicts pushed each other ever nearer to a radical brink. See Wilson, *Sense of the People*, 373–75.

38. Henry Laurens to George Appleby, Charleston, 26 September 1769, *PHL*, vol. 7.

39. For the details of this dispute, see Drayton, *Letters of Freeman Etc.,* (appendix) "The Mechanics of the General Committee to Drayton," 3 October 1769.

40. For an account of this dispute, see Nadelhaft, *Disorders of War*, 27–43, and Walsh, *Charleston's Sons of Liberty*, 81–87.

41. Presentments of the Charleston County Grand Jury, 23 April 1776, SCDAH.

42. Ibid.

43. Nash, *Urban Crucible*, 383–84.

## Conclusion

1. Defoe, "Tunbridge Wells," in *A Tour thro' the Whole Island of Great Britain*, 199; "Capt. Martin," in Merrens, *South Carolina Scene*, 230–31.

2. On the experience of the Revolution in South Carolina, see Olwell, *Masters, Slaves, and Subjects*, 221–70; Frey, *Water from the Rock*, 108–43; Klein, *Unification of a Slave State*, 78–148; Nadelhaft, *Disorders of War*; Walsh, *Charleston's Sons of Liberty*; Carp, *Rebels Rising*, 143–71.

3. It should be noted that this section does not purport to be an in-depth investigation of Charleston, or South Carolinian, society, during the Revolution. As Michael McDonnell has recently shown, with his study of class in Revolutionary Virginia, investigating the structure of South Carolinian society between 1779 and 1783 would require an entirely new book. See McDonnell, *Politics of War.*

4. Nadelhaft, *Disorders of War*, 48–50; Walsh, *Charleston's Sons of Liberty*, 80–81. John Paul Grimke, for example, sold seven lots of land during 1777, 1778, and 1779 (s.v. "Grimke,

John Paul," Index of Artisans, MESDA). Thomas Handlin, who had bought a lot on Friend Street in 1773 for SC£200, sold it for SC£5500 in 1777 (s.v. "Handlin, Thomas," Index of Artisans, MESDA).

5. Will of Joseph Roper, 1799, vol. 27, Book C, Charleston County Wills, CCPL. See also the wills of Hugh Cartwright, David Linn Wandow, James Irving, John Carr, Joshua Eden, Daniel Poyas, Joseph Roper, John Allen, James Mackie, William Roper, Richard Latham, Thomas Hutchinson, and Benjamin Wheeler, in Charleston County Wills, vols. 25, 26, and 27 (together covering the period 1793–1800). I am in no way suggesting here that middling sorts advocated an end to slavery. As the institution was the basis of their livelihoods, it is clear that they had as much invested in it as had the planters socially above them.

6. As quoted in Olwell, *Masters, Slaves, and Subjects,* 238.

7. For an account of Jeremiah's fate, see ibid., 234–36; Morgan, "Conspiracy Scares."

8. Presentments of the Charleston County Grand Jury, 21 February 1775, SCDAH. The information about this incident is noted to have come from Henry Peronneau Jr., who, in the same year, is recorded as a subscriber to Charleston's new Congregational Church, in "Cash Received and paid away on Account of the New Church in Archdale Street done by subscription," Circular Congregational Church (Charleston, S.C.), Records, 1732–1802, SCHS. For an account of the Lady Huntingdon episode, see Morgan, *Slave Counterpoint,* 424–25.

9. Walsh, *Charleston's Sons of Liberty,* 94–100; testimony of Thomas Doughty in the case of Wyatt vs. Richardson, Chancery Court Records, bundle 10, Box 1, 1797, SCDAH. There were a few "lucky" militiamen who had fought in defense of Charleston. Once the siege was over they were "paroled to their homes, and the greater part of the enemy officers were sent to Haddrell's Point, where they are permitted to go about the country within a radius of six miles"—a level of freedom that presumably would allow them to attempt to carry on business. See "Diary of Captain Ewald," in Uhlendorf, *Siege of Charleston,* 97.

10. Will of John Paul Grimke, 1790, vol. 23, Book B, 540, Charleston County Wills, CCPL.

11. As quoted in Nadelhaft, *Disorders of War,* 54–55.

12. On the patronage of Charleston businesses by British soldiers and plantation owners, see Eliza Wilkinson, diary, National Library of Scotland; Frey, *Water from the Rock,* 116. Containing details of disputes between lenders and borrowers, as well as the activities of Charleston's commissioners of markets, the Board of Police records also underlines the surprisingly large amount of business conducted in the city during the occupation. Minutes of the Charleston Board of Police, mss, National Archives. As the Ethiopa Ball staged by British soldiers demonstrates, social activities—if not always those approved by South Carolina's elites— continued despite the occupation. For details, see Olwell, *Masters, Slaves, and Subjects,* 255–56.

13. For the activities of Loyalist commissioners, see the minutes of the Board of Police, entries for 8 August 1780 (street repairs and cleaning), 27 October 1780 (care of the poor), 18 and 21 March 1781 (regulation of town bakers), 27 April 1781 (maintenance of good order in the market), 22 October 1781 (employment of slaves on fortifications and street cleaning) in Minutes, National Archives.

14. For detailed contents of estates of Charleston Loyalists, see Memorials of James Cook, vol. 87(1), reel 86; Gilbert Chalmers, vol. 97(2), reel 96; Daniel Manson, vol. 131(2),

reel 133; John Wyatt, vol. 132(2), reel 134; Robert Wells, reel 124, vol. 123; Thomas Harper, vol. 119(2); John Fisher, reel 129, vol. 127(2)-128(1); Robert Beard, James Begbie, Samuel Bonsall, vol. 25(2), Bundle 125, Loyalist Claims, LOC. See also Commissioners of Forfeited Estates, Commissioners of Forfeited Estates account book, 1782–1783, 34/405, SCHS.

15. *South Carolina Gazette and General Advertiser,* 8 July 1784; Testimony of Violetta Wyatt, case of Wyatt vs. Richardson, Chancery Court Records, bundle 10, Box 1, 1797, SCDAH. See also Commissioners of Forfeited Estates, Commissioners of Forfeited Estates account book, 1782–1783, 34/405, SCHS.

16. I find highly significant the fact that it was in 1784, following his split with the Charleston radicals, that Gadsden made his comment that South Carolina had "lost the harmony we were famous for." This perhaps suggests that his views were more linked with his personal situation in Low Country politics than with a realistic assessment of the level of harmony that had existed before the Revolution, when he had been a leading member of the radical faction.

17. As quoted in Nadelhaft, *Disorders of War,* 107.

18. This section draws heavily on the detailed account of the "Charleston opposition" provided in Nadelhaft, *Disorders of War,* 105–24.

19. In-depth accounts of this episode occur in Walsh, *Charleston's Sons of Liberty,* 119–20, and Nadelhaft, *Disorders of War,* 113–17. Pauline Maier also discusses this period of politics in South Carolina, but does not connect the Gillon faction to the urban middling sorts and their civic agenda. See Maier, "The Charleston Mob," 188–96. On a separate note, although gendered language does not seem to have played a large role in Low Country radical Whig ideology, it was a feature of this account of the disagreement between Captain Thompson and John Rutledge, and corresponds with a strand of rhetoric that Kathleen Wilson has identified in British urban radical politics. See Wilson, *Sense of the People,* 219–25.

20. Walsh, *Charleston's Sons of Liberty* 107–23, especially 120–21.

21. Testimony of Violetta Wyatt and George Flagg in the case of Wyatt vs. Richardson, Chancery Court Records, bundle 10, Box 1, 1797, SCDAH.

22. S.v., "Buckle, George," Index of Artisans, MESDA.

23. Company accounts of Wyatt, Richardson, and Richardson, included as evidence in the case of Wyatt vs. Richardson, Chancery Court Records, bundle 10, Box 1, 1797, SCDAH.

24. Testimony of James Allison, included as evidence in the case of Wyatt vs. Richardson, Chancery Court Records, bundle 10, Box 1, 1797, SCDAH.

25. See, for example, board of trustees meeting of 28 April 1786, College of Charleston trustee minutes vol. 1, 1785–1817, CC. The agreement is recorded in the Charleston County Register of Mesne Conveyance, Land Records, misc. part 87, Books R6-S6, 1796–1798, 246–51, SCDAH. For all transactions relating to Cannonborough, see "Cannon, Daniel," Index of Artisans, MESDA. The subsequent transformation of Cannonborough into a rich suburb is discussed in Poston, *Buildings of Charleston,* 617.

26. *Charleston Morning Post and Daily Advertiser,* 23 January 1786.

27. Advertisement of Thomas Bennett, *City Gazette and the Daily Advertiser,* 7 February 1795.

28. See tabular appendix

29. See Haggerty, "Trade and Trading Communities."

30. On the nature of a factor's work in Charleston, see Morgan, "Organization of the Colonial American Rice Trade."

31. See tabular appendix

32. Advertisement of John Speisseger, *Charleston Gazette and Daily Advertiser,* 20 November 1789; advertisement of Charles Stewart, *Charleston Gazette and Daily Advertiser,* 14 May 1795; and advertisement of Thomas Wallace, *Charleston Gazette and Daily Advertiser,* 3 April, 1790. For a discussion of the changing character of Charleston's merchant community during the Revolution, see Goloboy, "Success to Trade."

33. Records of the Charleston Orphan House, Charleston City Archive.

34. For rankings of American cities between 1790 and 1990, see Gibson, "Population of the 100 Largest Cities."

35. These sections on the economy rely heavily on Chaplin, *Anxious Pursuit,* 284–88 and 292–95.

36. For the story of William Ellison's life, see Johnson and Roark, *Black Masters;* Chaplin, *Anxious Pursuit,* 277–329; inventory of Thomas Baas, 18 August 1809, vol. D, 520, SCDAH.

37. See Klein, *Unification of a Slave State,* 276–82.

38. Ibid., 280.

39. Nadelhalft, *Disorders of War,* 23–25.

40. Klein, *Unification of a Slave State,* 259

41. Pease and Pease, *Web of Commerce,* 10 and 40–53.

# Bibliography

### Archival Sources

#### UNITED KINGDOM

*British Library, Manuscript Room*
"A Short Description of South Carolina," George Milligan Johnson, 1765

*British National Archives, London*
Colonial Records, Customs 1, Exports to Carolina from London and Outports, 1735–65
Minutes of the Charleston Board of Police, 1780–82

*National Archives of Scotland, Edinburgh*
Daybook of Alexander Nisbet and John Blackwood, 1721–35
Murray of Murraythwaite Muniments, 1747–63

*National Library of Scotland, Edinburgh*
Letters of Eliza Wilkinson: During the Invasion and Possession of Charleston, S.C., 1780–83

#### UNITED STATES

*Charleston City Archive*
Minutes of the Charleston Orphan House, 1790–1864

*Charleston County Public Library*
Charleston City Directory, 1782, 1790
Charleston County Wills, Inventories, and Miscellaneous Records, 1671–1807 (Works Progress Administration transcripts)

*Charleston Library Society*
Daybook of Thomas Elfe, 1765–75

*Charleston Museum*
Daybook of Nicholas de Longuemare, 1703–11

*Library Company of Philadelphia*
Letterbook of John Stevens, 1768–1770

*Library of Congress, Washington, DC*
Records of the Commission Appointed to Enquire into the Losses of American Loyalists (Great Britain), 1784–1790

*Museum of Early Southern Decorative Arts (MESDA), Winston-Salem, NC*
Index of Southern Artists and Artisans, entries for Charleston, SC, 1660–1800
Letterbook of Peter Manigault, 1763–73, transcribed by Maurice A. Crowse

*Newport Historical Society, Newport, RI*
Aaron Lopez papers, , 1764–67, box 650, folder 622

*New York Public Library, New York City*
Letterbook of William Wilson, 1757–60
Samuel and John Galloway Papers, 1754–64

*Special Collections of the Robert Scott Small Library, College of Charleston*
Account book of Henry Laurens, 1766–73
Trustee Minutes of the College of Charleston, Volume 1, 1785–1817

*South Carolina Department of Archives and History, Columbia, SC*
Chancery Court records, 1797
Charleston County Grand Jury Presentments, 1770–76
McCrady plat collection
Miscellaneous petitions to the South Carolina Legislature
South Carolina Judgment Rolls, 1730–1800
Journal of the Commissioner of Fortifications, 1755–64
Journal of the Public Accounts, Records of the Public Treasurers of South Carolina, Ledger A, 1759–68
Records of the South Carolina Treasury, Public Ledgers, 1775–77 and 1777–80

*South Carolina Historical Society, Charleston, SC*
Account book of James Laurens, 1772–79
Baker Family documents series, 1700—ca. 1935
Bills of the Commissioners for St. Michael's Church, 1751–63
Commissioners of Forfeited Estates account book, 1782–83
Daybook of Alexander Crawford, 1785–95
Daybook of James Poyas, 1764–66
Elizabeth Sindrey estate account book, 1705–21
Expense of building Mrs. Ann Middleton's house, 1799–1800
Isaac Hayne ledger, 1765–81
List of initial buyers of Charleston Grand Modell lots
Receipt book of Isaac Motte & Co., 1768–1815
Pinckney Family Papers, 1694–1847: receipts of Rawlins Lowndes
Records of the Circular Congregational Church, account ledger, 1777–1806
Vestry Minutes of St. Michael's Parish, 1758–97

*South Caroliniana Library, Columbia, SC*
Account book and letterbook of William Ancrum, 1776–80
Papers of Charles Pinckney, 1737–57
Records of the Fellowship Society, 1766–1800
Vestry Minutes of St. Philip's Parish (Works Progress Administration transcript)

*Southern Historical Collections, Chapel-Hill, NC*
Letterbook of Josiah Smith Jr., 1771–84

## Newspapers and Periodicals

*Caledonian Mercury*
*Charleston Gazette and Daily Advertiser,* 1792–1800
*City Gazette, or the Daily Advertiser,* Charleston, 1787–92
*Edinburgh Advertiser*
*The Gentleman's Magazine and Historical Chronicle,* London, 1731–1907
*Georgia Gazette,* Savannah, 1763–76.
*South Carolina Gazette,* Charleston, 1732–75.
*South Carolina Gazette and Country Journal,* Charleston, 1765–75
*South Carolina Gazette and General Advertiser,* Charleston, 1783–84.
*South Carolina Weekly Gazette,* Charleston, 1758–64.
*South Carolina and American General Gazette,* Charleston, 1764–81

## Other Sources

Anzilotti, Cara. "Autonomy and the Female Planter in Colonial South Carolina." *Journal of Southern History* 63 (1997): 239–68.

Appleby, Joyce. "The Social Consequence of American Revolutionary Ideals in the Early Republic." In *The Middling Sorts: Explorations in the History of the American Middle Class,* edited by Burton J. Bledstein and Robert D. Johnston, 31–49. New York: Routledge, 2001.

———. "The Vexed Story of Capitalism Told by American Historians." *Journal of the Early Republic* 21 (Spring 2001): 1–18.

Armitage, David. "Three Concepts of Atlantic History." In *The British Atlantic World, 1500–1800,* edited by David Armitage and Michael J. Braddick, 11–30. Basingstoke: Macmillan, 2002.

Bailyn, Bernard. *The Ideological Origins of the American Revolution.* Cambridge, MA: Belknap Press, 1967.

Barry, Jonathan. "Bourgeois Collectivism? Urban Association and the Middling Sort." In *The Middling Sort of People: Culture, Society, and Politics in England, 1550–1800,* edited by Jonathan Barry and Christopher Brooks, 84–113. Basingstoke: MacMillan, 1994.

———. "The Press and the Politics of Culture in Bristol, 1660–1775." In *Culture, Politics and Society in Britain, 1660–1800,* edited by Jeremy Black and Jeremy Gregory, 49–81. Manchester, U.K.: Manchester University Press, 1991.

Barry, Jonathan, and Christopher Brooks, eds. *The Middling Sort of People: Culture, Society, and Politics in England, 1550–1800.* Basingstoke: MacMillan, 1994.

Baumgarten, Linda. *What Clothes Reveal: The Language of Clothing in Colonial and Federal America.* New Haven, CT: Yale University Press, 2002.

Bebbington, D. W. *Evangelicalism in Modern Britain: A History from the 1730s to the 1980s.* London: Routledge, 1989.

Beeman, Richard. "Deference, Republicanism, and the Emergence of Popular Politics in Eighteenth-Century America." *William and Mary Quarterly,* 3rd ser., 49 (1992): 401–30.

Berg, Maxine. "Small Producer Capitalism in Eighteenth-Century England." *Business History* 35 (1993): 17–40.

———. "Women's Work, Mechanization, and the Early Phases of the Industrialization in

England." In *The Historical Meanings of Work*, edited by P. Joyce, 64–98. Cambridge: Cambridge University Press, 1987.

Berlin, Ira. *Many Thousands Gone: The First Two Centuries of Slavery in North America.* Cambridge, MA: Harvard University Press, 1998.

Berry, Helen. "Polite Consumption: Shopping in Eighteenth-Century England." *Royal Historical Society Transactions* 12 (2002): 375–95.

———. "Promoting Taste in the Provincial Press: National and Local Culture in Eighteenth-Century Newcastle upon Tyne." *British Journal for Eighteenth-Century Studies* 25 (2002): 1–17.

Bielinski, Stefan. "A Middling Sort: Artisans and Tradesmen in Colonial Albany." *New York History* 73 (1992): 261–90.

Blumin, Stuart M. *The Emergence of the Middle Class: Social Experience in the American City, 1760–1900.* Cambridge: Cambridge University Press, 1989.

Borsay, Peter. *The English Urban Renaissance: Culture and Society in the Provincial Town, 1660–1770.* Oxford: Oxford University Press, 1989.

———. "The Landed Elite and Provincial Towns in Britain, 1660–1800." *The Georgian Group Journal* 13 (2003): 281–94.

Braudel, Fernand. *The Structures of Everyday Life: The Limits of the Possible.* New York: Harper and Row, 1981.

Breen, T. H. *Marketplace of the Revolution.* New York: Oxford University Press, 2004.

———. *Tobacco Culture: The Mentality of the Great Tidewater Planters on the Eve of the Revolution.* Princeton, NJ: Princeton University Press, 1985.

Brewer, John, Neil McKendrick, and J. H. Plumb. *The Birth of a Consumer Society: The Commercialization of Eighteenth-Century England.* Bloomington: Indiana University Press, 1982.

Bridenbaugh, Carl. *Cities in Revolt: Urban Life in America, 1743–1776.* New York: Alfred A. Knopf, 1955.

———. *The Colonial Craftsman.* Mineola, NY: Dover, 1990.

———, ed. *Gentleman's Progress: The Itinerarium of Dr. Alexander Hamilton, 1744.* Pittsburgh: University of Pittsburgh Press, 1992.

Brown, Richard. *The South Carolina Regulators.* Cambridge, MA: Belknap Press, 1963.

Brown, Robert E. *Middle Class Democracy in Massachusetts.* Ithaca, NY: Cornell University Press, 1955.

Bullock, Steven C. "A Mumper among the Gentle: Tom Bell, Colonial Confidence Man." *William and Mary Quarterly,* 3rd ser., 55 (1998): 231–58.

Burnard, Trevor. *Creole Gentlemen: The Maryland Elite, 1691–1776.* New York: Routledge, 2002.

———. "'The Grand Mart of the Island': Kingston, Jamaica, in the Mid-Eighteenth Century and the Question of Urbanisation in Plantation Societies." In *A History of Jamaica, from Indigenous Settlement to the Present,* edited by Kathleen Monteith and Glen Richards, 225–41. Kingston: University of the West Indies Press, 2002.

Burton, E. Milby. *Charleston Furniture, 1700–1825.* Columbia: University of South Carolina Press, 1955.

Bushman, Richard L. *The Refinement of America: Persons, Houses, Cities.* New York: Vintage, 1992.

——. "Shopping and Advertising in Colonial American." In *Of Consuming Interests: The Style of Life in the Eighteenth Century*, edited by Cary Carson, Ronald Hoffman, and Peter J. Albert, 233–52. Charlottesville: University Press of Virginia, 1994.

Butler, Jon. *Becoming America: The Revolution before 1776*. New Haven, CT: Yale University Press, 2000.

Campbell, R. *The London Tradesman*. London, 1747.

Carp, Benjamin L. "Fire of Liberty: Firefighters, Urban Voluntary Culture, and the Revolutionary Movement." *William and Mary Quarterly*, 3rd ser., 58 (2001): 781–818.

——. *Rebels Rising: Cities and the American Revolution*. New York: Oxford University Press, 2007.

Carr, Lois Green, and Lorena S. Walsh. "The Planter's Wife: The Experience of White Women in Seventeenth-Century Maryland." *William and Mary Quarterly*, 3rd ser., 34 (1977): 542–71.

Carson, Cary, Ronald Hoffman, and Peter J. Albert, eds. *Of Consuming Interests: The Style of Life in the Eighteenth Century*. Charlottesville: University Press of Virginia, 1994.

Chalklin, C. W. *The Provincial Towns of Georgian England: A Study of the Building Process, 1740–1820*. London: Edward Arnold, 1974.

Chaplin, Joyce E. *An Anxious Pursuit: Agricultural Innovation and Modernity in the Lower South, 1730–1815*. Chapel Hill: University of North Carolina Press, 1993.

"Charter for the Province of Pennsylvania—1681." In *Sources and Documents of United States Constitutions*, edited by William F. Swindler, 8:255–62. Dobbs Ferry, NY, 1979. Available online at Avalon Project: Documents in Law, History, and Diplomacy, http://avalon.law.yale.edu/17th_century/pa01.asp.

Clark, Gregory. "Shelter from the Storm: Housing and the Industrial Revolution, 1550–1909." *Journal of Economic History* 62 (2002): 489–511.

Clark, Peter. *British Clubs and Societies, 1580–1800: The Origins of an Associational World*. Oxford: Oxford University Press, 2000.

——, ed. *The Cambridge Urban History of Britain*. Vol. 2, *1540–1840*. Cambridge: Cambridge University Press, 2000.

Clark, Peter, and R. A. Houston. "Culture and Leisure, 1700–1840." In *The Cambridge Urban History of Britain*, edited by Peter Clark, 2:575–614. Cambridge: Cambridge University Press, 2000.

Clowse, Converse. *Economic Beginnings in Colonial South Carolina, 1670–1730*. Columbia: University of South Carolina Press, 1971.

——. *Measuring Charleston's Overseas Commerce, 1717–1767: Statistics from the Port's Naval Lists*. Washington, DC: University Press of America, 1981.

Cobau, Judith. "The Precarious Life of Thomas Pike, a Colonial Dancing Master in Charleston and Philadelphia." *Dance Quarterly* 17 (1994): 229–62.

Coclanis, Peter, ed. *The Atlantic Economy during the Seventeenth and Eighteenth Centuries: Organization, Operation, Practice, and Personnel*. Columbia: University of South Carolina Press, 2005.

——. *The Shadow of a Dream: Economic Life and Death in the South Carolina Low Country, 1670–1920*. New York: Oxford University Press, 1989.

——. "The Sociology of Architecture in Colonial Charleston: Pattern and Process in an Eighteenth-Century Southern City." *Journal of Social History* 18 (1985): 607–23.

Cohen, Hennig, ed. "Four Letters from Peter Timothy, 1755, 1768, 1771." *South Carolina Historical Magazine* 55 (1954): 160–65.

Cohen, Patricia Cline. "Reckoning with Commerce: Numeracy in Eighteenth Century America." In *Consumption and the World of Goods*, edited by John Brewer and Roy Porter, 320–34. New York: Routledge, 1993.

Cooper, David, ed. *The Statutes-at-Large of South Carolina*. Vol. 2. Columbia: A. S. Johnston, 1841.

Corfield, P. J. *The Impact of English Towns, 1700–1800*. Oxford: Oxford University Press, 1982.

DalLago, Enrico. "The City as Social Display: Landed Elites and Urban Images in Charleston and Palermo." *Journal of Historical Sociology* 14 (2001): 374–96.

Daniels, Christine. "Wanted: A Blacksmith Who Understands Plantation Work: Artisans in Maryland, 1700–1810." *William and Mary Quarterly*, 3rd ser., 50 (1993): 743–67.

Dantas, Mariana L. R. "Black Townsmen: A Comparative Study of Persons of African Origin and Descent in Slavery and Freedom in Baltimore, Maryland, and Sabara, Minas Gerais, 1750–1810." PhD diss., Johns Hopkins University, Baltimore, 2004.

Davidoff, Leonore, and Catherine Hall. *Family Fortunes: Men and Women of the English Middle Class, 1780–1850*. 2nd ed. London: Routledge, 1992.

D'Cruze, Shani. "Middling Sorts in Eighteenth Century Colchester: Independence, Social Relations, and the Community Broker." In *The Middling Sort of People: Culture, Society, and Politics in England, 1550–1800*, edited by Jonathan Barry and Christopher Brooks, 181–207. Basingstoke: Palgrave-Macmillan, 1994.

"Deference or Defiance in Eighteenth-Century America? A Round Table." *Journal of American History* 85 (June 1998): 13–97.

Defoe, Daniel. *The Complete English Tradesman*. London, 1726. Edinburgh 1839 edition accessed online at http://www.gutenberg.org/etext/14444.

———. *A Tour Thro' the Whole Island of Great Britain*. London, 1725.

de Vries, Jan. "The Industrial Revolution and the Industrious Revolution." Papers presented at the 53rd Annual Meeting of the Economic History Association. *Journal of Economic History* 54 (June 1994): 249–70.

Dixon, Caroline Wyche. "The Miles Brewton House: Ezra Waite's Architectural Books and Other Possible Design Sources." *South Carolina Historical Magazine* 82 (1981): 118–43.

Doerflinger, Thomas. *A Vigorous Spirit of Enterprise: Merchants and Economic Development in Revolutionary Philadelphia*. Chapel Hill: University of North Carolina Press, 1986.

Downes, Kerry. *Christopher Wren*. London: Allen Lane, 1971.

Drayton, William Henry. *The Letters of Freeman, Etc.: Essays on the Nonimportation Movement in South Carolina*. Collected by William Henry Drayton Weir, edited with an introduction and notes by Robert M. Weir. Columbia: University of South Carolina Press, 1977.

Earle, Carville. *The Evolution of a Tidewater Settlement System: All Hallow's Parish, Maryland, 1650–1783*. Chicago: University of Chicago Press, 1975.

Earle, Carville, and Ronald Hoffman. "Urban Development in the Eighteenth-Century South." *Perspectives in American History* 10 (1976): 7–78.

Earle, Peter. *The Making of the English Middle Class: Business, Society, and Family Life in London, 1660–1730.* Berkeley: University of California Press, 1989.

Edelson, S. Max. "Affiliation without Affinity: Skilled Slaves in Eighteenth-Century South Carolina." In *Money, Trade, and Power: The Evolution of South Carolina's Plantation Society,* edited by Jack P. Greene, Randy J. Sparks, and Rosemary Brana-Shute, 217–55. Columbia: University of South Carolina Press, 2001.

———. *Plantation Enterprise in Colonial South Carolina.* Cambridge, MA: Harvard University Press, 2006.

———. "Planting the Low Country: Agricultural Experience and Economic Enterprise in the Lower South, 1695–1785." PhD diss., Johns Hopkins University, Baltimore, 1999.

Edgar, Walter B., and N. Louise Bailey, eds. *Biographical Dictionary of the South Carolina House of Representatives.* Vol. 2, *The Commons House of Assembly, 1692–1775.* Columbia: University of South Carolina Press, 1977.

Ernst, Joseph A., and H. Roy Merrens. "Camden's Turrets Pierce the Skies! The Urban Process in the Southern Colonies during the Eighteenth Century." *William and Mary Quarterly,* 3rd ser., 30 (1973): 549–74.

Estes, Rosemary Niner. "Daniel Cannon: A Revolutionary 'Mechanick' in Charleston." *Journal of Early Southern Decorative Arts* 9 (1983): 1–31.

Evelyn, John. *The Diary of John Evelyn.* Edited by John Bowle. Oxford: Oxford University Press, 1983.

Farmer, Charles J. "Persistence of Country Trade: The Failure of Towns to Develop in Southside Virginia during the Eighteenth Century." *Journal of Historical Geography* 14 (1988): 331–41.

*The Federal and State Constitutions, Colonial Charters, and Other Organic Laws of the States, Territories, and Colonies Now or Heretofore Forming the United States of America.* Compiled and edited under the act of Congress of June 30, 1906 by Francis Newton Thorpe. Washington, DC: Government Printing Office, 1909.

Frey, Sylvia. *Water from the Rock: Black Resistance in a Revolutionary Age.* Princeton, NJ: Princeton University Press, 1991.

"The Fundamental Constitutions of Carolina: March 1, 1669." Available online at the Avalon Project: Documents in Law, History, and Diplomacy. http://avalon.law.yale.edu/17th_century/nc05.asp.

"Fundamental Orders of 1639." [Connecticut.] In *Documentary Source Book of American History, 1606–1898,* by William MacDonald, 36–38. New York: Macmillan, 1908. Available online at the Avalon Project: Documents in Law, History, and Diplomacy. http://avalon.law.yale.edu/17th_century/order.asp/.

Gallay, Allan. *The Formation of a Planter Elite: Jonathan Bryan and the Southern Colonial Frontier.* Athens: University of Georgia Press, 1989.

———. "Jonathan Bryan's Plantation Empire: Land, Politics, and the Formation of a Ruling Class in Colonial Georgia." *William and Mary Quarterly,* 3rd ser., 45 (1988): 253–79.

———. "The Origins of Slaveholders' Paternalism: George Whitefield, the Bryan Family, and the Great Awakening in the South." *Journal of Southern History* 53 (1987): 369–94.

Garden, Alexander. *A brief account of the deluded Dutartres, extracted from a sermo[n] preached by the Rev. Mr. Alexander Garden A.M., at Charlestown, in South-Carolina.* New-Haven, 1762.

———. *Regeneration and the testimony of the spirit: Being the substance of two sermons lately preached in the Parish Church of St. Philip, Charles-town, in South-Carolina: Occasioned by some erroneous notions of certain men who call themselves Methodists.* Boston, 1741.

———. *Six letters to the Rev. Mr. George Whitefield.* Boston, 1740.

Genovese, Elizabeth Fox. *Within the Plantation Household: Black and White Women of the Old South.* Chapel Hill: University of North Carolina Press, 1988.

Gilbert, A. D. *Religion and Society in Industrial England: Church, Chapel, and Social Change, 1740–1914.* London: Longman, 1976.

Gilje, Paul A. *Liberty on the Waterfront: American Maritime Culture in the Age of Revolution.* Philadelphia: University of Pennsylvania Press, 2004.

Goloboy, Jennifer. "'Success to Trade': Charleston's Merchants in the Revolutionary Era." PhD diss., Harvard University, 2003.

Great Britain, and Danby Pickering. *The Statutes at Large from the Twelfth Year of King Charles II to the Last Year of King James II, Inclusive, to Which is Prefixed, Table Containing the Titles of All the Statutes during that Period.* Vol. 8 of *The Statutes at Large, from Magna Charta to the End of the 11th Parliament of Great Britain, [1225]-1761.* Cambridge, 1763.

Greene, Jack P. *Imperatives, Behaviors, Identities: Essays in Early American Cultural History.* Charlottesville: University Press of Virginia, 1992.

———. *Pursuits of Happiness: The Social Development of Early Modern British Colonies and the Formation of American Culture.* Chapel Hill: University of North Carolina Press, 1988.

———. *The Quest for Power: The Lower Houses of Assembly in the Southern Royal Colonies, 1689–1776.* Chapel Hill: University of North Carolina Press, 1963.

———. "Search for Identity: An Interpretation of the Meanings of Selected Patterns of Social Response in Eighteenth-Century America." *Journal of Social History* 3 (1969–70): 189–220.

Greene, Jack P., Rosemary Brana-Shute, and Randy J. Sparks, eds. *Money, Trade, and Power: The Evolution of South Carolina's Plantation Society.* Columbia: University of South Carolina Press, 2001.

Haan, Richard L. "'The Trade do's not Flourish as Formerly': The Ecological Origins of the Yamassee War of 1715." *Ethnohistory* 28 (1982): 341–58.

Haggerty, Sheryllynne. "Trade and Trading Communities in the Eighteenth-Century Atlantic: Liverpool and Philadelphia, 1760–1810." PhD diss., Liverpool University, 2002.

———. *The British Atlantic Trading Community, 1760–1810: Men, Women, and the Distribution of Goods.* Leiden: Brill, 2006.

Haley, K. H. D. *The First Earl of Shaftesbury.* Oxford: Oxford University Press, 1968.

Hancock, David. *Citizens of the World: London Merchants and the Integration of the British Atlantic Community, 1735–1785.* Cambridge: Cambridge University Press, 1997.

———. "Rethinking the Economy of British America." In *The Economy of Early America: Historical Perspectives and New Directions,* edited by Cathy Matson, 71–106. University Park: Pennsylvania State University Press, 2006.

Hart, Oliver. *Dancing Exploded: A sermon, shewing the unlawfulness, sinfulness, and bad consequences of balls, assemblies, and dances in general. Delivered in Charlestown, South-Carolina, March 22, 1778.* Charlestown, 1778.

Hartz, Louis. *The Liberal Tradition in America.* New York: Harcourt, Brace and World, 1955.

Hatfield, April L. *Atlantic Virginia: Intercolonial Relations in the Seventeenth Century.* Philadelphia: University of Pennsylvania Press, 2004.

Hemphill, C. Dallett. *Bowing to Necessities: A History of Manners in America, 1620–1860.* New York: Oxford University Press, 1999.

———. "Manners and Class in the Revolutionary Era: A Transatlantic Comparison." *William and Mary Quarterly,* 3rd ser., 63 (2006): 345–72.

Henretta, James. "Families and Farms: Mentalité in Pre-Industrial America." *William and Mary Quarterly,* 3rd ser., 35 (1978): 3–32.

———. *Salutary Neglect: Colonial Administration under the Duke of Newcastle.* Princeton, NJ: Princeton University Press, 1972.

Herman, Bernard L. "The Charleston Single House." In *The Buildings of Charleston: A Guide to the City's Architecture,* edited by Jonathan H. Poston, 37–41. Columbia: University of South Carolina Press, 1997.

———. "Slave and Servant Housing in Charleston, 1770–1820." *Historical Archaeology* 33 (1999): 88–101.

———. *Town House: Architecture and Material Life in the Early American City, 1780–1830.* Chapel Hill: University of North Carolina Press, 2005.

Hewatt, Alexander. *An Historical Account of the Rise and Progress of the Colonies of South Carolina and Georgia.* London: A. Donaldson, 1779.

Hirsch, Arthur Henry. *The Huguenots of Colonial South Carolina.* With a new introduction by Bertrand van Ruymbeke. 2nd ed. Columbia: University of South Carolina Press, 1999.

Holton, Woody. *Forced Founders: Indians, Debtors, Slaves, and the Making of the American Revolution in Virginia.* Chapel Hill: University of North Carolina Press, 1999.

Hood, Adrienne. *The Weaver's Craft: Cloth, Commerce, and Industry in Early Pennsylvania.* Philadelphia: University of Pennsylvania Press, 2003.

Hudson, Pat. *The Genesis of Industrial Capital: A Study of the West Riding Wool Textile Industry, c. 1750–1850.* Cambridge: Cambridge University Press, 1986.

Humphrey, Samuel A. *Thomas Elfe, Cabinetmaker.* Charleston, SC: Wyrick and Co., 1996.

Hunt, Margaret. *The Middling Sort: Commerce, Gender, and the Family in England, 1680–1780.* Berkeley: University of California Press, 1996.

Hunter, Phyllis Whitman. *Purchasing Identity in the Atlantic World: Massachusetts Merchants, 1670–1780.* Ithaca, NY: Cornell University Press, 2001.

Innes, Joanna, and Nicholas Rogers. "Politics and Government, 1700–1840." In *The Cambridge Urban History of Britain,* vol. 2, *1540–1840,* edited by Peter Clark, 529–75. Cambridge: Cambridge University Press, 2000.

Innes, Stephen. *Creating the Commonwealth: The Economic Culture of Puritan New England.* New York: W. W. Norton, 1995.

———, ed. *Work and Labor in Early America.* Chapel Hill: University of North Carolina Press, 1988.

Isaac, Rhys. *The Transformation of Virginia, 1740–1790.* Chapel Hill: University of North Carolina Press, 1982.

Johnson, Michael P., and James L. Roark. *Black Masters: A Free Family in the Old South.* New York: W. W. Norton, 1984.

Johnson, Samuel. *A Dictionary of the English Language.* London, 1755.

Jones, Alice Hanson. *The Wealth of a Nation To Be: The American Colonies on the Eve of the Revolution.* New York: Columbia University Press, 1980.

Jones, E. L., and M. E. Falkus. "Urban Improvement and the English Economy in the 17th and 18th Centuries." *Research in Economic History* 4 (1979): 199–248.

"Journal of Josiah Quincy, Jr., 1773." *Proceedings of the Massachusetts Historical Society,* 3rd ser., 49 (1916), 424–81.

Kierner, Cynthia A. *Beyond the Household: Women's Place in the Early South, 1700–1835.* Ithaca, NY: Cornell University Press, 1998.

———. "Hospitality, Sociability, and Gender in the Southern Colonies." *Journal of Southern History* 62 (1996): 449–80.

———. *Traders and Gentlefolk: The Livingstons of New York, 1675–1790.* Ithaca, NY: Cornell University Press, 1992.

King, Boston. "Memoirs of the Life of Boston King, A Black Preacher." *The Methodist Magazine,* March—June 1798. Available at http://antislavery.eserver.org/narratives/boston_king/.

Kirkham, P. A. "Samuel Norman: A Study of an Eighteenth-Century Craftsman." *Burlington Magazine* 4 (1972): 501–13.

Klein, Rachel N. *Unification of a Slave State: The Rise of the Planter Class in the South Carolina Backcountry, 1760–1808.* Chapel Hill: University of North Carolina Press, 1990.

Kupperman, Karen Ordahl. *The Jamestown Project.* Cambridge, MA: Harvard University Press, 2007.

Landsman, Ned. *From Colonials to Provincials; American Thought and Culture, 1680–1760.* New York: Twayne, 1997.

Langford, Paul. *A Polite and Commercial People: England, 1727–1783.* Oxford: Oxford University Press, 1989.

Langley, Batty. *The Builder's Jewel, or, The Youth's Instructor, and Workman's Remembrancer.* London, 1741.

Langley, Clara A., ed. *South Carolina Deed Abstracts, 1719–1772.* 4 vols. Easley, SC: Southern Historical Press, 1983.

Langton, John. "Urban Growth and Economic Change: From the Late Seventeenth Century to 1841." In *The Cambridge Urban History of Britain,* Vol. 2, *1540–1840,* edited by Peter Clark, 453–90. Cambridge: Cambridge University Press, 2000.

Latham, Robert, and Williams Matthews, eds. *The Diary of Samuel Pepys: A New and Complete Transcription.* Vol. 7, *1666.* London: Bell, 1972.

Laurens, Henry. *The Papers of Henry Laurens.* Edited by Philip M. Hamer. 16 vols. Columbia: University of South Carolina Press, [1968]—2003.

Lemire, Beverly. *Fashion's Favorite: The Cotton Trade and the Consumer in Britain, 1660–1800.* Oxford: Oxford University Press, 1991.

———. "The Theft of Clothes and Popular Consumerism in Early Modern England." *Journal of Social History* 24 (1990): 255–76.

Little, Thomas J. "'Adding to the Church Such as Shall be Saved': The Growth in Influence of Evangelicalism in Colonial South Carolina, 1740–1775." In *Money, Trade, and Power: The Evolution of South Carolina's Plantation Society,* edited by Jack P. Greene, Randy J. Sparks, and Rosemary Brana-Shute, 363–82. Columbia: University of South Carolina Press, 2001.

Littlefield, Daniel C. *Rice and Slaves: Ethnicity and the Slave Trade in Colonial South Carolina.* Urbana: University of Illinois Press, 1981.

———. "The Slave Trade to Colonial South Carolina: A Profile." *South Carolina Historical Magazine* 91 (1990): 68–99.

Lockridge, Kenneth. "Land, Population, and the Evolution of New England Society, 1630–1790." *Past and Present* 39 (1968): 62–80.

———. *A New England Town: The First Hundred Years: Dedham, Massachusetts, 1636–1736.* Expanded ed. New York: W. W. Norton, 1985.

Lounsbury, Carl. *From Statehouse to Courthouse: An Architectural History of South Carolina's Colonial Capitol and Charleston County Courthouse.* Columbia: University of South Carolina Press, 2001.

Maier, Pauline. "The Charleston Mob and the Evolution of Popular Politics in Revolutionary South Carolina, 1765–1784." *Perspectives in American History* 4 (1970): 173–96.

———. *From Resistance to Revolution: Colonial Radicals and the Development of American Opposition to Britain.* New York: W. W. Norton, 1972.

Mancall, Peter C., Joshua L. Rosenbloom, and Thomas Weiss. "Indians and the Economy of Eighteenth-Century Carolina." In *The Atlantic Economy during the Seventeenth and Eighteenth Centuries: Organization, Operation, Practice, and Personnel,* edited by Peter Coclanis, 297–322. Columbia: University of South Carolina, 2005.

Martin, John Frederick. *Profits in the Wilderness: Entrepreneurship and the Founding of Towns in New England in the Seventeenth Century.* Chapel Hill: University of North Carolina Press, 1991.

Martin, Jonathan D. *Divided Mastery: Slave Hiring in the American South.* Cambridge, MA: Harvard University Press, 2004.

Matson, Cathy, ed. *The Economy of Early America: Historical Perspectives and New Directions.* University Park: Pennsylvania State University Press, 2006.

———. *Merchants and Empire: Trading in Colonial New York.* Baltimore: Johns Hopkins University Press, 1998.

McClain, Molly, and Alessa Ellefson. "A Letter from Carolina, 1688: French Huguenots in the New World." *William and Mary Quarterly,* 3rd ser., 69 (2007): 377–94.

McCrady, Edward. *The History of South Carolina under the Royal Government, 1719–1776.* New York: The Macmillan Company; London: Macmillan & Co., Ltd., 1899.

McCurry, Stephanie. *Masters of Small Worlds: Yeoman Households, Gender Relations, and the Political Culture of the Antebellum South Carolina Low Country.* New York: Oxford University Press, 1995.

McCusker John J., and Russell R. Menard. *The Economy of British America, 1607–1789, with Supplementary Bibliography.* Rev. ed. Chapel Hill: University of North Carolina Press, 1991.

———. *Rum and the American Revolution: The Rum Trade and the Balance of Payment of the Thirteen Continental Colonies.* New York: Garland, 1989.

McDonnell, Michael. *The Politics of War: Race, Class, and Conflict in Revolutionary Virginia.* Chapel Hill: University of North Carolina Press, 2007.

McInnes, Angus. "The Emergence of a Leisure Town: Shrewsbury, 1660–1760." *Past and Present* 120 (1998): 53–87.

McKellar, Elizabeth. *The Birth of Modern London: The Development and Design of the City, 1660–1720.* Manchester: Manchester University Press, 1999.

McKendrick, Neil. "Josiah Wedgwood: An Eighteenth-century Entrepreneur in Salesman-ship and Marketing Techniques." *Economic History Review* 12 (1960): 408–33.

Menard, Russell R. "Economic and Social Development of the South." In *Cambridge Economic History of the United States,* vol. 1, *The Colonial Era,* edited by Stanley L. Engerman and Robert E. Gallman, 249–95. New York: Cambridge University Press, 1996.

———. "Financing the Low Country Export Boom: Capital and Growth in Early South Carolina." *William and Mary Quarterly,* 3rd ser., 51 (1994): 659–76.

———. "From Servants to Slaves: The Transformation of the Chesapeake Labor System." *Southern Studies* 16 (1977): 355–90.

———. "Slavery, Economic Growth, and Revolutionary Ideology in the South Carolina Low-country." In *The Economy of Early America: The Revolutionary Period, 1763–1790,* edited by Ronald Hoffman, John J. McCusker, Russell R. Menard, and Peter J. Albert, 244–74. Charlottesville: University Press of Virginia, 1988.

Menard, Russell R., and David B. Ryden. "South Carolina's Rural Land Market: An Analysis of Property Sales, 1720–1775." *Social Science History* 29 (2005): 599–623.

Mercantini, Jonathan. *Who Shall Rule at Home? The Evolution of South Carolina Political Culture, 1748–1776.* Columbia: University of South Carolina Press, 2007.

Merrell, James H. *The Indians' New World: Catawbas and Their Neighbors from European Contact through the Era of Removal.* Chapel Hill: University of North Carolina Press, 1989.

Merrens, H. Roy, ed. *The Colonial South Carolina Scene.* Columbia: University of South Carolina Press, 1977.

Merrens, H. Roy, and George D. Terry. "Dying in Paradise: Malaria, Mortality, and the Perceptual Environment in Colonial South Carolina." *Journal of Southern History* 50 (1984): 542–46.

Merrill, Michael. "Putting 'Capitalism' in its Place: A Review of the Recent Literature." *William and Mary Quarterly,* 3rd ser., 52 (1995): 315–26.

Micklus, Robert. "'The History of the Tuesday Club': A Mock Jeremiad of the Colonial South." *William and Mary Quarterly,* 3rd ser., 40 (1983): 42–61.

Middleton, Simon. *From Privileges to Rights: Work and Politics in Colonial New York City.* Philadelphia: University of Pennsylvania Press, 2006.

Middleton, Simon, and Billy G. Smith. "Class in Early America: An Introduction." *William and Mary Quarterly,* 3rd Ser., 63 (2006): 211–20.

Migliazzo, Arlin C. "A Tarnished Legacy Revisited: Jean Pierre Purry and the Settlement of the Southern Frontier, 1718–1736." *South Carolina Historical Magazine* 92 (1991): 232–52.

Morgan, Edmund. *American Slavery, American Freedom: The Ordeal of Colonial Virginia.* New York: W. W. Norton, 1975.

Morgan, Kenneth. *Bristol and the Atlantic Trade in the Eighteenth Century.* Cambridge: Cambridge University Press, 1993.

———. "The Organization of the Colonial American Rice Trade." *William and Mary Quarterly,* 3rd ser., 50 (1995): 433–52.

———. "Slave Sales in Colonial Charleston." *English Historical Review* 113 (1998): 905–27.

Morgan, Philip D. "Black Life in Eighteenth-Century Charleston." *Perspectives in American History,* n.s., 1 (1984): 187–232.

———. "Black Society in the Low Country, 1760–1810." In *Slavery and Freedom in the Age of the American Revolution*, edited by Ira Berlin and Ronald Hoffman, 83–142. Charlottesville: University Press of Virginia, 1983.

———. "Conspiracy Scares." *William and Mary Quarterly*, 3rd ser., 59 (2002): 159–167.

———. *Slave Counterpoint: Black Culture in the Eighteenth-Century Chesapeake and Low Country*. Chapel Hill: University of North Carolina Press, 1998.

Morris, Christopher, ed. *The Illustrated Journeys of Celia Fiennes, 1685–c. 1712*. London: Macdonald, 1982.

Morris, Richard B. *Government and Labor in Early America*. New York: Columbia University Press, 1946.

Morris, Thomas D. *Southern Slavery and the Law, 1619–1860*. Chapel Hill: University of South Carolina Press, 1996.

Mowl, Tim, and Brian Earnshaw. *John Wood: Architect of Obsession*. Hersham, Surrey, U.K.: Millstream Press, 1988.

Mui, Hoh Cheung, and Lorna H. Mui. *Shops and Shopkeeping in Eighteenth-Century England*. London: Routledge, 1989.

Mulcahy, Matthew. "The Great Fire of 1740 and the Politics of Disaster Relief in Colonial Charleston." *South Carolina Historical Magazine* 99 (1998): 135–57.

Nadelhaft, Jerome J. *The Disorders of War: The Revolution in South Carolina*. Orono: Maine University Press, 1981.

Nash, Gary B. "Artisans and Politics in Eighteenth-Century Philadelphia." In *The Origins of Anglo-American Radicalism*, edited by Margaret Jacob and James Jacob. Winchester, MA: Allen and Unwin, 1984.

———. *First City: Philadelphia and the Forging of Historical Memory*. Philadelphia: University of Pennsylvania Press, 2001.

———. "The Framing of Government in Pennsylvania: Ideas in Contact with Reality." *William and Mary Quarterly*, 3rd ser., 33 (1966): 183–209.

———. "Poverty and Poor-relief in Pre-Revolutionary Philadelphia." *William and Mary Quarterly*, 3rd ser., 43 (1976): 3–30.

———. *Quakers and Politics: Pennsylvania, 1681–1726*. Princeton, NJ: Princeton University Press, 1968.

———. *Race, Class, and Politics: Essays on American Colonial and Revolutionary Society*. Urbana: University of Illinois Press, 1986.

———. "The Social Evolution of Preindustrial American Cities, 1700–1820." *Journal of Urban History* 13 (1987): 115–45.

———. *The Urban Crucible: Social Change, Political Consciousness, and the Origins of the American Revolution*. Cambridge, MA: Harvard University Press, 1979.

Nash, R. C. "The Organization of Trade and Finance in the Atlantic Economy: Britain and South Carolina, 1670–1775." In *Money, Trade, and Power: The Evolution of South Carolina's Plantation Society*, edited by Jack P. Greene, Randy J. Sparks, and Rosemary Brana-Shute, 74–107. Columbia: University of South Carolina Press, 2001.

———. "South Carolina and the Atlantic Economy in the Late Seventeenth and Eighteenth Century." *Economic History Review* 45 (1992): 677–702.

———. "Urbanization in the Colonial South: Charleston, South Carolina, as a Case Study." *Urban History* 19 (1992): 3–29.

Newell, Margaret E. *From Dependency to Independence: Economic Revolution in Colonial New England.* Ithaca, NY: Cornell University Press, 1998.

Norton, Mary Beth. "The Evolution of White Women's Experience in Early America." *American Historical Review* 89 (1984): 593–619.

O'Brien, Patrick, and Roland Quinault, eds. *The Industrial Revolution and British Society.* Cambridge: Cambridge University Press, 1993.

O'Connor, Ellen Hartigan. "Collaborative Consumption and the Politics of Choice in Early American Port Cities." In *Gender, Taste, and Material Culture in Britain and North America, 1700–1830,* edited by Amanda Vickery and John Styles, 125–50. New Haven, CT: Yale University Press, 2006.

———. "The Measure of the Market: Women's Economic Lives in Charleston, South Carolina, and Newport, Rhode Island, 1750–1820." PhD diss., University of Michigan, 2003.

Olwell, Robert. *Masters, Slaves, and Subjects: The Culture of Power in the South Carolina Low Country, 1740–1790.* Ithaca, NY: Cornell University Press, 1998.

Pearson, Edward. "Planters Full of Money: The Self-Fashioning of the Eighteenth-Century South Carolina Elite." In *Money, Trade, and Power: The Evolution of South Carolina's Plantation Society,* edited by Jack P. Greene, Randy J. Sparks, and Rosemary Brana-Shute, 299–321. Columbia: University of South Carolina Press, 2001.

Pease, Jane H., and William H. Pease. *The Web of Commerce: Private Values and Public Styles in Boston and Charleston, 1828–1853.* New York: Oxford University Press, 1985.

Pencak, William. "Social Structure in Revolutionary Boston: Evidence from the Great Fire of 1760." *Journal of Interdisciplinary History* 10 (1979): 267–78.

Perkins, Edward J. "The Entrepreneurial Spirit in Colonial America: The Foundations of Modern Business History." *Business History Review* 63 (1989): 160–86.

Piker, Joshua. *Okfuskee.* Cambridge, MA: Harvard University Press, 2004.

Pocock, J. G. A. *The Machiavellian Moment: Florentine Political Thought and the Atlantic Republican Tradition.* Princeton, NJ: Princeton University Press, 1975.

Port, M. H., ed. *The Commissions for Building Fifty New Churches: The Minute Books, 1711–1727, a Calendar.* London: London Record Society, 1986.

Poston, Jonathan H., ed. *The Buildings of Charleston: A Guide to the City's Architecture.* Columbia: University of South Carolina Press, 1997.

Price, Jacob M. "Buchanan & Simson, 1759–1763: A Different Kind of Glasgow Firm Trading to the Chesapeake." *William and Mary Quarterly,* 3rd ser., 40 (1983): 3–41.

———. "Economic Functions and the Growth of American Port Towns in the Eighteenth Century." *Perspectives in American History* 8 (1974): 123–86.

———. "The Last Phase of the Virginia-London Consignment Trade: James Buchanan & Co., 1758–1768." *William and Mary Quarterly,* 3rd ser., 43 (1986): 64–98.

Pringle, Robert. *The Letterbook of Robert Pringle.* Edited by Walter B. Edgar. 2 vols. Columbia: University of South Carolina Press, 1972.

Ramsay, David. *The History of South Carolina, from First Settlement in the Year 1670, to the Year 1808.* Charleston: Published by David Longworth for the author, 1809.

Ramsey, William L. "Something Cloudy in their looks": The Origins of the Yamasee War Reconsidered." *Journal of American History* 90 (2003): 44–75.

Richardson, David. "The British Slave Trade to Colonial South Carolina." *Slavery and Abolition* 12 (1991): 125–72.

Rilling, Donna. *Making Houses, Crafting Capitalism: Master Builders in Philadelphia, 1790–1850.* Philadelphia: University of Pennsylvania Press, 1999.

Rock, Howard, and Paul Gilje, eds. *American Artisans: Crafting a Social Identity.* Baltimore: Johns Hopkins University Press, 1995.

Rogers, George C., Jr. *Charleston in the Age of the Pinckneys.* Norman: University of Oklahoma Press, 1980.

Rogers, Nicholas. "The Middling Sort in Eighteenth-Century Politics." In *The Middling Sort of People: Culture, Society, and Politics in England, 1550–1800,* edited by Jonathan Barry and Christopher Brooks, 159–81. London: MacMillan, 1994.

Roper, L. H. *Conceiving Carolina: Proprietors, Planters, and Plots, 1662–1729.* New York: Palgrave, 2004.

———. "The 1701 Act for the Better Ordering of Slaves": Reconsidering the History of Slavery in Proprietary South Carolina." *William and Mary Quarterly,* 3rd ser., 64 (2007): 395–417.

Rozbicki, Michal J. *The Complete Colonial Gentleman: Cultural Legitimacy in Plantation America.* Charlottesville: University Press of Virginia, 1998.

———. "The Curse of Provincialism: Negative Perceptions of Colonial American Plantation Gentry." *Journal of Southern History* 63 (1997): 727–52.

Russo, Jean B. *Free Workers in a Plantation Economy: Talbot County, Maryland, 1690–1759.* New York: Garland, 1989.

Ryan, Mary P. *Cradle of the Middle Class: The Family in Oneida County, New York, 1790–1865.* Cambridge: Cambridge University Press, 1981.

Salinger, Sharon V. *To Serve Well and Faithfully: Labor and Indentured Servitude in Pennsylvania, 1682–1800.* Cambridge: Cambridge University Press, 1987.

Salinger, Sharon V., and Charles Weatherell. "Wealth and Renting in Pre-Revolutionary Philadelphia." *Journal of American History* 71 (1985): 826–40.

Salley, A. S., Jr., ed. *Marriage Notices in the South Carolina Gazette and Its Successors.* Baltimore: Genealogical Publishing Co., 2003.

Salmon, Marylynn. "Women and Property in South Carolina: The Evidence from Marriage Settlements, 1730 to 1830." *William and Mary Quarterly,* 3rd ser., 39 (1982): 655–85.

Saunders, Katherine. "'As regular and fformidable as any such woorke in America': The Walled City of Charles Town." In *Another's Country: Archeological and Historical Perspectives on Cultural Interactions in the Southern Colonies,* edited by J. W. Joseph and Martha Zierden, 198–214. Tuscaloosa: University of Alabama Press, 2002.

Scott, Kenneth. "Sufferers in the Charleston Fire of 1740." *South Carolina Historical Magazine* 64 (1963): 203–11.

Sekora, John. *Luxury: The Concept in Western Thought, Eden to Smollett.* Baltimore: Johns Hopkins University Press, 1977.

Sellers, Charles. *The Market Revolution in Jacksonian America, 1815–1849.* New York: Oxford University Press, 1994.

Sellers, Leila H. *Charleston Business on the Eve of the Revolution.* Chapel Hill: University of North Carolina Press, 1934.

Shammas, Carole. "Anglo-American Household Governance in Comparative Perspective." *William and Mary Quarterly*, 3rd ser., 52 (1995): 104–44.

———. *A History of Household Government in America*. Charlottesville: University of Virginia Press, 2002.

———. *The Pre-Industrial Consumer in Britain and America*. New York: Oxford University Press, 1990.

Shields, David S. "Mean Streets, Mannered Streets: Charleston." In "The Early Cities of the Americas," edited by Gary B. Nash. Special issue, *Common-Place* 3 (2003). Online at *http://www.common-place.org/vol-03/no-04/charleston/*.

———. *Civil Tongues and Polite Letters in British America*. Chapel Hill: University of North Carolina Press, 1997.

Simmonds, Lorna Elaine. "The Afro-Jamaican and the Internal Marketing System: Kingston, 1780–1834." In *Jamaica in Slavery and Freedom: History, Heritage, Culture*, edited by Kathleen Monteith and Glen Richards, 274–90. Mona, Jamaica: University Press of the West Indies, 2002.

Simons, Harriet P., and Albert Simons. "The William Burrows House of Charleston." *Winterthur Portfolio* 3 (1967): 172–203.

Simpson, William. *The Practical Justice of the Peace and Parish Officer of His Majesty's Province of South Carolina*. Charleston: Robert Wells, 1761.

Sirmans, M. Eugene. *South Carolina Politics under the Royal Government, 1729–1776*. Chapel Hill: University of North Carolina Press, 1966.

Smith, Billy G. "Inequality in Late Colonial Philadelphia: A Note on Its Nature and Growth." *William and Mary Quarterly*, 3rd ser., 41 (1984): 629–45.

———. *The Lower Sort: Philadelphia's Laboring People, 1750–1800*. Ithaca, NY: Cornell University Press, 1990.

Smith, Josiah. *The Burning of Sodom with its moral causes: Improv'd in a sermon preach'd at Charlestown, South Carolina, after a most terrible fire, which broke out on Nov 18 1740. And in a very short time laid the fairest and richest parts of town in ashes, and consum'd the most valuable effects of the merchants and inhabitants*. Boston: D. Fowle for Eleazer Phillips in Charlestown, SC, 1741.

Smith, S. D. "Gedney Clarke of Salem and Barbados: Transatlantic Super-Merchant." *New England Quarterly* 76 (2003): 499–551.

———. "The Market for Manufactures in the Thirteen Colonies, 1698–1776." *Economic History Review* 48 (1995): 575–90.

Smollett, Tobias. *The Expedition of Humphry Clinker*. Oxford: Oxford University Press, 1998.

Sobel, Mechal. *The World They Made Together: Black and White Values in Eighteenth-Century Virginia*. Princeton, NJ: Princeton University Press, 1987.

South Carolina. General Assembly. Commons House. *The Journal of the Commons House of Assembly*. Vol. 4, *Sept. 14, 1742–Jan. 27, 1744*. Edited by J. H. Easterby. Columbia: South Carolina Archives Department, 1954.

———. *The Journal of the Commons House of Assembly*. Vol. 10, *23 Apr. 1750–31 Aug. 1751*. Edited by J. H. Easterby. Columbia: Published for the South Carolina Department of Archives and History by the University of South Carolina Press, 1974.

Starr, Rebecca. *A School for Politiks: Commercial Lobbying and Political Culture in Early South Carolina.* Baltimore: Johns Hopkins University Press, 1998.

Steele, Ian K. "The British Parliament and the Atlantic Colonies to 1760: New Approaches to Enduring Questions." *Parliamentary History* 14 (1995): 29–46.

Steen, Carl. "Pottery, Intercolonial Trade, and Revolution: Domestic Earthenwares and the Development of an American Social Identity." *Historical Archeology* 33 (1999): 62–72.

Stobart, Jon. "An Eighteenth-Century Revolution? Investigating Urban Growth in North West England, 1664–1801." *Urban History* 23 (1996): 26–47.

———. "Leisure and Shopping in the Small Towns of Georgian England: A Regional Approach." *Journal of Urban History* 31 (2005): 479–503.

———. "Shopping Streets as Social Space: Leisure, Consumerism, and Improvement in an Eighteenth-Century Town." *Urban History* 25 (1998): 3–21.

Stockes, Melvyn, and Stephen Conway, eds. *The Market Revolution in America: Social, Political, and Religious Expressions, 1800–1880.* Charlottesville: University Press of Virginia, 1996.

Stumpf, Stuart O. "A Case of Arrested Development: Charles' Town's Commercial Life, 1670–1690." *Southern Studies* 20 (1981): 361–77.

———. "South Carolina Importers of General Merchandise, 1735–1764." *South Carolina Historical Magazine* 84 (1983): 1–10.

———. "Trends in Charleston's Interregional Import Trade, 1735–1764." *Southern Studies* 23 (1984): 243–65.

Sturtz, Linda. *Within Her Power: Propertied Women in Colonial Virginia.* New York: Routledge, 2002.

Sugarman, David, and Ronnie Warrington. "Land Law, Citizenship, and the Invention of 'Englishness': The Strange World of the Equity of Redemption." In *Early Modern Conceptions of Property,* edited by John Brewer and Susan Staves, 111–43. New York: Routledge, 1996.

Sung Bok Kim. *Landlord and Tenant in Colonial New York: Manorial Society, 1664–1775.* Chapel Hill: University of North Carolina Press, 1978.

Sweet, Rosemary. *The English Town, 1680–1840: Government, Society, and Culture.* Harlow, U.K.: Pearson Education, 1999.

———. *The Writing of Urban Histories in Eighteenth-Century England.* Oxford: Oxford University Press, 1997.

"A Symposium on Charles Sellers' 'The Market Revolution in Jacksonian America, 1815–1849.'" *Journal of the Early Republic* 12 (1992): 445–76.

Tadmor, Naomi. "The Concept of the Household-Family in Eighteenth-Century England." *Past and Present* 151 (1996): 111–40.

Thompson, E. P. *The Making of the English Working Class.* New York: Vintage, 1966.

Thorp, Daniel B. "Doing Business in the Backcountry: Retail Trade in Colonial Rowan County, North Carolina." *William and Mary Quarterly,* 3rd ser., 48 (1991): 387–408.

Uhlendorf, Bernard A., trans. and ed. *The Siege of Charleston, with an Account of the Province of South Carolina: Diaries and Letters of Hessian Officers from the von Jungkenn Papers in the William L. Clements Library.* Ann Arbor: University of Michigan Press, 1938.

Ulrich, Laurel Thatcher. *Good Wives: Image and Reality in the Lives of Women in Northern New England, 1650–1750*. New York: Vintage, 1991.

United States. Bureau of the Census. *Heads of Families at the First Census of the United States, Taken in the Year 1790. South Carolina*. Washington, DC: Government Printing Office, 1908.

Urdank, Albion M. "The Consumption of Rental Property: Gloucestershire Plebeians and the Market Economy, 1750–1860." *Journal of Interdisciplinary History* 21 (1990): 261–81.

van Ruymbeke, Bertrand. "The Huguenots of Proprietory South Carolina: Patterns of Migration and Integration." In *Money, Trade, and Power: The Evolution of South Carolina's Plantation Society*, edited by Jack P. Greene, Rosemary Brana-Shute, and Randy J. Sparks, 26–48. Columbia: University of South Carolina Press, 2001.

Vickers, Daniel. "Competency and Competition: Economic Culture in Early America." *William and Mary Quarterly*, 3rd ser., 47 (1989): 3–29.

Wade, Richard C. *Slavery in the Cities*. New York: Oxford University Press, 1964.

Waldstreicher, David. *In the Midst of Perpetual Fetes: The Making of American Nationalism, 1776–1820*. Chapel Hill, University of North Carolina Press, 1997.

———. "Reading the Runaways: Self-Fashioning, Print Culture, and Confidence in Slavery in the Eighteenth-Century Mid-Atlantic." *William and Mary Quarterly*, 3rd ser., 56 (1999): 243–72.

Walsh, Claire. "Shops, Shopping, and the Art of Decision Making in Eighteenth-Century England." In *Gender, Taste, and Material Culture in Britain and North America, 1700–1830*, edited by John Styles and Amanda Vickery, 151–78. New Haven, CT: Yale University Press, 2006.

Walsh, Lorena S. "Provisioning Tidewater Towns." *Explorations in Early American Culture* 4 (2000): 46–80.

Walsh, Richard. *Charleston's Sons of Liberty: A Study of the Artisans, 1763–1789*. Columbia: University of South Carolina Press, 1959.

Waterhouse, Richard "The Development of Elite Culture in the Colonial American South: A Study of Charles Town, 1670–1770." *Australian Journal of Politics and History* 28 (1982): 391–404.

———. "Economic Growth and Changing Patterns of Wealth Distribution in Colonial Low Country South Carolina." *South Carolina Historical Magazine* 89 (1988): 203–17.

———. *A New World Elite: The Making of a Merchant and Planter Class in South Carolina, 1670–1770*. New York: Garland, 1989.

Weatherill, Lorna. *Consumer Behaviour and Material Culture in Britain, 1660–1760*. London: Routledge, 1996.

Weir, Robert M. "'The Harmony We Were Famous For': An Interpretation of Pre-Revolutionary South Carolina Politics." *William and Mary Quarterly*, 3rd ser., 26 (1969): 473–501.

———. "Shaftesbury's Darling: British Settlement in the Carolinas at the Close of the Seventeenth Century." In *The Oxford History of the British Empire*, vol. 1, *The Origins of Empire: British Overseas Enterprise to the Close of the Seventeenth Century*, edited by Nicholas P. Canny, 375–97. Oxford: Oxford University Press, 1998.

Welch, Pedro L. V. *Slave Society in the City: Bridgetown, Barbados, 1680–1834*. Kingston, Jamaica: Ian Randle Publishers, 2003.

Wells, Louisa Susanna. *Journal of a Voyage from Charlestown to London.* New York: New York Historical Society, 1906.

Whitefield, George. *George Whitfield's Journals.* Edinburgh: Banner of Truth Trust, 1978.

Wilson, Kathleen. *The Sense of the People: Politics, Culture, and Imperialism in England, 1715–1785.* Cambridge: Cambridge University Press, 1995.

———. "Urban Culture and Political Activism in England: The Example of Voluntary Hospitals." In *The Transformation of Political Culture in Late Eighteenth-Century England and Germany,* edited by Eckhart Hellmuth, 165–84. Oxford: Oxford University Press, 1989.

Wood, Betty. "White Society and the Informal Slave Economies of Lowcountry Georgia, ca. 1763–1830." *Slavery and Abolition* 11 (1990): 313–31.

Wood, Bradford. *This Remote Part of the World: Regional Formation in the Lower Cape Fear, North Carolina, 1725–1775.* Columbia: University of South Carolina Press, 2004.

Wood, Gordon S. *The Radicalism of the American Revolution.* New York: Vintage, 1993.

Wood, Peter H. *Black Majority: Negroes in Colonial South Carolina from 1670 through the Stono Rebellion.* New York: W. W. Norton, 1974.

Wren, Stephen. *Parentalia; or, Memoirs of the Family of the Wrens.* London: Gregg Press, 1965.

Wright, Conrad Edick, and Katheryn P. Viens, eds. *Entrepreneurs: The Boston Business Community, 1700–1850.* Boston: Northeastern University Press, 1997.

Wulf, Karin. *Not All Wives: Women of Colonial Philadelphia.* Ithaca, NY: Cornell University Press, 2000.

# Index

*Italics indicate tables or figures.*

269